DECISIONS AT CHANCELLORSVILLE

OTHER BOOKS IN THE COMMAND DECISIONS IN AMERICA'S CIVIL WAR SERIES

Decisions at Stones River
Matt Spruill and Lee Spruill

Decisions at Second Manassas
Matt Spruill III and Matt Spruill IV

Decisions at Chickamauga
Dave Powell

Decisions at Chattanooga
Larry Peterson

Decisions of the Atlanta Campaign
Larry Peterson

Decisions of the 1862 Kentucky Campaign
Larry Peterson

Decisions at The Wilderness and Spotsylvania Court House
Dave Townsend

Decisions at Gettysburg, Second Edition
Matt Spruill

Decisions of the Tullahoma Campaign
Michael R. Bradley

Decisions at Antietam
Michael S. Lang

Decisions of the Seven Days
Matt Spruill

Decisions at Fredericksburg
Chris Mackowski

Decisions at Perryville
Larry Peterson

Decisions of the Maryland Campaign
Michael S. Lang

Decisions at Shiloh
Dave Powell

Decisions at Franklin
Andrew S. Bledsoe

Decisions of the 1862 Shenandoah Valley Campaign
Robert Tanner

Decisions at Kennesaw Mountain
Larry Peterson

Decisions of the Vicksburg Campaign
Larry Peterson

DECISIONS AT CHANCELLORSVILLE

The Sixteen Critical Decisions
That Defined the Battle

Sarah Kay Bierle

Maps by Alex Mendoza

COMMAND DECISIONS
IN AMERICA'S CIVIL WAR
Matt Spruill and Larry Peterson,
Series Editors

The University of Tennessee Press / Knoxville

Copyright © 2025 by The University of Tennessee Press / Knoxville.
All Rights Reserved.
First Edition.

All photographs courtesy of the author unless otherwise indicated.

Library of Congress Cataloging-in-Publication Data

Names: Bierle, Sarah Kay author | Mendoza, Alexander, 1970- illustrator
Title: Decisions at Chancellorsville : the sixteen critical decisions that defined the battle / Sarah Kay Bierle ; maps by Alex Mendoza. Other titles: Command decisions in America's Civil War
Description: First edition. | Knoxville : University of Tennessee Press, [2025] | Series: Command decisions in America's Civil War series | Includes bibliographical references and index. | Summary: "Having won a considerable victory at Fredericksburg only months earlier, Gen. Robert E. Lee would again be tested by Gen. Joseph Hooker and the Federal Army at Chancellorsville. Hooker and the bulk of his army crossed the Rappahannock River at dawn on April 27, 1863, in conjunction with cavalry raids from Maj. Gen. George Stoneman. But Lee boldly divided his army, leaving a small force to defend Fredericksburg and attacking Hooker with the remainder of the Army of Northern Virginia. As the battle wore on, Lee launched multiple attacks on Hooker's defenses resulting in massive casualties for both sides. Lee divided his army again, sending Gen. Thomas 'Stonewall' Jackson's corps on a flanking maneuver that infamously resulted in the general's injury by friendly fire and eventual death. Though the Confederate Army's victory was assured, Lee equated the loss of Stonewall Jackson to the loss of his right hand, and as many months later Lee would find his army in a tide-turning defeat at the Battle of Gettysburg"—Provided by publisher.
Identifiers: LCCN 2025003884 (print) | LCCN 2025003885 (ebook) | ISBN 9781621909569 paperback | ISBN 9781621909583 Adobe PDF | ISBN 9781621909576 Kindle edition
Subjects: LCSH: Chancellorsville, Battle of, Chancellorsville, Va., 1863 | Command of troops—Case studies Classification: LCC E475.35 .B54 2025 (print) | LCC E475.35 (ebook) | DDC 973.7/33—dc23/eng/20250416
LC record available at https://lccn.loc.gov/2025003884
LC ebook record available at https://lccn.loc.gov/2025003885

To Chris Kolakowski,
who took a chance and voted to mentor a young woman
to help her become a better writer, a stronger researcher,
and . . . a historian.

CONTENTS

Preface	xiii
Acknowledgments	xix
Introduction	1
Chapter 1. Before the Battle: January–April 1863	11
Chapter 2. The Battle Begins: May 1, 1863	33
Chapter 3. The Battle's Surprises: May 2, 1863	59
Chapter 4. Battle to the East: May 3, 1863	83
Chapter 5. A Fateful Day: May 3, 1863	107
Chapter 6. Final Moves: May 4–6, 1863	127
Chapter 7. Aftermath and Conclusions	133
Appendix I. Battlefield Guide to the Critical Decisions at Chancellorsville	143
Appendix II. Chancellorsville and the Lost Cause	193
Appendix III. Union Order of Battle	199
Appendix IV. Confederate Order of Battle	219
Notes	229
Bibliography	243
Index	249

ILLUSTRATIONS

Photographs

George McClellan	6
Robert E. Lee and generals, 1862	7
Battle of Fredericksburg	8
Ambrose Burnside	12
Mud March	14
Pres. Abraham Lincoln	15
William B. Franklin	17
Joseph Hooker	18
Robert E. Lee	20
James Longstreet	21
Winter camp with snow	24
Union winter camps	25
Joseph Hooker on horseback	27
Thomas J. Jackson	34
Richard Anderson	35
Chancellorsville House	42
Henry Slocum	47
George Meade	47
George Sykes	47
Virginia Wilderness	51
J. E. B. Stuart	52

Robert E. Lee and Stonewall Jackson	53
Oliver O. Howard	61
Union cavalry	66
Eleventh Corps refugees and reinforcements	69
Stonewall Jackson wounded at Chancellorsville	73
A. P. Hill	75
Robert Rodes	76
J. E. B. Stuart	78
Jubal Early	86
John Sedgwick	87
William Barksdale	88
John Sedgwick and staff	93
Casualties in Sunken Road	97
Robert E. Lee at Chancellorsville, 1900	100
Salem Church, National Park Service	104
Daniel Sickles	108
Jonathan Letterman	114
Darius Couch	117
Henry Hunt	121
Union artillery	125
Winter camp cabin	146
Hamilton's Crossing	148
Zoan Church Ridge earthworks	150
First day at Chancellorsville Battlefield view	154
Chancellor House foundations	158
Lee-Jackson Bivouac Site	161
Jackson Trail	164
Flank attack fields	165
Mountain Road	169
Hazel Grove cannon toward Fairview	173
Cannon and lunette at Fairview	175
Trenches at Last Line	179
Sunken Road	182
Marye's Heights slope	184
Salem Church	186
Twenty-Third New Jersey Monument, Salem Church	188
Rappahannock River	191

Maps

Western Theater, 1862	2
Eastern Theater, 1862	4
Hooker's Campaign	29
Confederates Turn and Fight	39
Battle Map, May 1, 1863	43
Defensive Lines at Chancellorsville, May 2	49
Flank March and Divided Army	56
Eleventh Corps Position	64
Jackson Operations, May 2	70
Position of Lee's Army Night of May 2–3	77
Positions on May 3	85
Battle of Second Fredericksburg	95
East and West, May 3	103
Battle of Salem Church	105
Hazel Grove	111
Retreating from Chancellorsville	123
Tour Stops	144

PREFACE

The cry of a bird pierces the woods, cutting over the sound of the nearby traffic. The canopy of the trees lets in the light, probably more than the forest limbs of 1863 did. The trail winds toward a clearing, allowing a modern hiker to break into the opening. Ahead lies the foundation remains of the Chancellor House. Across the highway, the battery of silent cannons placed by the National Park Service keep guard at Fairview, eternally waiting for an artillery barrage from Hazel Grove beyond. One hundred sixty years ago, this crossroads clearing hosted the command headquarters of the Federal Army of the Potomac. Just over a mile away, the commander of the Confederate Army of Northern Virginia plotted an attack that sealed his place in military history while simultaneously destroying his victorious force.[1]

The Battle of Chancellorsville, fought May 1–6, 1863, pitted two armies against each other in what would be the costliest battle up to that time in the American Civil War. The Army of the Potomac had struggled through a depressing winter to emerge emboldened, encouraged, and determined to win. The new commander, Gen. Joseph "Fighting Joe" Hooker, promised a victory, and his soldiers eyed the elusive prize—a decisive defeat delivered to the Confederates in Virginia. Meanwhile, the Army of Northern Virginia, with Gen. Robert E. Lee commanding, entered the Chancellorsville fight desperate to destroy Hooker's army and perhaps tempt the aloof European powers to the side of the rebellious Southern states.

Why do battles unfold in particular ways? Why did a numerically stronger army with nearly all the military advantages settle at a crossroads in a densely wooded area and hand the military initiative to the enemy? What or who influenced one general to risk it all in a bold attack that divided his army and placed its soldiers in an incredibly vulnerable situation?

Walking through the preserved land of Chancellorsville Battlefield makes many historians and visitors ponder a simple question: Why? The first time I visited Chancellorsville—at age fourteen—I narrowly focused on two valid issues: why Stonewall Jackson impulsively advanced beyond his lines to scout, and what would have happened if he had not been shot. Years later, when I came to live in central Virginia, I approached Chancellorsville with more nuanced questions.

The fight that erupted in the Virginia Wilderness around the Chancellorsville clearing marked these armies' first full combat in the Old Dominion since President Lincoln had shifted the North's war aims. Four months earlier, on January 1, 1863, the Emancipation Proclamation promised freedom to thousands of enslaved men, women, and children within the Confederacy. US armies now had to subdue Confederate armies, capture more territory from rebelling states, and enforce that promise of freedom as a sign of the power of the American government. Hooker's predecessor had failed to give the northern home front confidence in the strength of the Federal army to achieve victories. The Confederates recognized the war was changing and knew everything would be different if their enemy secured battlefield victories. The stakes were high in the spring of 1863, and the common soldiers on both sides readied for a decisive combat. Few realized the enormous loss that their units would suffer in a struggle for victory that seemed hollow when the fighting concluded.

Oftentimes, history plainly records *what* happened. *Why* events happened in a certain way can be more elusive, affected by factors including personalities, circumstances, politics, logistics, topography, and leadership. Officers made decisions with far-reaching impact. Why did they choose one option over another? How did that decision affect the entire battle?

My goal with this volume is to show that the Battle of Chancellorsville did not leave either army the victim or victor of random events. The attacks and defenses, the "surprises" and retreats, the victory and defeat did not happen as accidents. Events occurred because of command decisions—sometimes reached at the armies' headquarters, sometimes made by officers or men taking initiative on the front lines. Some of these decision moments impacted the entire battle, possibly even the course of the Civil War in the East. At the top of the decision hierarchy, a select number of choices shaped the way the campaign and battle unfolded. These were the critical decisions.

Preface

Critical decisions cover the entire spectrum of war: strategy, operations, tactics, organization, personnel, and logistics. Initially some decisions appear to be minor, but they actually are critical decisions that had a major impact in shaping events.

Through the pages of this book, I'll share accounts of men deciding, battling, dying, or surviving as a starting point to reexamine the whys of this costly combat. Decisions have outcomes, and critical decisions influence everything. The critical decision methodology allows someone who has an understanding of what happened to move to the next level and ask why events happened or what caused them to happen. When the critical decision concept is understood, it can be applied to any battle or campaign in any war.

It is important that you, the reader, understand the concept of a critical decision. Otherwise, this book will appear to be only a short and selected narrative history of Chancellorsville. This work instead offers a new concept, exploring why the battle and campaign developed as they did—*the why instead of the what*.

As defined in the Command Decisions in America's Civil War series, a critical decision has such magnitude that it shaped events immediately thereafter, and also the entire battle from that point forward. If a critical decision had not been made or had been decided in any other way, the Battle of Chancellorsville would have been irrevocably different.

The following chart illustrates the decision hierarchy. At the bottom are the many and various decisions. Above those are fewer important decisions, and at the top are a very few critical decisions.

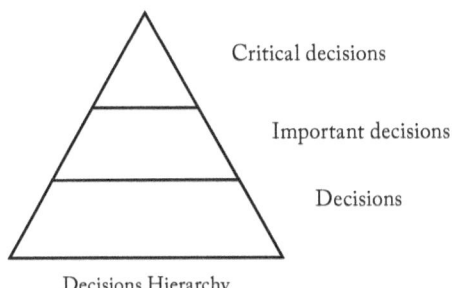

Decisions Hierarchy

Leadership involves decisions, and these occur at multiple levels during a battle, ranging across many parts of military life and the concept of war. Strategic decisions call for broad, often large-scale actions and significant outcomes. Tactical decisions are a more specific means of carrying out a particular strategy. Organizational and personnel decisions involve placing people in the right places at the right time or failing to properly deploy strengths and skills. Logistical decisions may enhance or entirely cripple the power of a unit or an army. All these types of decisions and many others may factor into a critical decision. However, a critical decision is the hinge, the moment where everything changes. Once this choice is made, nothing will be the same, and there can be no turning back.

Working with the series' definition of the term, I have noted sixteen critical decisions for the Battle of Chancellorsville. US Army major general Joseph Hooker or other Union officers made nine of these critical decisions, while Confederate general Robert E. Lee or his officers made six. The difference in numbers stems from Hooker's choices to give up his military advantages and initiative, handing opportunity to Lee to react. Lee still had to choose his response, and some of these moments became crucial decisions. Hooker had rebuilt the Army of the Potomac and had promised victories, but in the end, Lee won a Pyrrhic victory at the Chancellorsville Crossroads.

The sixteen critical decisions for the Battle of Chancellorsville are grouped into six specific categories and time periods:

Before the Battle: January–April 1863
    Lincoln Appoints Hooker
    Lee Sends Longstreet's Corps Away
    Hooker Determines His Offensive Strategy
The Battle Begins: May 1, 1863
    Lee Decides to Turn and Fight
    Hooker Pulls Back
    Lee Decides to Allow Jackson to Initiate a Flank Attack
The Battle's Surprises: May 2, 1863
    Hooker Decides the Confederates Are Retreating
    Jackson Plans to Cut Off the Federals from US Ford
    Lee Puts J. E. B. Stuart in Command of the Second Corps
Battle to the East: May 3, 1863
    Griffin Grants a Temporary Truce
    Sedgwick's Troops Move Forward
    Lee Divides His Army Again
A Fateful Day: May 3, 1863
    Hooker Orders Sickles to Abandon Hazel Grove
    Union Officers Do Not Replace Hooker after His Injury
    Hooker Brings Hunt from the Rear
Final Moves: May 4–6, 1863
    Hooker Retreats

The goal of this book is to examine the moments, conditions, and situations surrounding these critical decisions, as well as the other possible options available to the decision makers. This is not a traditional narrative history for the Battle of Chancellorsville.

In the research, thought process, and writing of this book, I have relied heavily on primary sources to construct the scenarios of the decisions, sifting for details of the what that impacted the ultimate why of the battle. In some instances, you will notice different spelling and grammar in the primary source quotes; these are the words and writings as the soldiers penned them.

It is impossible to return to the blazing woods around the Chancellorsville clearing and observe the critical decision moments and their impact. However, using military papers and other primary sources, it is possible to reconstruct some of the details concerning these moments, and to better appreciate or understand critical decisions that affected the lives of soldiers and reverberated across North and South with startling and tragic consequences. Critical decisions acted like crossroads, and there would be no return from them.

ACKNOWLEDGMENTS

What a delight to be able to extend sincere thanks to colleagues, advisers, and friends for their assistance with this project!

Chris Mackowski asked whether I might be interested in learning more about the Command Decisions in America's Civil War series and introduced me to the series editors. He graciously reviewed my early lists of critical decisions, offering advice and a few ideas. Thank you, Chris.

Chris Kolakowski is one of the mentors I call when considering new book projects. I'm grateful for his good questions that focus my perspective around new opportunities. Chris, thanks for being part of my own critical decisions for research, writing, and publishing over the years. Thank you for your guiding advice for learning and building a career in the history field.

Series editors Matt Spruill and Larry Peterson offered excellent feedback and suggestions and were enduringly patient as I navigated career changes during research and writing. I appreciate their guidance, encouragement, and kindness, as well as the chance they gave me to grow as a writer through this project.

Thomas Wells and the University of Tennessee Press are in the front ranks of academic publishing about Civil War history. I thank them for the opportunity to publish this book.

Sincere thanks to Gregory Mertz for his insightful notes and suggestions that improved and clarified parts of the manuscript.

I appreciate the staff, librarians, and archivists at The Huntington Library who preserve a treasure trove of Civil War documents, including Gen. Joseph Hooker's papers.

I'm grateful that my parents, Shawn and Susan Bierle, allowed me to visit Chancellorsville Battlefield during our family's East Coast adventures in 2008. The drizzly day with the dogwoods blooming in the woods is embedded in my mind, along with the history of this place. Thank you to the National Park Service for helping to protect this landscape, and for providing the frontline interpreters who helped a teenager find the places written about in the history books.

Brennan McAuley, a good friend and former law enforcement ranger at Fredericksburg and Spotsylvania National Military Park, informed me of wandering bears frequenting the Chancellorsville trails and other safety considerations during some of my research time.

Finally, to my friends and colleagues at the American Battlefield Trust and the Central Virginia Battlefields Trust, thank you for the work that you do to preserve more land at Chancellorsville Battlefield. Here's to more acreage and continuing interpretation of this land and the stories of the soldiers and civilians in this critical fight.

May the readers of this book be challenged to think about decisions and outcomes, and may they find their own moments of connecting with history through more research and walking the battlefields of Chancellorsville, Second Fredericksburg, and Salem Church. Thank you for adding this volume to your reading list or library.

INTRODUCTION

Pvt. John Haley of the Seventeenth Maine Infantry stood in formation on April 9, 1863, waiting for Pres. Lincoln to pass his regiment, which had been detailed to escort duty for the chief executive's visit. The review offered a welcome break from the winter of picket duty, camp boredom, drilling, and changing camp locations. However, the spring warmth and the arrival of political dignitaries also heralded a new season of military campaigning. As he briefly observed the president's sorrowful expression, Haley thought, "He is probably aware that a battle cannot long be deferred."[1]

That spring, leaders and common soldiers on both sides were keenly aware that spring meant breaking winter camps and campaigning toward new battles. Those combats could deliver the decisive victory that had thus far eluded the Union and Confederate armies as they approached the third spring of war. Decisive military victory would allow the winning side to fulfill the political aims of this conflict and secure either state sovereignty or the concept of union.

In 1861, the exuberant volunteers in their multicolored uniforms thought one battle would decide the war. The reality set in after the First Battle of Bull Run in July 1861. The Confederates won that battle, but not decisively enough to finish the war and secure the independence of the seceded states.[2] Both sides turned to recruiting larger volunteer armies, and the US Navy scrambled to enforce a blockade of the Southern coastline.

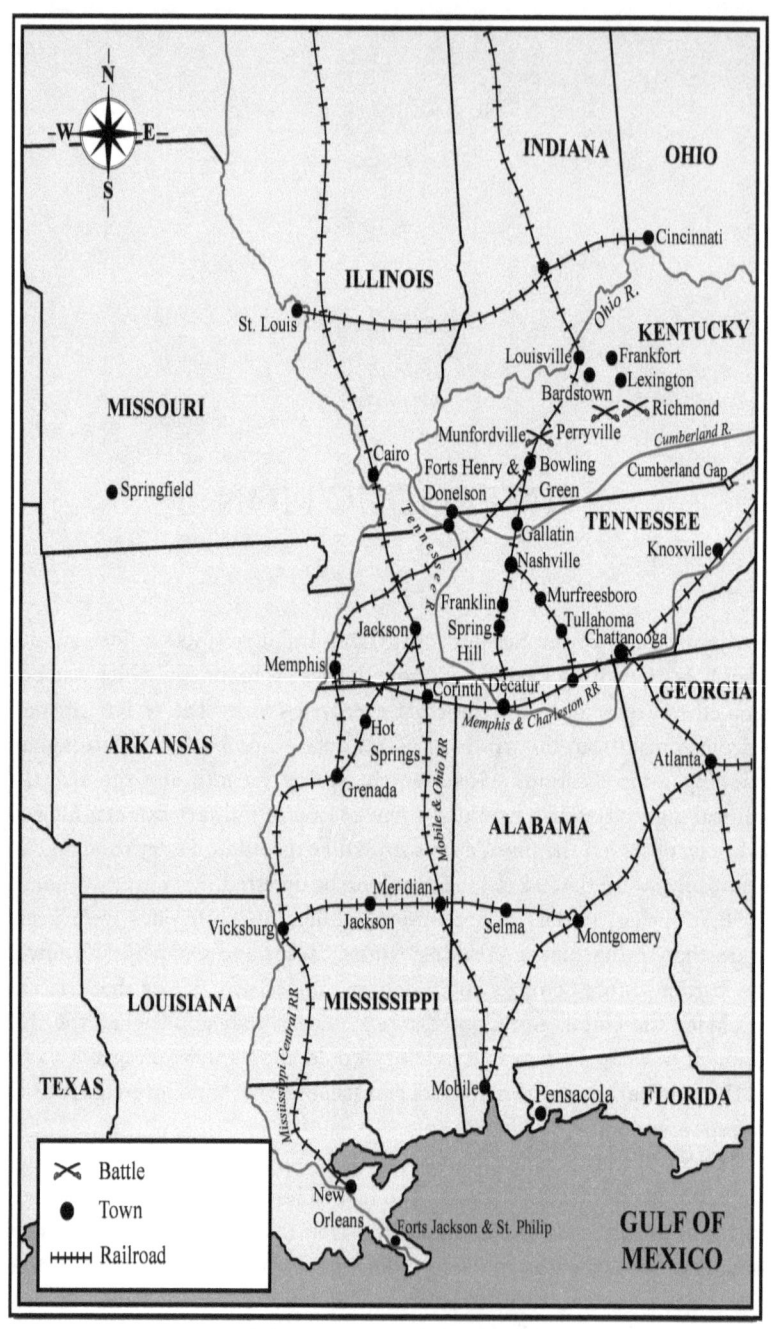

The Western Theater

Early in 1862, attention turned to the Western Theater, as the Union Anaconda Plan started squeezing and capturing Confederate strongholds along the rivers. Forts Henry and Donelson surrendered in February, opening parts of the Tennessee River, keeping the border state of Kentucky under Union control, and allowing Union troops to occupy Nashville, Tennessee. Along the Tennessee River on April 6–7, 1862, near Pittsburg Landing, the Confederates launched a surprise attack in the Battle of Shiloh. A counterattack turned Shiloh into a Union victory, but the high casualties stunned the entire American populace.[3]

While Union campaigns ground to a halt in Virginia during the spring and summer, the Federals' successes continued in the West and Deep South. The Confederates lost Fort Pulaski on April 11, 1862, allowing Union troops access to the mouth of the Savannah River. By May 1, Union navy and army forces captured New Orleans, one of the most important port cities in the Confederacy. Access to New Orleans from the south allowed the Federal brown-water navy to pursue riverine warfare and probe deeper into Confederate territory along the Mississippi River. When the Union fully controlled that major waterway, the Confederacy would be divided, leaving Texas, Louisiana, Arkansas, and Missouri (border state) isolated from the other seceded states.[4]

In the fall of 1862, Gen. Braxton Bragg and Maj. Gen. Edmund Kirby Smith led two Confederate armies into Kentucky. They hoped to regain territory between the Tennessee River and the Appalachian Mountains, install a Confederate-supporting governor, and further convince the border state to join the Southern rebellion. The Battle of Perryville on October 8, 1862, added a western tactical victory to the Confederates' tally sheet. However, Union Maj. Gen. Don C. Buell claimed the strategic victory, effectively preventing Bragg's and Smith's forces from uniting. Thwarted in their prime objectives, the Confederates retreated to Tennessee, leaving Kentucky in Union hands.[5]

Despite the successes throughout the year, the Union cause in the West faced challenges by the end of 1862. Maj. Gen. Ulysses S. Grant and more than thirty thousand Union soldiers attempted to move directly to Vicksburg, Mississippi, one of the last Confederate strongholds on the Mississippi River. The Battle of Chickasaw Bayou at the end of December 1862 and Confederate operations against Grant's supply depot at Holly Springs stalled that attempt, forcing Grant to reconsider his approach to Vicksburg and eventually fight a prolonged campaign and siege in 1863.[6] Back in Tennessee, the Battle of Stones River pitted Gen. Braxton Bragg's Confederates against Maj. Gen. William Rosecrans's Union soldiers from December 31, 1862 to January 2, 1863. The Federals won, but their Army of the Cumberland was so battered

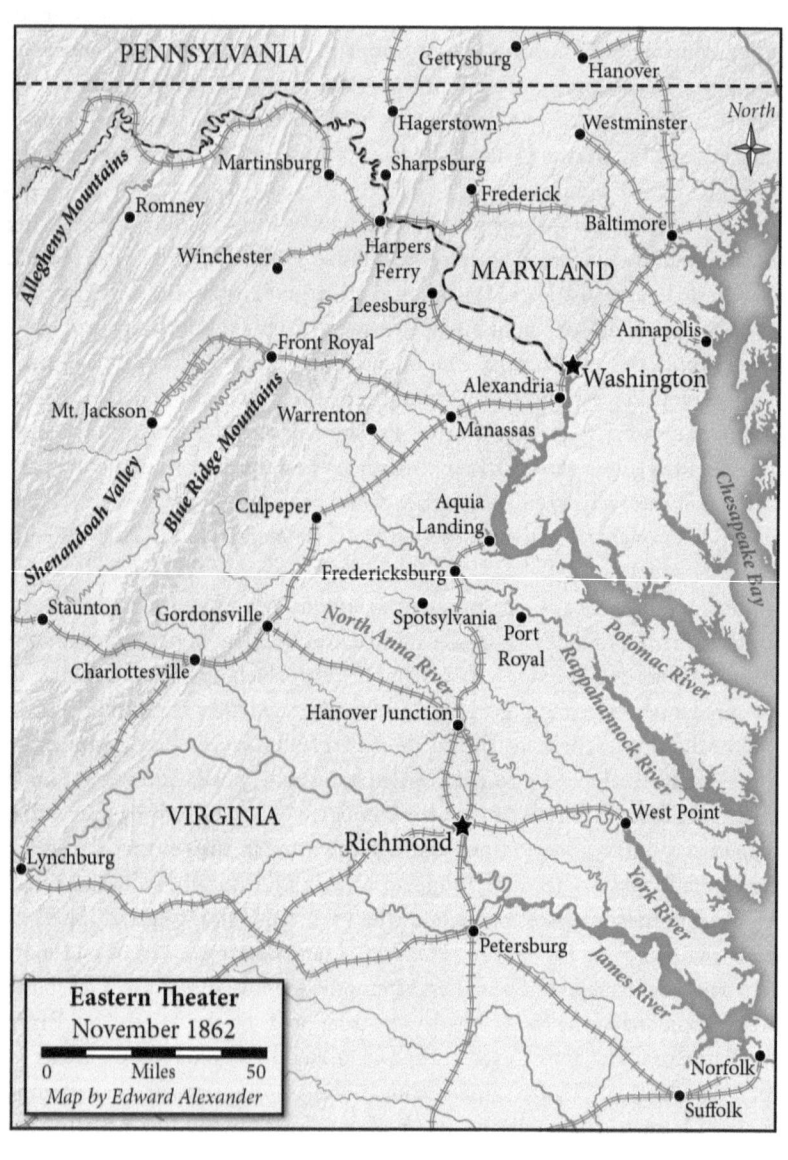

that it would be nearly six months before Rosecrans effectively took the field again, leaving military actions and the quest for a decisive victory at a standstill in Tennessee.[7]

The Union's victories in the Western Theater contrasted sharply with its defeats in Virginia, generally encompassing the Eastern Theater of the Civil War. Confederates pointed to Virginia and their triumphs in that state as hopeful signs, even as they lost territory in the West. Many Southerners also hoped that a large victory in Virginia would increase the possibilities of capturing the Federal capital of Washington, DC, or bring recognition of Confederate sovereignty from European powers.

While Forts Henry and Donelson in Tennessee surrendered during February 1862, the Union Army of the Potomac readied to take the field. Maj. Gen. George B. McClellan presented his finalized plans for a grand campaign in the east. Several small Union armies would operate in western Virginia and the Shenandoah Valley. Meanwhile, for the main focus of his strategy, McClellan planned to transfer more than 100,000 troops—the majority of the Army of the Potomac—to the Virginia Peninsula. The soldiers would land at Fortress Monroe, march up the Peninsula, and capture Richmond, the capital of the Confederacy.

McClellan moved his army to the Peninsula. A combination of excessive cautiousness, inflated reports of Confederate defenders, and political squabbling stalled his advance.[8] Approximately ninety-four thousand Confederates under Gen. Joseph E. Johnston's command were positioned to defend Richmond, and they fought delaying actions and battles along the Peninsula.

In the Shenandoah Valley, Union forces enjoyed initial successes and partially secured a large swath of territory in the northern part of the region. However, in May 1862 Confederate Maj. Gen. Thomas J. Jackson—nicknamed "Stonewall"—punched back. A series of rapid maneuvers over five weeks resulted in five notable battles (McDowell, Front Royal, First Winchester, Cross Keys, and Port Republic) and numerous skirmishes. At the end of Jackson's 1862 Valley Campaign, he had defeated three Union armies, much to the embarrassment and concern of Maj. Gen. McClellan and President Lincoln.[9]

Meanwhile, on the Virginia Peninsula, Gen. Joseph Johnston was wounded during the Battle of Seven Pines on May 31. Confederate Pres. Jefferson Davis appointed Gen. Robert E. Lee to take command of the Confederate army and the defense of Richmond. With McClellan's army within ten miles of Richmond, Lee inherited a massive challenge.[10] McClellan's delays worked to Lee's advantage, giving him time to bring Jackson and Confederate troops from the Shenandoah Valley. Reinforced, Lee took the offensive

Introduction

Maj. Gen. George B. McClellan (Union) commanded the Army of the Potomac for the majority of 1862. Library of Congress.

at the end of June.[11] The Seven Days Battles started on June 26, 1862, and lasted until July 2. Places like Mechanicsville, Gaines's Mill, Golding's Farm, Savage Station, Glendale, and Malvern Hill became the scenes of intense fighting, as Lee strategically pushed McClellan east across the Chickahominy River and then south toward the James River. Bewildered and demoralized, McClellan conducted what he termed a "change of base" to Harrison's Landing on the James River. Most of his Army of the Potomac idled away the summer weeks there, waiting to return to battle or leave the swampy Peninsula. The Seven Days Battles elevated Lee to heroic status in the Confederacy and forged the Army of Northern Virginia into an organized and distinctive fighting force.[12]

McClellan lingered on the Peninsula, arguing long distance with Lincoln and other authorities in Washington. Less than pleased with Gen. McClellan's retreat from the borders of Richmond, Lincoln pinned new hopes on Maj. Gen. John Pope, who took command of the Union Army of Virginia. Pope plunged into central Virginia and opened a new chapter of warfare; he allowed his army to live off the land and bring a form of total war to the adjacent Southern civilians. To counter Pope's position in central Virginia and threats to railroad lines, Lee detached Jackson to threaten him. The Battle of Cedar Mountain on August 9 halted Pope's southward advance. Pope placed his army along the Rappahannock River, hoping to use the natural river boundaries for his protection.[13]

Gen. Lee marched northward from Richmond with Maj. Gen. James Longstreet's troops to reinforce Jackson. On August 25 Lee sent Jackson on a turning movement around Pope's right (west) flank. Pope had lost contact with Jackson, and on August 27, he was surprised to find a major stockpile of his army's supplies at Manassas Junction going up in the flames as Jackson suddenly attacked his rear supply lines. Jackson "disappeared" once more, only to strike at Pope's army again on August 28, 1862, starting the Second Battle of Bull Run (Manassas). Lee and Longstreet rushed reinforcements into the multiday battle, resulting in a rout of Pope's army.[14] A follow-up battle at Chantilly on September 1 further demoralized Pope's Army of Virginia; the unit continued retreating to Washington, DC, uniting with elements of McClellan's force that had finally been transported off the Peninsula.

Taking advantage of recent successes and searching for a decisive victory that would give the Confederacy control of the Federal capital or recognition from England or France, Lee turned his Army of Northern Virginia northward into Maryland. Pres. Lincoln put McClellan back in command and tasked him with defeating Lee and stopping the Maryland invasion. Once again, McClellan took his time. His delay allowed the Confederates to split their force, capture the Union garrison at Harpers Ferry, fight at South Mountain, and eventually reassemble the majority of the Army of Northern Virginia in the farmland along Antietam Creek and around the village of Sharpsburg. The Battle of Antietam on September 17, 1862—the single bloodiest day in US history—resulted in 22,727 casualties. The fierce fighting ended in a tactical draw, but this was a strategic victory for McClellan, as Lee withdrew from Maryland.[15]

Gen. Robert E. Lee and Confederate generals of the Army of Northern Virginia had won many battlefield victories during 1862 and hoped for a decisive fight in 1863. Library of Congress.

Introduction

It was enough of a Union victory that Lincoln decided to issue the Emancipation Proclamation. On January 1, 1863, enslaved persons in states still in rebellion would be "henceforth and forever free." Lincoln thus added a new objective to the Union war aims. Slavery had been a cause of the war, and with his proclamation, the president made both the end of slavery and national reunification the stated objectives. Not all Union soldiers reacted positively to the announcement. Confederates responded predictably, believing that the Federal government meant to destroy their society and "way of life" by ending their "peculiar institution" that had kept millions of individuals in racial slavery for nearly 250 years.[16]

Lincoln needed another Union victory to add weight to the words he would sign into official war aims on January 1, 1863. McClellan found numerous excuses to avoid attacking Lee in northern Virginia during the autumn of 1862. By November 5, Lincoln had had enough. He removed McClellan from command, and two days later put Maj. Gen. Ambrose Burnside in charge of the Army of the Potomac. A reluctant army leader, Burnside nevertheless put forward a new plan to advance rapidly toward Richmond using the Richmond, Fredericksburg & Potomac Railroad as his supply route through the eastern part of Virginia. His plan stalled at Fredericksburg, where he waited for pontoon bridges to cross his army, artillery, and supply wagons over the Rappahannock River.

This Currier & Ives illustration of the Battle of Fredericksburg in December 1862 emphasizes the repeated charges that Union brigades made toward the Confederate defensive position at Marye's Heights. Library of Congress.

Burnside's delay allowed the Confederates to discover his movement and advance toward Richmond. Longstreet, Lee, and Jackson marched to Fredericksburg, setting up a defensive position on the southern bank of the Rappahannock River and extending the Confederate picket line twenty miles downriver to avoid a surprise crossing. On December 11, Burnside's engineers began to lay the pontoon bridges, and the Battle of Fredericksburg opened. Contested river crossings, urban street fighting, artillery barrage, and intentional destruction of civilian property characterized the first two days of fighting. By December 13, Lee had consolidated the Army of Northern Virginia's defensive line, and Burnside had formed plans for the Army of the Potomac to attack. Unclear orders and limited grasp of the actual situation unfolding on the battlefield resulted in uncoordinated Union attacks that devolved into hopeless, repeated assaults, resulting in approximately 12,500 Union casualties compared to 6,000 Confederate losses. Under the cover of darkness, Burnside eventually withdrew the Union survivors. He then turned to face his subordinate generals' dissension and blame, Lincoln's disappointment, and the weight of grief from the Northern home front.[17] A Union victory to add power to the Emancipation Proclamation would not come from the Eastern Theater.

Though the Confederates claimed victory at Fredericksburg, Lee's disappointment was evident. For Lee, 1862 had been a highly successful year on the battlefield, but he had failed to secure a victory that completely destroyed a Union army. Nor had a rebel win helped the Confederacy gain bargaining power to form a separate nation and preserve slavery.[18]

As 1863 dawned over Washington, DC, Richmond, and the winter encampments of the Army of the Potomac and Army of Northern Virginia, the pressure for a decisive victory increased. The stakes had been raised, and with abolition added to the Union war aims, progressive European powers were losing interest in aiding the Confederacy. Even as generals and soldiers waited out the winter months in their tents or improvised cabins, they knew that 1863 could be a turning point for their causes. With the promise of freedom raising the political stakes, and with neither side willing to back down or negotiate, it fell to the generals and the common soldiers to decide the outcome of the war on the battlefield.

The critical decisions for the next campaign and battle would be fueled by political pressure, battlefield circumstance, and reactionary steps to military threats or opportunities. The events would not be random, but rather the result of a few critical decisions that would spark or influence the chain of events of the Battle of Chancellorsville.

As the Army of the Potomac and Army of Northern Virginia continued their bloody quest for a decisive victory, Chancellorsville would be added to the war timeline as the next major moment in Virginia. The battle could not be long deferred, and the results of the critical decisions would be shocking to the politicians, the generals, the soldiers, and the home front.

As Pvt. John Haley returned to camp after the presidential review, he deemed that April day's events preparation for the next battle. His experiences and the accounts of victories or setbacks that he read about in the newspapers laid the groundwork for 1863. With much at stake, and with the knowledge that it was the common soldier's duty to carry out the objectives and face the results of the high command decisions, Haley experienced a grim foreshadow, "a feeling of uneasiness and horrible uncertainty possessed me."[19]

CHAPTER 1

BEFORE THE BATTLE

JANUARY–APRIL 1863

If you have skipped the preface, please return and explore the definition of a critical decision to fully understand the purpose and interpretation presented in this book.

As detailed in the introduction, the prior events and decisions on the Civil War timeline impacted the scenarios and choices that occurred during the Chancellorsville Campaign. Pressure on the Union and Confederate army commanders to secure a decisive victory and bring their opponent to surrender or negotiate increased as President Lincoln formally added emancipation of enslaved people within the Confederacy to the Union's war aims. The Union Army of the Potomac needed a major victory in Virginia to add weight to the president's Emancipation Proclamation, while the Confederate Army of Northern Virginia had to both defend Richmond and seek victory that would gain independence for the seceded states and perhaps lead to recognition from a European power. As the curtain of history rose on the year 1863, the stakes stood high, but the gamblers still had to place their bets on military leadership.

Before the armies engaged in combat, three critical decisions were made. These decisions gave one army a new commander, reduced the operational strength of the other army, and laid out the initial offense plan for the Federal campaign.

Lincoln Appoints Hooker

Situation

Pvt. Charles Engel of the 137th New York Infantry wrote despairingly to his wife on January 26, 1863, "O Charlotte you cant think what a job it is for an army to move when it is so mudey [*sic*].... Words cant describe the sene. Every horse and mule and man covered with mud. Wagons broke and tiping over in the mud. Mud is no name for it. I wish you could see where we come through."[1]

Engle described the bloodless but appropriately named Mud March of January 1863, following the Battle of Fredericksburg in December 1862. His words echoed the feelings of frustration and that enveloped the commander, officers, and soldiers of the Union's Army of the Potomac, including the new general who took command the day before Engle penned his letter.

Fredericksburg had been a horrifying Union defeat, hardly the hoped-for eastern victory to support the president's Emancipation Proclamation. Even before the survivors in blue had resettled in camps on the north side of the Rappahannock River, the army's generals turned on one another, looking for a scapegoat for the futile attacks. Maj. Gen. Ambrose Burnside, a reluctant army commander since his appointment on November 7, 1862, faced the reality of his battlefield loss, and to his credit, he initially took responsibility. "For

Maj. Gen. Ambrose Burnside had experienced defeat and difficulties at Fredericksburg and in the Mud March. Library of Congress.

the failure in the attack I am responsible.... That you left the whole management in my hands, without giving me orders, makes me more responsible," Burnside wrote to General-in-Chief Henry Halleck.[2]

However, simply taking responsibility for the defeat would not be enough. Since December 1861, the congressional Joint Committee on the Conduct of the War regularly investigated generals and tried to discover the reasons for military failures. Members of the committee interviewed Burnside and the generals who commanded the Grand Divisions, Generals Sumner, Franklin, and Hooker.[3] Looming over them all was the joint committee's ongoing investigation of Fitz John Porter, a favorite from the days when Maj. Gen. George B. McClellan commanded the Army of the Potomac. Porter, who had fallen from favor and faced a court-martial, was likely to be scapegoated for the Union defeat at Second Bull Run the previous August.

While the Union soldiers built winter huts and picketed the freezing banks of the Rappahannock, the generals of the Army of the Potomac grumbled against Burnside. Most were willing to blame Burnside, but a few offered plots against their peers. Maj. Gen. William B. Franklin and Maj. Gen. Joseph Hooker—commanders of the Left and Center Grand Divisions, respectively—criticized one another for the loss at Fredericksburg. With unclear orders and little initiative of his own, Franklin had failed to carry out the main assault on December 13. Meanwhile, Hooker's troops had been involved in repeated diversion attacks meant to support Franklin; Hooker finally protested to Burnside, begging him to halt the assaults against the murderous Confederate position at Marye's Heights. Gen. Franklin, with his henchman Maj. Gen. William "Baldy" Smith, prepared a letter to President Lincoln suggesting that the army return to the James River and try again to capture Richmond by way of operations on the Virginia Peninsula—like Gen. McClellan had tried during the previous summer.[4] It was part of a military and political scheme to get McClellan restored to command of the army.

Threatened from multiple sides and uncomfortable with the division among the headquarters, Burnside offered his resignation to President Lincoln on January 1, 1863. Lincoln refused to accept, but he also failed to approve Burnside's next proposed military advance. Frustrated, Burnside returned to the Rappahannock and complained to a few of the generals he thought he could trust.[5]

Deciding that inactivity would be one of the worst choices, Burnside issued orders for his Grand Divisions to march upriver, cross at Banks' Ford, and attack the Confederates at Fredericksburg from the west. Weather conspired against him. Rain turned the Virginia roads into a quagmire. Wagons

Illustrator Alfred Waud sketched this scene of Union troops on January 21, 1863, during the infamous Mud March. Library of Congress.

got stuck. Pontoon bridges needed to cross the river were suctioned into the mud. Union soldiers staggered through the mire. Morale did not improve when Federals saw the enemy's signs mocking their standstill.[6] Literally unable to move soldiers, cannon, wagons, or bridges, Burnside ordered the troops to slog back to their camps.

Like Pvt. Engels and many other soldiers, Maj. Gen. John F. Reynolds, commanding the First Corps in Franklin's Grand Division, reported on the infamous Mud March. He told his sisters, "We are now 'stuck in the mud' unable to get up our artillery or supplies and Burnside goes to Washington to know what to do!! If we do not get some one soon who can command an army without consulting 'Stanton and Hallock' at Washington, I do not know what will become of this army."[7] Other generals, like Hooker, were less private in their disgust at Burnside's decisions.

Burnside had rushed off to the White House carrying an ultimatum: General Orders No. 8. Lincoln had to permit the following conditions laid out in No. 8 or else Burnside would resign. First, "being guilty of unjust and unnecessary criticisms of the actions of his superior officers . . . and having, by the general tone of his conversation, endeavored to create distrust in the minds of officers," Gen. Hooker had to be dismissed from command. Second,

Pres. Abraham Lincoln navigated politics while searching for a Union general who would win battlefield victories. Library of Congress.

Sixth Corps division commander Brig. Gen. W. T. H. Brooks also had to be removed for "using language tending to demoralize his command." Third, Sixth Corps Generals Newton and Cochrane would be dismissed for approaching the president with "criticisms upon the plans of their commanding officer." Fourth, six other generals, including Franklin, would be deemed of "no further service to this army" and "relieved from duty."[8]

Lincoln received Burnside's communications on January 24, 1863, and told the general that he would inform him of the decision on the following day.

Options

Pres. Lincoln, Secretary of War Edwin Stanton, and General-in-Chief Henry Halleck had three viable options: Keep Burnside in command and dismiss the "problem generals," place Franklin in command, or put Hooker in command. Their choice would signal their assessment of Burnside's leadership and the military cabals that had formed among the generals. The critical decision of supporting or selecting the Army of the Potomac's commander would set the course for the spring campaign in Virginia.

Option 1: Keep Burnside in Command

If the decision-makers kept Burnside in command, they would essentially endorse his actions, showing confidence in his leadership despite his defeats. Burnside's list of generals for removal was lengthy and would create leadership changes and disgruntles soldiers losing some commanders they liked. His changes would also affect Northern politics and the home front; the November 1862 elections had already shown an erosion of support for the Republican Party among the voting populace, and the removal and promotion of generals had political implications.

Keeping Burnside and following his demands could continue the Army of the Potomac's tradition of the commanding general dictating and the president reacting. This arrangement had been problematic the previous summer with Maj. Gen. McClellan and the Peninsula Campaign. A list of demands from a victorious general might be easier to consider, but if the Lincoln administration sided with Burnside, it opened the door to more political criticism. The administration needed wins, not excuses or demands. Thus far, Burnside had not delivered victories and morale of the army had sunk to all-time low.

Option 2: Place Franklin in Command

Though part of the dissension chorus against Burnside, Maj. Gen. William Franklin had approached Lincoln with a plan. His plan lacked originality—a return to the Virginia Peninsula to attack Richmond that had been tried the previous summer—but he offered an offensive solution along with his list of complaints. Franklin's battlefield record was mixed. Commanding the Sixth Corps since March 1862, he had advocated retreating from Richmond during the Seven Days Battles. He also failed to strike at the divided Confederate army at Harpers Ferry during the Maryland Campaign. During the Battle of Antietam, Franklin wanted to attack aggressively, but he had been ordered to keep his corps in reserve. The Battle of Fredericksburg had been a debacle for him, but he quickly blamed Burnside.

Appointing Franklin to command would be reinstating a McClellan supporter who lacked battlefield victories or consistent aggressive initiative. Lincoln needed triumphs on the battlefield to back up the Emancipation Proclamation and lay the groundwork for his presidential campaign for the following year. Giving Franklin the post would reward the disloyalty he had exhibited after Fredericksburg, promote a general with a mediocre record, and continue the McClellan style of politics and leadership that the Army of the Potomac had experienced for a year.

Maj. Gen. William B. Franklin (Union) angled for the role of commander of the Army of the Potomac during the winter of 1863. Library of Congress.

Option 3: Place Hooker in Command

Maj. Gen. Joseph Hooker was part of the military cabal against Burnside, and his removal ranked first on Burnside's list of demands. But Hooker had a battlefield reputation weighing in his favor. Commanding a division during the Peninsula Campaign, he led at the front and earned the nickname Fighting Joe Hooker when a newspaper correspondent accidentally omitted punctuation. His men followed him willingly and liked his flair for command. By the Battle of Antietam, Hooker led the First Corps of the Army of the Potomac and pressed a ferocious but costly attack through the Cornfield, opening the day of fighting. Under Burnside, he commanded the Center Grand Division (the Third and Fifth Corps), and his troops made continued assaults against the high ground of Marye's Heights during the Battle of Fredericksburg. In 1862, Hooker had proved that he could fight. Wounded in combat at Antietam and respected by many of the troops, the outspoken and aggressive major general stood in contrast to the other complainers.

However, appointing Hooker would not only reward his complaining and his disloyalty to Burnside and, but it would also risk future political troubles. Hooker had declared a dictatorship the solution to Union victory, a strong suggestion that he did not care for how the Lincoln administration operated the war. His aggressiveness and ambition might aim further than army command and threaten the idea of a constitutional republic.

Before the Battle

Maj. Gen. Joseph Hooker (Union) had been an aggressive leader during 1862 battles and promised to lead the Army of the Potomac to victory in the spring of 1863. Library of Congress.

Decision

Lincoln placed Hooker in command of the Army of the Potomac. Appointing McClellan supporters could perpetuate the leadership and political difficulties that had existed for the past year. Lincoln needed victories, and he took a risk and appointed an aggressive commander to seek them. However, the president acknowledged Hooker's poor behavior and his talk about dictatorship, telling him, "Only those generals who gain successes, can set up dictators. What I now ask of you is military success, and I will risk the dictatorship."[9]

Results/Impact

On January 25, 1863, General Orders No. 20 relieved Burnside, Sumner, and Franklin from command and appointed Hooker to head the Army of the Potomac. By the following day, the orders were in effect and the soldiers began to hear the news.[10]

Hooker spent the next weeks working to restore the morale of the army, reverse the high desertion rate, and prepare the troops to fight in the next campaign. He improved the food supply for the men, implemented a system of furloughs, and brought in new staff leadership.[11] By spring, Hooker had restored the fighting spirit within the Army of the Potomac, and the soldiers readied to "go forward, and give us victories," as Lincoln had directed the new commanding general upon his appointment.[12]

Pvt. Charles Engel of the 137th New York Infantry, who had written with despair to his wife after the Mud March, sent a different story by April 13, 1863. His determination had been revived, and he—like thousands of others—was ready to seek victory through battle once again: "I heard today that the front army was moving. I guess there will be some fighting done soone. I heard they was going to get reenforcements from Washington and leave us here. I hope they will. Generl Hooker seas he is agoing to put a change in the war one way or the other within ninety days. I hope he will. If I have got to fight I want to do it now. You musent be afraid about my going into the battle."[13]

Lee Sends Longstreet's Corps Away

Situation

Reflecting on Gen. Robert E. Lee's character in the postwar era, staff officer Walter H. Taylor noted, "His army demanded his first thought and care; to his men, to their needs, he must first attend.... Duty first, was the rule of his life, and his every thought, word, and action, was made to square with duty's inexorable demands."[14] Duty and the means of keeping an army together and ready for action hallmarked the winter of 1862–63 for the Confederate commander. He faced a difficult decision prompted by the logistical situation that would impact his available fighting numbers in his first major battle of 1863.

Since taking command and creating the Army of Northern Virginia, Gen. Robert E. Lee had been fighting for a decisive victory, and he had totaled an impressive score on the battlefield thus far. He had driven McClellan from the gates of Richmond, beaten Pope at Second Manassas, fought McClellan to a standstill at Antietam, and witnessed the slaughter of Union troops at Fredericksburg. Still, Lee had not brought a Union army to its knees, nor had he captured a strategic point that would make Northern politicians agree to peace or convince a European power to side with the Confederacy.

Lee's campaign and battle record surpassed the other Confederate army commanders and rose above the rotating list of commanders at the Army of the Potomac's headquarters. But Lee lacked the logistical infrastructure to fully support his army and his victories. Logistics influences decisions in every war, but the need for food and the need to protect the farms of Virginia had already factored into the general's strategic decisions in the 1862 Maryland Campaign.

Following the Confederate victory at Fredericksburg, Lee faced difficulties

Gen. Robert E. Lee (Confederate) commanded the Army of Northern Virginia and knew the high stakes for a decisive battlefield victory by the spring of 1863. Library of Congress.

—even as the Southern home front sang his praises. The morale of his army stayed strong, but how could he logistically keep his troops together? How could he feed the men and the horses through the cold months and be ready to fight again in the spring campaign? The Army of Northern Virginia totaled a little more than ninety-one thousand soldiers as 1863 dawned, too many for the region of Fredericksburg to support.[15] Lee spent the winter of 1862–63 refining his command structure and shifting troops to strategic areas that could also feed and shelter these portions of his army. Promotions came, elevating officers to fill the vacancies caused by the 1862 battles, and the Confederate artillery was reorganized and assigned.[16] The Confederate cavalry undertook several winter raids and clashed with the emboldened Union cavalry at Kelly's Ford on March 17, 1863.

Keeping many of the cavalry units spread out across central Virginia had the advantages of allowing troops to quickly assemble for raids, covering the outer perimeters of the Confederate lines, and shifting the burden of finding forage for the horses to different counties. Looking for new areas to provide forage for the teams of horses, Lee had ordered his artillery units farther to the rear even before the end of 1862.

Options

To solve the dilemma of supplies and position a significant force to threaten or check Federals massing for a new campaign, Lee had several possible options: send Longstreet's Corps away, send Jackson's Corps into a semi-independent command, or relocate the Army of Northern Virginia. His choice would also signal the trust that he placed in his corps commanders. Whom would he keep close, and whom would he dispatch to another location? Small Union armies situated along the southeastern coast of Virginia in the vicinity of Suffolk and in the northern portion of the Shenandoah Valley were points to watch or confront. Lee needed to send a portion of his army somewhere that was far enough away to relieve the supply situation, strategic in military purpose, and yet close enough for good communications and a relatively quick reunion of the total army.

Option 1: Send Longstreet's Corps Away.

Previously in 1862, Lee had kept Longstreet and his corps close. Most notably, during the march that culminated with the Battle of Second Manassas (August 28–30, 1862), Lee had stayed with Longstreet on the journey from

Lieut. Gen. James Longstreet—known as "Lee's Warhorse"—dependably commanded the First Corps of the Army of Northern Virginia. Library of Congress.

Richmond to Manassas. However, he had dispatched Jackson to begin the campaign and execute long marches that set the stage for the battle. Lee had accepted Longstreet's concept for a defensive line and battle at Fredericksburg. While the two men's working relationship differed from the near mythical partnership of Lee and Jackson, the army commander and his First Corps general had consistently worked well together. Only later, in the post-Gettysburg and postwar eras, would stories of differences or hard feelings arise.

Sending Longstreet to an alternate location would remove nearly twenty thousand experienced combat troops from the Fredericksburg area and basically create a semi-independent command.[17] Longstreet seemed open to the idea and had actually been hinting since October 1862 that his corps could be shifted to the Western Theater or another location. In February 1863, as Union troops gathered near Suffolk, Virginia, Longstreet renewed the idea that he and his corps could be spared from the winter camps on the Rappahannock to pursue another military objective. Their removal to another region would also allow them to gather food and forage in a different region, taking some of the strain off central Virginia. Giving Longstreet a semi-independent command was far from a banishment. Instead, Lee would be fulfilling the Old Warhorse's idea and showing his trust in his corps commander to operate separately.

Option 2: Unleash the Second Corps of the Army of Northern Virginia

In some respects, sending Jackson and his corps into a semi-independent command seemed like the most natural option. Jackson's history of successfully planning and maneuvering on his own while coordinating overall strategy with Lee, stretched back to the 1862 Shenandoah Valley Campaign. Though he underperformed during the Seven Days Battles, Jackson redeemed himself with the bold strike at the Union army, resulting in the Battle of Cedar Mountain, and with his swift responses at Second Manassas and Chantilly. During the 1862 Maryland Campaign, Lee had sent Jackson on long marches with campaign objectives, trusting that he could return to the main army in time for a full-scale battle. Jackson had not disappointed Lee.

Tugging at stoic Stonewall's heartstrings came the stories of Union occupation of the crossroads city of Winchester, in the northern portion of the Shenandoah Valley. The previous winter, Jackson had stayed in that small brick city, befriending many of the inhabitants. It had been the scene of one of his great victories and "liberations" when he recaptured the town on May 25, 1862, during the First Battle of Winchester. Now, in the winter of 1862–63, Union Gen. Robert Milroy and approximately seven thousand troops occupied Winchester and the surrounding region, enforcing emancipation and bringing a harsher form of warfare to coerce the rebellious civilians into loyalty, submission, or at least civility. Returning to the Shenandoah Valley and liberating Winchester would be an option Jackson could appreciate, and it would return a significant Confederate force to the valley region, putting additional pressure on the Federal capital, Washington, DC. Ideally, Jackson could gather food and forage stored on the farms in the rich agricultural region.

Option 3: Relocate the Army of Northern Virginia

Prior to the Battle of Fredericksburg in December 1862, Lee had contemplated setting up a defensive line at the North Anna River, approximately thirty miles closer to Richmond than Fredericksburg.[18] Establishing a winter camp line at the North Anna River would give up a larger swath of Virginia territory to Union control. However, it would also put the Confederate army closer to the capital and to the railroad hubs at Petersburg, Danville, and Lynchburg. A location nearer the railroads could mean a better supply system, and the possibility of temporarily and rotationally relocating divisions by rail into southern Virginia or even North Carolina.

This option did not readily offer an opportunity to threaten a Union force, but it could allow the army to spread out more and reassemble more quickly due to the better transportation options. Strategically, Lee would still hold a strong defensive line north of Richmond and could range his cavalry to the west, protecting his link to the middle Shenandoah Valley. If he launched an offensive campaign in the spring, he could potentially swing part of his army northward through central Virginia or the Shenandoah Valley and aim toward the Federal capital, similar to the maneuver in the Second Manassas Campaign of the previous year.

Decision

Lee accepted Longstreet's request to move away from the Rappahannock camps and confront the gathering Union forces at Suffolk. On February 18, 1863, the orders were issued, and Longstreet had new independent objectives: cover Richmond from attack from the southeast, gather forage and food, remain in contact with and support of Lee, and capture the Union troops at Suffolk, Virginia.

Results/Impact

On February 25, 1863, Longstreet was appointed to command the Department of Virginia and North Carolina, which encompassed the territory between

Winter snows blanketed the Union and Confederate camps during the early months of 1863. Library of Congress.

Richmond, Virginia, and the Cape Fear River in North Carolina.[19] In theory, by ranging his troops south of Richmond and east toward Suffolk, Longstreet would only be a few days' trip from the rest of the army. Moreover, he would still be in regular communication with Lee, able to reunite with the general should a unified Confederate army be needed to confront Hooker or to launch a spring offensive campaign of its own.

Sending Longstreet to Suffolk divided the Army of Northern Virginia, reducing Lee's available troops to about 60,200. Any choice to divide the army meant that the independent command might be engaged with Union forces and unable to easily return to support Lee against Hooker. However, Lee retained Anderson's and McLaws's Divisions from Longstreet's Corps, and he could stay in constant communication with Longstreet thanks to working telegraph lines. Still, if the Union army swiftly hatched and enacted a plan, Lee could be forced to fight a battle with nearly half of his infantry absent. He ultimately hoped to reunite the army in the spring, when the pastures and fields had enough grass to feed the thousands of horses and mules, thereby reducing the need for railroad-transported food.

On March 4, 1863, Walter H. Taylor wrote to his sweetheart, giving a glimpse of the attitudes at Lee's headquarters. As he pointed out, the officers knew that another campaign loomed, and Longstreet had already departed: "Mr. F. J. Hooker is quiet. In a few weeks now we will be again active—and, though I dread the awful consequences of battle, I dare say it will be well for us when it comes."[20]

Hooker Determines His Offensive Strategy

Situation

Capt. Henry L. Abbott of the Twentieth Massachusetts rushed back to his regiment from furlough, anxious not to miss the spring campaign. He arrived in time and explained the situation to his father on April 20, 1863: "We found it [the army] stationary still. The rebels know as well as you at home that we are under marching orders with eight days' rations. The roads of course are a subterfuge, & as I can hardly suspect Hooker of the same stupidity as Burnside, I think the thing must be purposedly let out to play some game."[21]

Abbott numbered among the soldiers who had enjoyed furloughs, improved food, and rising morale in the winter camps in Stafford County, Virginia, since Maj. Gen. Joseph Hooker had been placed in command. As the spring air warmed and the worst of the seasonal rains passed, Hooker faced the challenge of forming his campaign plan and turning his bold words to the politicians into victorious actions. In addition to reorganizing and reinspiring the Army of the Potomac, Hooker filled the command vacancies, and his

The cabins of the Thirty-Seventh New York Infantry Regiment exemplify some of the shelters where Union soldiers lived during the early months of 1863. Library of Congress.

army would go into action with new commanders in nineteen brigades, four divisions, and four corps.[22]

Unlike his predecessors, Hooker had spent the early spring employing intelligence gatherers who brought back fairly accurate information, different from the inflated numbers delivered to McClellan the previous spring. Through the work of scouts and spies and observations by the Balloon Corps, Hooker and his staff developed an accurate understanding of the major road networks in central Virginia, the number of troops in Lee's army, and the location of each of the divisional camps across the Rappahannock River. Hooker was aware that Lee faced supply difficulties, and he could use that situation to his advantage. Also, through his spies and by simply keeping up with the Southern newspapers, Hooker knew that Longstreet had been detached from the Army of Northern Virginia and had carried out the Siege of Suffolk during April 1863. These pieces of information would shape the Union commander's decisions for the spring campaign.

Hooker also had a new military power at his disposal: effective Union cavalry. In the early months of 1863, Federal horsemen had been fighting back effectively against Confederate ones. Partly due to increasing skill and good leadership and partly due to Hooker's insistence that these troops do something to curb the bold Confederate winter raids, the Union cavalry could be deployed as a fighting force. Traditionally, cavalry hovered in advance of an army, scouting and screening. However, the Battle of Kelly's Ford (March 17, 1863) and an attempted though aborted raid later in the spring convinced Hooker that he could consider detaching his cavalry and dispatching the men to harass or block the Confederates.

Planning the spring campaign was not entirely up to Gen. Hooker. He had to make sure his plans were approved by the president and secretary of war, and he would need some level of consensus from his corps commanders. Several options could not be considered due to past history and Hooker's own temperament. Returning by river to the Virginia Peninsula and advancing on Richmond to repeat McClellan's 1862 attempt was a no go. Staying in the winter camps, which covered the main approach to Washington, DC, and waiting for Lee to make a move also did not fit with Hooker's plans; doing so would have handed the military initiative to Lee from the beginning.

One of the biggest obstacles to Hooker lay in front of his army: the Rappahannock River. To attack or maneuver against Lee's force, Hooker had to get his troops across this body of water. The river narrowed farther upstream and widened below Fredericksburg. Fording places existed upstream, but the farther in that direction a military force went, the more likely it was to have to cross the Rappahannock and Rapidan Rivers on its route south or east. More river crossings meant more pontoon bridges.

Maj. Gen. Joseph Hooker promised an energetic campaign with the reinvigorated Army of the Potomac. Library of Congress.

As Hooker contemplated his options, the reality that his army could be separated by miles of territory and riverbank presented communication challenges. Hooker thus turned to innovative solutions. First, the Balloon Corps might be able to assist with observation. Second, telegraph wire could be run along the northern side of the riverbank and connected to the portions of the army crossing the river at different points. In theory, the high-view observations and quick telegraph communication could give Hooker and the Army of the Potomac a technological edge as they marched to battle.

To win decisively, Hooker needed to either force Lee to retreat and give up strategic ground or outmaneuver Lee and spring a surprise attack on the Confederate capital, Richmond. Lee had reduced his fighting force by nearly twenty thousand troops when he sent Longstreet south, but the rebel commander still held a solid position. Spread out along the Rappahannock River and with Confederate cavalry ranging to Culpeper and beyond, Lee's camps centered around the formidable high ground that had created a position of slaughter for the Union army during the Battle of Fredericksburg. Hooker did not want to repeat that disaster. Lee's position also easily covered the overland advances on Richmond, and he could shift his army if Hooker tried a wide flanking movement.

Hooker needed to devise a strategy that got his army to the south side of the Rappahannock River, ideally without battling during the crossing. Then, he had options: force Lee to battle, or pin Lee in place and turn on Richmond.

Hooker outnumbered Lee with nearly 134,000 men, and on paper the odds rested in his favor.

Options

With his superior numbers, improved intelligence, technological innovations, and emboldened cavalry, Hooker could choose from several alternatives as he planned a military offensive for his spring campaign. He could move the army downstream to cross below Fredericksburg, or he could move upstream to cross and attempt to march toward the Confederate rear. A final possibility was to divide his army and attempt to pin his enemy and force a battle. Hooker's choice would set the course for his troops and ideally bring the decisive Union victory needed in the Eastern Theater. Where he crossed the Rappahannock River would be the first important part of his decision. Then Hooker would have to decide whether his object was to fight Lee or to simply hold Lee and outmarch him to Richmond.

Option 1: Move the Union Army Downstream on the Rappahannock

One option that Pres. Lincoln initially seemed to favor was moving the Army of the Potomac downstream from Fredericksburg. This called for moving the army along the Rappahannock to a point beyond the Confederate camps on the opposite side, then crossing—ideally, unopposed—at a wide point of the river. With heavy artillery to cover the crossing, and possibly even with support from Union gunboats navigating the river below Fredericksburg, the Confederates could be held at bay, hopefully avoiding a repeat of the December disasters. Once across, the Union army could march on the Confederates' position and take the high ground in the flank or strike at the limited railroad lines supplying Lee's army. Cutting the railroad lines could put Hooker in the position to battle on ground of his choosing or make a dash toward Richmond.[23]

Several drawbacks presented themselves with this possibility. First, moving downstream would open the Union army's supply base at Aquia Landing to raiding—something that the active Confederate cavalry would likely discover and take advantage of. Second, shifting the army that far south along the Rappahannock peninsula would start to uncover Washington, DC, making it vulnerable to a Confederate attack. The defenses of Washington would protect the capital. But they would not do so indefinitely, and not if Lee decided to strike north and leave his own capital undefended for the sake of a decisive blow to Northern morale.

The downstream option presented intriguing opportunities to quickly cut

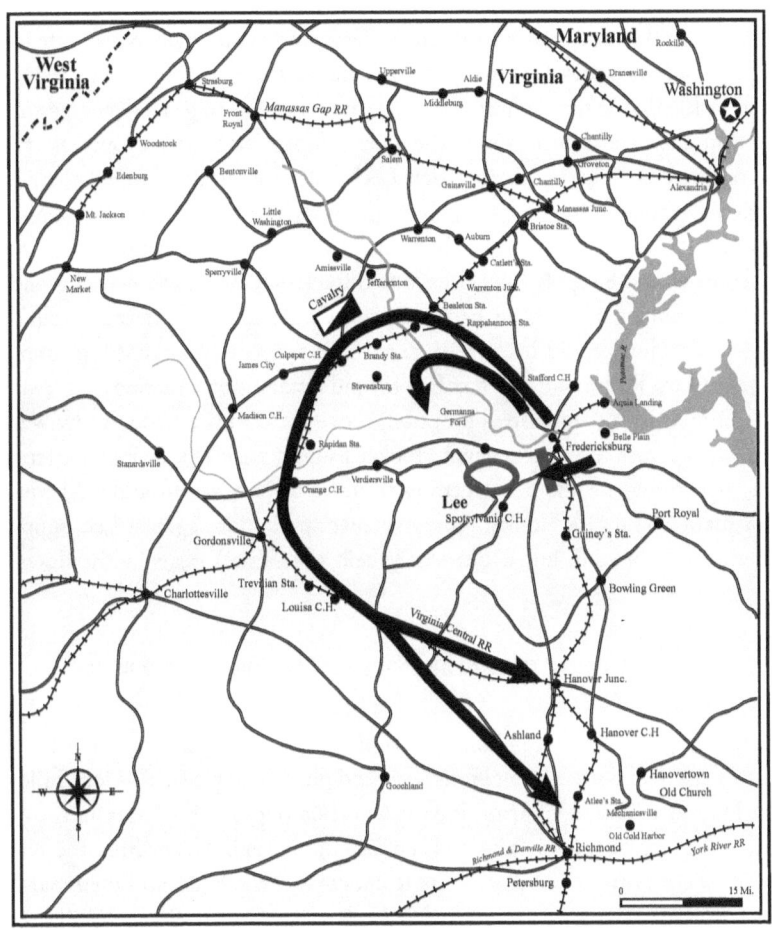

Hooker's Campaign

Lee's supply lines and threaten Richmond, but would these be worth the risk of making the Federal capital vulnerable or jeopardizing the Army of the Potomac's supply base?

Option 2: Move the Union Army Upstream on the Rappahannock

Places like Kelly's Ford offered good crossing locations and were conducive to pontoon bridges. Moving the Federals upstream and crossing the Rappahannock would put distance between the Union army and the Confederate infantry. Union cavalry could advance first and establish a cleared zone, reducing the likelihood that infantry would fight infantry during the river crossing.

Once on the south side of the river, Hooker had several options. He could turn east and try to approach Lee's rear, forcing the Confederates to fight on ground of his choosing. He could swing the army south, threatening Gordonsville, a major railroad hub, and then turn east toward Richmond to threaten more supply lines. Lee would likely fall back toward Richmond, possibly forcing Hooker to battle on the Confederates' preferred ground. However, Hooker and his cavalry could also concentrate on cutting supply lines toward Richmond and box Lee toward a starvation situation.

Similar to the downstream option, moving the entire Union army west and then across the river opened Hooker's supply base to attack and offered an opportunity for the Confederates to move toward Washington. Moving upstream would give Hooker more maneuvering options against Lee, supply lines, or Richmond, but it ultimately held the same threats as the downstream plan.

Option 3: The Union Army Divides to Attack Lee on Two Fronts and Threatens Richmond

A third option was a combination of plans and concepts to get the army across the river with minimal resistance and pin Lee in place. This idea called for Hooker to divide his army, leaving a portion opposite Fredericksburg and then crossing in that vicinity to keep Lee's attention. Meanwhile, the majority of the army would march upstream, cross at the fords, and then march east on the major roads to approach Lee's army from the rear. While the infantry completed these deceptions and marches, the cavalry would take a sweeping route toward Richmond with orders to destroy the railroad tracks that provided vital supplies and possible reinforcements to Lee's army. Union Brig. Gen. George Stoneman had already attempted a raid toward Richmond with ten thousand cavalry in mid-April, but he had been turned back by poor weather.

This ambitious plan had risks. At times, more than twenty miles would separate the portions of the Union army, forcing soldiers to rely on the communication and observation innovations. The timing of the diversions, crossings, and marches would have to be carefully coordinated, and there would be little room for changes. The concept of sending the cavalry to destroy the railroad and threaten Richmond looked excellent on paper as a final component for Lee's discomfiture. Even so, it would deprive Hooker of much-needed scouting and real-time intelligence that cavalry traditionally provided to a marching force.

Decision

Hooker chose the third option: to divide his army, threaten Lee on two fronts, and strike at his supply lines. He put much faith in his cavalry raid, anticipating that Lee would fall back as soon as his logistics were threatened and before fully realizing that the Union army was divided. On April 19, 1863, Pres. Lincoln and Secretary of War Stanton heard and agreed to Hooker's plan.

In the final stages of preparing for the spring campaign, Hooker ordered Gen. John Sedgwick of the Sixth Corps to demonstrate at Fredericksburg with forty thousand men and eventually cross the river to threaten Lee's front. Meanwhile, Hooker and the other corps would complete the double envelopment: forty-two thousand soldiers from the Fifth, Eleventh, and Twelfth Corps would cross the Rappahannock River upstream at Kelly's Ford, while ten thousand men from the Second Corps would cross at United States Ford. The infantry would head east, crossing the Rapidan River, pressing through seventy square acres of land known as the Wilderness, and threatening Lee's rear. At the same time, Gen. George Stoneman would take his cavalry strike force toward the railroad and Richmond.

Results/Impact

The results of Hooker's decision for his offensive military strategy set the stage for the Battle of Chancellorsville and put Lee in the reactionary position for the opening movements of the campaign. The initiative rested with the Union army.

However, Hooker's complicated plan lay open to difficulties, as he placed the river and miles of land between the two portions of his infantry army. The distance and the lack of cavalry to guide and screen the infantry would severely limit Hooker's ability to coordinate attacks and keep Lee on the defensive. The cavalry raid toward Richmond and the Confederate railroad would not be as effective as Hooker anticipated and, in hindsight, it might have been better to keep most of the cavalry operating with the infantry forces.

A couple of weeks after his anticipation of the spring plans, Henry Abbott reflected on Hooker's decisions for the Army of the Potomac with dissatisfaction. The young officer would complain, "What appeared to be an error in dividing the army into halves has really turned out so & not to be strategy, as everyone had to think at first."[24] Before the marches and crossings began, there was uncertainty within the ranks about Hooker's grand plan. Those misgivings would prove true, as Lee once again read the situation and reacted with unpredictable boldness.

The three critical decisions in the weeks leading to the Chancellorsville Campaign—Hooker's appointment to command, Longstreet's temporary departure from the Army of Northern Virginia, and Hooker's offensive strategy—laid the groundwork for the battle that would unfold in the first week of May 1863.

CHAPTER 2

THE BATTLE BEGINS

MAY 1, 1863

With a new commander taking the campaign field for the first time, the Union's Army of the Potomac prepared to battle the Confederate Army of Northern Virginia, which had already been forced to divide its strength due to logistics. Maj. Gen. Hooker had planned an offensive campaign to put pressure on Gen. Lee and force him to fight or retreat.

The military plans started to unfold at the end of April 1863, and the first large-scale clash of the campaign took place on May 1, as the Union army's vanguard units tried to leave the Virginia Wilderness. Three critical decisions were made on this day. These decisions made the passive Confederates the aggressor in their tactics, forced the Union to give up military advantage of terrain and initiative, and divided the Confederate army for a risky flank attack.

Lee Decides to Turn and Fight

Situation

"That sounds as though something stirring were on foot," Lieut. Gen. Thomas Jonathan "Stonewall" Jackson remarked to his wife while preparing to follow the military summons that had disturbed their early morning hours.[1] Soon, the Confederate commander of the Second Corps of the Army of Northern

Lieut. Gen. Thomas J. Jackson—nicknamed "Stonewall"—commanded the Second Corps of the Army of Northern Virginia. National Archives.

Virginia learned that the Yankees were crossing the Rappahannock at multiple points. With the arrival of that news, Jackson realized that the anticipated spring campaign had begun with a Union offensive, and he needed to send his beloved wife and baby girl farther south to safety. Jackson had enjoyed ten days of active fatherhood as his family visited him at the Yerby plantation in the last days of April 1863. Now, military necessity loomed, and like thousands of other soldiers, Jackson would have to prepare for the coming battle.

By the time Jackson arrived at his headquarters and later consulted with Gen. Robert E. Lee, the conundrum was emerging to their view. Where was Hooker's main attack heading? Where should they place the bulk of their army to counter Hooker's offensive? The Confederate generals considered the information received on the previous day. They knew that on April 28 two pontoon bridges had been laid just south of Fredericksburg on the Rappahannock, and Union troops had begun to cross.[2] The new morning messages sent from the west informed them that Union troops had started crossing the Rappahannock at Kelly's Ford.

Throughout April 29, reports still confirmed Union crossings and activity along the Rappahannock River south of Fredericksburg, but other reports from Confederate cavalry general J. E. B. Stuart told Lee and Jackson that their enemy also maneuvered farther to the west. The troops crossing at Kelly's Ford had started marching east and crossed the Rapidan River at Germanna Ford. Simultaneously, another Union force crossed the Rappahannock River

May 1, 1863

at Ely's Ford. The two columns seemed to be converging to meet near the Chancellorsville Crossroads and heading toward Fredericksburg to threaten the Confederate rear.[3] Meanwhile, Jackson sent orders to his corps to prepare. Lee would have to decide where the main threat was aimed, but when that had been determined, Jackson planned to move quickly.

The main Confederate army waited for Lee's orders to deploy, but the general positioned some of his infantry to fight delaying skirmishes and keep him informed. During the evening of April 29, Lee ordered Maj. Gen. Richard Anderson to pull the remainder of his division from United States Ford (just above Fredericksburg) and march west to observe, delay, and report on the Union advance. Anderson would meet with two of his brigade commanders—Brig. Gens. Mahone and Posey—whose troops had already fallen back from other posts along the river and congregated near the Chancellorsville Crossroads.[4]

As night fell on April 29, the expectancy of coming battle strained Jackson's Corps. Jedidiah Hotchkiss, chief topographical engineer on Stonewall's staff, penned a few lines to his wife, Sarah, foreshadowing the battle: "Tomorrow, O! tomorrow, Death will hold high carnival."[5] The tragic carnival was delayed yet another day, but by April 30, Union movements gave Lee more clues to make his deployment decisions. Maj. Gen. Anderson retreated approximately three miles to a piece of high ground:

Maj. Gen. Richard H. Anderson commanded one of the divisions of the Confederate First Corps and remained with Lee in central Virginia. His troops were among the first to engage advancing Union brigades in the Chancellorsville Campaign. Public domain.

Zoan Church Ridge. Here, he positioned his brigades to cover the Orange Turnpike, leading to Fredericksburg, and Mine Road, meeting the turnpike from the north.[6] His division prepared to confront two-thirds of the Union army converging at the Chancellorsville Crossroads and fanning out to create a line advancing east.

Skirmishing and sounds of fighting drifted back to Lee, Jackson, and the Confederate Second Corps. Along the Rappahannock to their immediate front, the Union elements commanded by Maj. Gen. John Sedgwick waited quietly. Suddenly, a commotion rippled through Jackson's Corps. A Confederate captain later remembered events: "As we listened to the cannonade great commotion could be seen in our neighboring camps—couriers riding rapidly in every direction. One soon pays his respects to us with orders to be ready to move at a moment's warning. Blankets are soon rolled, swords buckled on, haversacks filled with uncooked rations, rifles in hand we take our position to await the inevitable order which is quickly received to march."[7]

Lee would decide whether to send, keep, or divide Jackson's Corps and set the stage for the battle. Hooker wanted to force Lee to react, and now that time had come.

Options

After evaluating the situation for nearly two days to ideally avoid a premature movement, Lee prepared to make his choice and his major opening move of the spring campaign. Hooker had started the game of war with an offensive move, and Lee readied to block with a defensive one. He had three options, including several ways that could quickly turn a defense into an offense if the Union actions allowed. Lee could watch and attack Sedgwick's command in front of him along the Rappahannock River. Alternatively, he could start a major retreat of all his forces in central Virginia and set up a defensive line farther south. Finally, he could send Jackson's Corps west to fight the Union troops advancing from that direction.

Option 1: Attack Sedgwick's Command

Maj. Gen. John Sedgwick paraded approximately forty thousand Union troops under Lee's and Jackson's noses after crossing the Rappahannock River about one mile below Fredericksburg. The Confederates eyed the situation through their field glasses and waited. Memories of the Battle of Fredericksburg lingered in the minds of both Federals and rebels. The Confederates still held the high ground over the sloping plain that had been killing fields during the December 1862 battle. Time passed, and Sedgwick's force seemed more interested in demonstrating than attacking.

Stonewall Jackson proposed a Confederate offensive to push the Union troops back across the river. Lee gave Jackson permission to send scouts and investigate this potential situation on April 29. Any Confederate attack would come under fire from the Union artillery batteries still positioned across the river on Stafford Heights. An assault would commit all or at least a large portion of Jackson's Corps, leaving a limited reserve to counter the Union movement from the west. If Sedgwick put up prolonged resistance, this fight could allow Hooker to close quickly on the Confederate rear.

By the end of April 29, Jackson's initial enthusiasm for fighting Sedgwick had begun to fade.[8] The option still lay on the table. If Lee moved all or the bulk of his army to the west, he risked leaving Sedgwick's force in his rear, unfought and still on the south side of the river. Lee had known John Sedgwick in the United States Army before the Civil War, and he did not credit him with quick or bold movements. This knowledge of Sedgwick's character factored into Lee's decision. If he chose to not take the bait for a fight, Lee strongly believed that Sedgwick could be evaded.

Option 2: Turn West and Fight Hooker

Lee considered another option: ignore Sedgwick and send Jackson's Corps toward the west. By the night of April 30, four Union corps—approximately seventy thousand men—had moved into the Virginia Wilderness and formed advancing columns facing east or in reserve to support the advance. A six-mile front of Union troops readied to emerge from the dense woods and limiting plank roads, bursting into the open ground. Between them and Fredericksburg sat Anderson's Division and most of McLaws's Division reinforcing along Zoan Church Ridge.

If Jackson's Corps headed west, the Confederates could fight defensively along the ridge, blocking the main roads toward Fredericksburg. Hooker's ability to swing south would be limited by the dense terrain, and Lee would still hold the advantage of interior lines, allowing him to move troops to meet threats. The danger of leaving Sedgwick's force unopposed or only with a small Confederate force in position might be mitigated if that Union commander acted with the deliberateness and precision that Lee remembered from past years. If the Confederates could either draw Hooker into a quick battle or find an opportunity for their own offensive strike, they could potentially neutralize the threat from the west, leaving Sedgwick to be dealt with later or to simply retreat across the river.

Hooker had the bulk of the Army of the Potomac on his roundabout march. He was the commander, and he had been boasting about his spring successes. The movement across the upstream fords and through the Virginia

Wilderness looked like the more potent threat. Lee did not have much respect for Hooker or his abilities, but he suspected that "Fighting Joe" might move with greater speed than "Uncle John" Sedgwick.

Option 3: Fall Back and Set Up a Defensive Line

The reports of the Union movements near Fredericksburg and from the west looked like an offensive double envelopment as they developed on the maps. Hooker was trying to trap Lee's force. A third option differed from choosing which Union element to fight: Lee could retreat.

Falling back from the vicinity of Fredericksburg and pulling the few infantry brigades and the cavalry from the Wilderness region could allow Lee to consolidate his force and prepare for battle on ground of his choosing. If Hooker used the few major roads within the Wilderness to pursue Lee's retreating army south, Lee could potentially set up a strike or trap to meet Hooker's men as they emerged from the tangled woods, perhaps near Spotsylvania Court House. Or Lee could retreat farther toward the North Anna River and set up a strong defensive line there.

With thousands of troops still absent from the Army of Northern Virginia in Longstreet's Suffolk excursion, Lee was outnumbered. If he retreated along the railroad line, he might be closer to reuniting his army if Longstreet headed north to a new position above Richmond. Withdrawing from the trap that Hooker seemed to be creating could allow Lee to reposition, reunite his army, and foil the Union plans. He could slip south and prepare for a large battle on satisfactory ground. With luck, the movement might disconcert and delay Hooker, which could allow Longstreet to quickly rejoin Lee. A reunited Confederate army could either fight a major defensive battle, or it could divide and maneuver similar to the Second Manassas Campaign of the previous summer.

Decision

Lee decided to turn and fight Hooker. He would wait to deal with Sedgwick later in the campaign. However, Lee decided to leave Maj. Gen. Jubal Early's division of Jackson's Corps and a brigade from McLaws's Division (Barksdale's Brigade)[9] in the defensive lines near Fredericksburg. These troops were to watch Sedgwick and act as a warning barrier in case that general decided to fight or try to advance to join Hooker in the west.

Results/Impact

With this decision to divide his forces and send the majority west to fight Hooker as he advanced out of the Wilderness, Lee kept interior lines for his

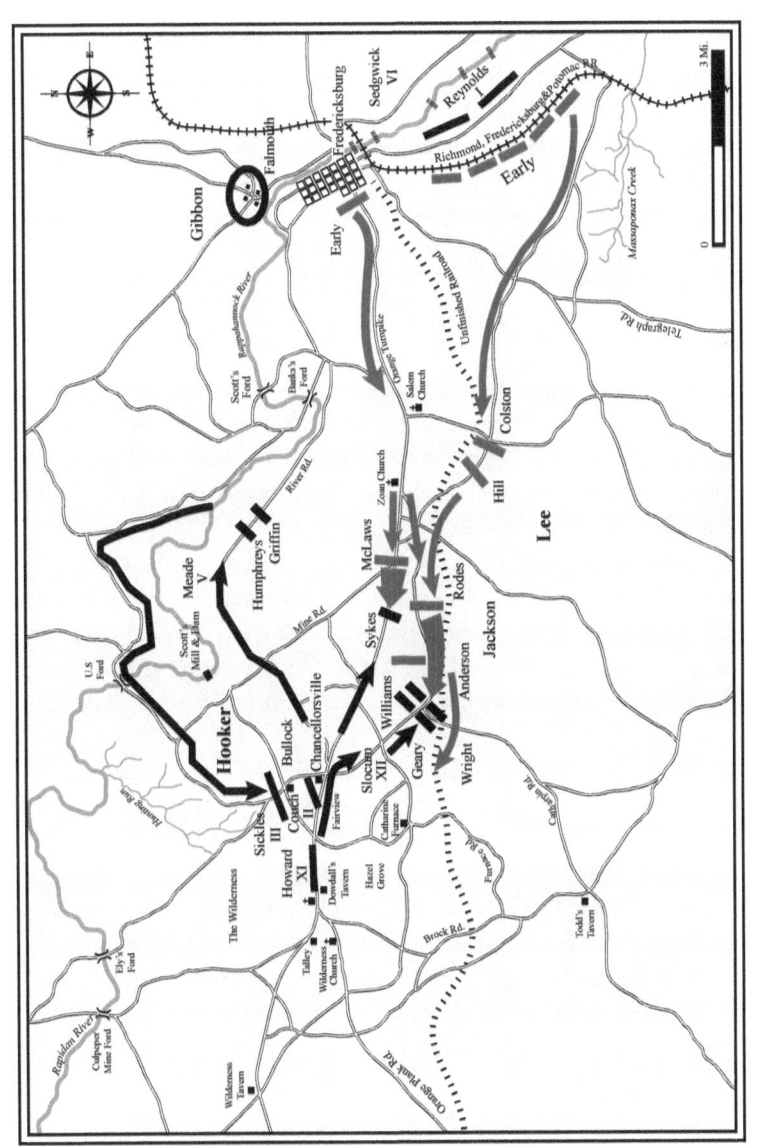

Confederates Turn and Fight

army and put confronting troops in front of both Union elements. He would put the fighting pressure on the Union corps with Hooker and simply watch and hold Sedgwick in place.

Lee issued orders for McLaws's Division (minus Barksdale's Brigade) and Jackson's Corps (minus Early's Division) to march west.[10] Not only did Lee plan to send the bulk of his fighting force toward Hooker, he would also send Jackson to take command of the field from Maj. Gen. Anderson. Lee trusted Jackson to read the battlefield and take appropriate measures for the fight. If there had to be a Confederate defense along Zoan Church Ridge, Jackson could make that decision. However, if there was any hesitation from Hooker's corps or any advantage to exploit for the Confederates to take the offensive, Jackson would seize that.

The orders to head west prompted a night march for Jackson's Corps. William Calder, a soldier in the Second North Carolina Infantry, remembered, "We had no idea where we were going. A soldier never knows where he is going, nor what he is going to do, until the moment for action comes. They have only to trust in their commanders. . . . On we went through mud and over stumps, stumbling about in the dark, to the great danger of our heads and shins."[11]

As a cloudy daylight broke on May 1, 1863, Jackson's rebels realized they marched to the west. Some, like Calder, glimpsed Stonewall as he rode along the gray column to follow through on Lee's decision: "The old hero came dashing by his horse at full speed, and hat in hand, followed by a single courier. He cast his eyes from one side of the road to the other, his head working, as if it were on wires."[12]

Jackson reached Zoan Church Ridge a little after 8:00 a.m. and found Gen. Anderson's men digging trenches on the high ground.[13] Assessing the situation, Jackson ordered the entrenching to halt.[14] He did not fault Anderson for the defensive plan. However, Jackson knew he was bringing forty thousand more troops to the field, and he saw an opportunity to fight back as Hooker's men tried to leave the Wilderness. Lee's decision to turn to the west and send Jackson to take senior command of the unfolding battlefield would shake Hooker's plans, forcing that Union general to rethink everything he had previously arranged.

Hooker Pulls Back

Situation

In the ranks of the Seventeenth United States Infantry, Lieut. Stanley Abbot faced his first battle. The twenty-one-year-old had longed to be a soldier, and he went against his family's wishes to join the US Regulars. A few weeks earlier Abbot had written in his diary, "The time approaches when I shall be able to know of what stuff I am made. At present I am in a curious state of doubt whether I am a hero or a coward."[15] Brig. Gen. Sykes's division deployed in line of battle on May 1, 1863, advancing against the Confederates who had hurried west from Fredericksburg to confront the lead elements of the Union army. By the end of the day, Abbot knew his character had stood the test of battle, but the Union generals and decision-makers would be in a "curious state of doubt" regarding their next actions.

May 1, 1863, dawned with morning fog and clouds obscuring the view. As intelligence officers tried to discover whether the Confederates stayed near the city or moved west, aerial observations from Thaddeus Lowe's Balloon Corps had limited results. In the Union marching columns, enthusiasm still surged. Both the encircling movement toward the west and the river crossing had proceeded smoothly in the previous days.

The Fifth Corps, Eleventh Corps, and Twelfth Corps had started their march west on April 27 and 28. These three corps, totaling approximately forty-two thousand men, crossed Kelly's Ford on the Rappahannock River on pontoon boats and then turned south and east. They crossed the Rapidan River at Germanna and Ely's Fords and marched along converging roads into the Virginia Wilderness, rendezvousing at the Chancellorsville Crossroads on April 30. Meanwhile, two divisions of the Second Corps (approximately ten thousand men) crossed the Rappahannock at United States Ford and also headed toward the crossroads. The Union Third Corps and the remaining division of the Second Corps had waited in their camps on the north side of the Rappahannock, staged between Sedgwick moving on Fredericksburg and Hooker arriving at Chancellorsville. Pleased with his strategys' progress and the lack of significant Confederate resistance, Hooker summoned the Third Corps on the night of April 30–May 1 to cross at United States Ford and join the troops near Chancellorsville. By morning, Hooker had approximately seventy thousand soldiers around or within marching distance of the crossroads in the Virginia Wilderness. He rested his army and prepared to leave the tangled acres of dense woods on May 1.

Lead units of the Union army had started arriving at the Chancellorsville Crossroads around noon on April 30. Generals congratulated one another, and arriving soldiers cheered while bands played. The Union army was on campaign and had successfully moved to trap the Confederates or force them to turn and fight. A march of approximately three and a half miles farther east would allow Union units to secure some open farm fields and reach Zoan Church Ridge, which marked the border of the Wilderness. However, Hooker kept the divisions stacking around Chancellorsville.

This painting created after the Civil War depicts the large house at the Chancellorsville Crossroads; Hooker established his headquarters here for most of the battle days. Library of Congress.

He issued a congratulatory order to his soldiers and settled in for the night, encouraged by the enthusiasm and high morale in his army. Hooker's statement read, in part: "It is with heartfelt satisfaction the commanding general announces to the army that the operations of the last three days have determined that our enemy must either ingloriously fly, or come out from behind his defenses and give us battle on our own ground, where certain destruction awaits him. The operations of the Fifth, Eleventh, and Twelfth Corps have been a succession of splendid achievements."[16] In the darkness, a few corps and division commanders shook their heads, puzzled at the delay in the dense woods.

By morning on May 1, 1863, Confederates strengthened a defensive line along the high ground at Zoan Church Ridge. Then, Lieut. Gen. Stonewall Jackson arrived with reinforcements and prepared to fight offensively to halt or delay the Union advance.

The Union troops seeking to leave the Wilderness region that day stretched across a six-mile front, though not a continuous battle line. Parallel roads assisted with the forward movement. Part of the Fifth Corps headed north and east along the River Road, and this element was the most separated along the advancing front. From the Chancellorsville Crossroads, the Orange Turnpike headed directly east, and soldiers from the Fifth Corps pressed forward along this route too, following the road that led directly toward Zoan Church Ridge. The Orange Plank Road swung south of the Orange Turnpike and ran

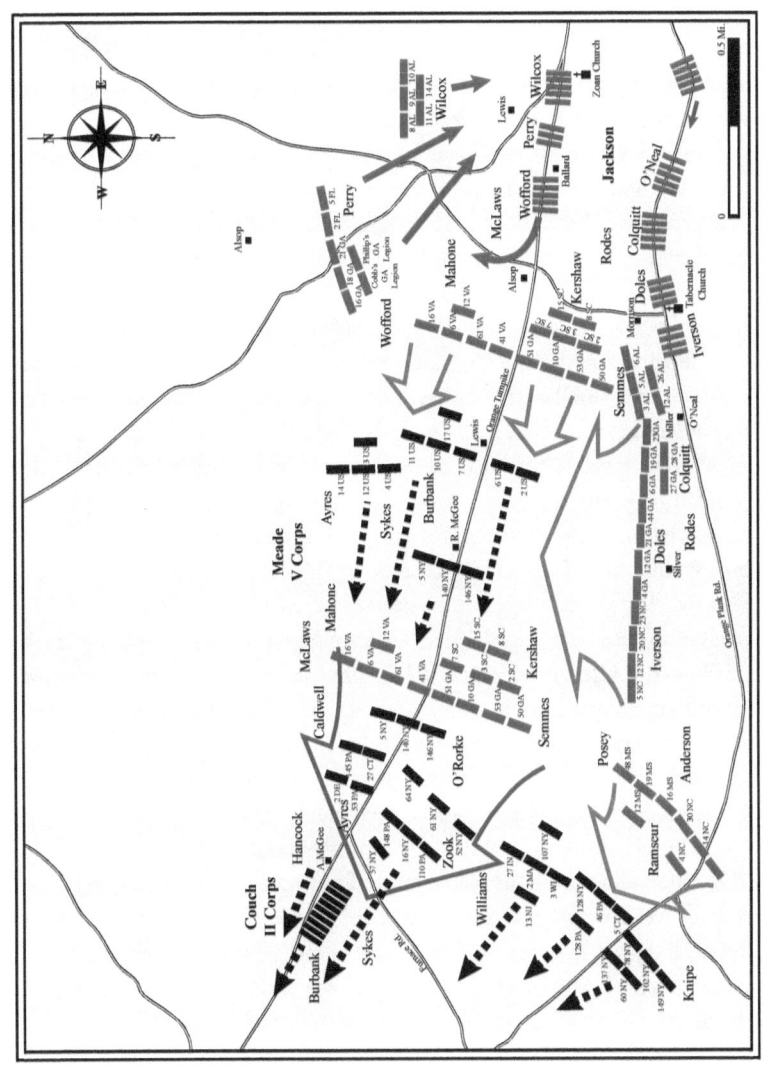

May 1, 1863

parallel to it, providing a good alternate route to move troops. Divisions of the Twelfth Corps headed out along Orange Plank Road.[17]

The Fifth Corps' and Twelfth Corps' brigades ran into Jackson's advancing Confederates. Along the Orange Turnpike, Anderson's Division deployed, and brigades clashed with Union cavalry from the Eighth Pennsylvania. The cavalrymen fought a delaying action, allowing Union infantry to charge into the farm fields. Here, a brigade of United States Regulars rushed into the fight. Stanley Abbot later wrote about a Confederate soldier he encountered during the fighting, reporting the rebel saying "that he knew we were regulars because we deployed by regt. And double quicked straight at them, giving them no time to [aim] their artillery with effect. The volunteers, he said, 'creep up. You ran.'"[18] Farther south along the Orange Plank Road, separated by nearly a mile of rough terrain at the farthest point from the turnpike, McLaws's Division tangled with the Twelfth Corps. Confederate cavalry commanded by Maj. Gen. J. E. B. Stuart came into position, covering Jackson's left flank and ensuring that no surprises came from that direction.

Though the Confederates opposed the Union advance, Hooker's men still had numerical advantage and, particularly along the Orange Turnpike, topographical advantage. A series of rising ridges culminating at McGee Ridge gave the Union infantry the benefit of high ground. Soldiers from the Second Corps arrived to reinforce the Fifth Corps, and the generals on the field had hopes of victory or at least a "fair fight."

Meanwhile, Hooker sat at his newly established headquarters in the Chancellor House. (Though called Chancellorsville, the dwelling at the Chancellorsville Crossroad was one large house, owned by the Chancellor family and used as an inn for many previous years.) Messages flew along the temporary telegraph lines on the Stafford side of the river, carrying reports from the observation balloons that ascended as the day's weather improved.[19] Some messages carried the rumor that elements of Longstreet's command were returning,[20] and Hooker started to worry about his divided force.[21] He relied on reports and did not ride out to the fighting lines, according to known primary sources. A commanding general's place is at headquarters and not on a skirmish line, but Hooker could have gone and viewed the fighting or ridden closer to the battle lines to understand the situation before making his next decision. Instead, he stayed at headquarters and blindly faced a choice about the direction of the battle.

Options

Maj. Gen. Joseph Hooker had three options on the afternoon of May 1, 1863. His advancing columns were fighting Confederates, and the outcome looked uncertain. The Twelfth Corps along the Orange Plank Road held its own. The Fifth Corps along the Orange Turnpike had been forced back and took up a strong defensive position on high ground, with reinforcements from that corps and from the Second Corps arriving to strengthen the soldiers' line.

Hooker's enemy had decided to turn and fight. Now, Hooker had to choose his next move. Three main options held possibilities and disadvantages. First, Hooker could continue the fight and push toward Fredericksburg, carrying out his original campaign plan. Second, he could hold the ground already obtained and order Sedgwick to advance from his inactive position south of Fredericksburg. Third, Hooker could wait and form a defensive line, letting the Confederates batter themselves against artillery and earthworks.

Option 1: Fight and Continue Advancing toward Fredericksburg

Although the Confederates had pushed back the Union lines, Hooker had plenty of troops who had not yet engaged in combat during this campaign. The Second Corps had already started sending units to reinforce the Fifth Corps. The Eleventh Corps sat in reserve, and the Third Corps was en route to join the rest of the troops near Chancellorsville.

Hooker's plans called for a quick advance to place his army in the rear of the Confederates near Fredericksburg. He had already delayed inexplicably on April 30, allowing the lead elements to pause for half a day and spend the night near the Chancellorsville Crossroads instead of immediately pressing farther east and getting out of the forested region. Confederate reinforcements had arrived to oppose the advance on May 1, but Hooker could choose to follow the original plan. Putting more Union troops into the battle lines and ordering an advance toward Fredericksburg would allow Hooker to keep the initial scheme, using more of his available force to carry it out.

Option 2: Fight on the Ground Already Obtained and Order
Sedgwick to Advance

Perhaps worried about the number of Confederates opposing him or being drawn into a trap, Hooker could bring General Sedgewick into a more active role. Sedgwick had already crossed the Rappahannock River south of Fredericksburg, and his troops served as a distraction. Knowing that the Confederates had turned to fight, Hooker could order the corps with him to engage and hold its current fighting lines. Meanwhile, he could order Sedgwick to advance. Placed in a vise, Lee would either fight divided, battle on two sides, or try to slip out of the trap.

This option had the disadvantage of taking more time to send the message to Sedgwick and wait for his action to begin. But the concept would advantageously keep the offensive and action with Hooker and the Union army, and Lee and the Confederates would still be forced to react.

Option 3: Stop and Create a Defensive Line

A third option would be to put aside the original plan to advance and to create a defensive line instead. Hooker had enough troops to create a strong defensive position. Memories of the Confederates' defensive positions at Antietam in September 1862 and Fredericksburg in December 1862 still lingered in the minds of Union soldiers and commanders; as Hooker had been present at both battles, perhaps they affected his memory, too. Creating a defensive line with artillery and infantry could force Lee to charge his army to destruction while the Union troops fought somewhat protected.

While there are advantages to a strong defensive position and forcing an enemy to attack it, this option had two distinct disadvantages. First, setting up a defensive position in the Union's current location meant staying in the Wilderness region, where the dense forest would severely limit visibility, mobility, and operations. Second, setting up a defensive line and not ordering any other operations handed the initiative to the Confederates and would place the Union army and Sedgwick's detachment into a reactive mode.

Decision

Hooker's options to reinforce and advance according to the original plan, pause and order Sedgwick to move, or halt and set a defensive position came as a result of his troops' positions and the Confederates' determined fighting on May 1. Hooker chose Option 3, to stop and set up a defensive position. However, he went further in the disadvantageous choice: ordering the Fifth Corps, elements of the Second Corps, and the Twelfth Corps to retreat. Falling back deeper into the Wilderness, Hooker ordered these corps to set up a defensive line around the Chancellorsville Crossroads and in the perimeter woods.

Results/Impact

Hooker sent messengers to carry his orders to the fighting generals: disengage from the battle, retreat to the Chancellorsville clearing, and set up a defensive position. The corps and division commanders reacted swiftly and with fury.

Maj. Gen. Henry Slocum, commanding the Twelfth Corps, heard the orders to stop the advance from staff officer Washington A. Roebling. The general called the messenger a liar, saying, "Nobody but a crazy man would

May 1, 1863

Maj. Gen. Henry Slocum (Union) commanded the Twelfth Corps of the Army of the Potomac. Library of Congress.

give such an order when we have victory in sight!" Then Slocum threatened to shoot Roebling if the information proved false.[22] After confirming the order and personally protesting to Hooker, Slocum obeyed and turned his column back into the Wilderness.

On the Fifth Corps' line, Major Generals Sykes and Meade were also upset. Sykes's troops had been fighting well, and he saw they held a strong position. He wanted reinforcements, not a retreat. Meade, along the River Road, had not yet fought Confederates that day and thought it would be better to keep advancing. The Fifth Corps' divisions followed Hooker's orders,

Maj. Gen. George G. Meade (Union) led the Fifth Corps of the Army of the Potomac. Library of Congress.

Maj. Gen. George Sykes (Union) commanded the Second Division of the Fifth Corps during the Battle of Chancellorsville. Library of Congress.

but Meade's recorded grumbling spoke for officers and soldiers: "If we can't hold the top of a hill, we certainly can't hold the bottom of it."[23]

The Second Corps, which had begun deploying troops to reinforce Sykes, experienced confusion. Hooker's chief engineer, Brig. Gen. G. K. Warren, suggested that these troops hold their position. However, Gen. Darius Couch, commanding the Second Corps, decided to obey Hooker's orders and ordered the withdrawal. In a flurry of messages, Hooker seemed to change his mind, perhaps influenced by Warren's firsthand knowledge. It was too late.[24] As soon as the Union line started falling back, the Confederates pressed their advantage.

Despite their anger or confusion, the generals obeyed and sent the orders down their chain of command. The Union troops retreated, and the Confederates followed, gaining valuable high ground along the Orange Turnpike and pushing into the area of Catharine Furnace off the Orange Plank Road.

The Union line encircled the Chancellorsville Crossroads. Facing Fredericksburg and intersecting over the Orange Turnpike, the Second Corps took position, and regiments started digging trenches.[25] The Twelfth Corps faced south, crossing the Orange Plank Road as it turned toward the crossroads. The Third Corps moved into position on the Twelfth's right, pushing from a plantation farm called Fairview toward high ground called Hazel Grove, and blocking that vital place from Confederate control. Out to the west, the Eleventh Corps camped on comparatively open ground along the Orange Turnpike, forming the right flank of the Union's curving line. After the battle, General Hancock—whose division had been reinforcing Sykes—testified calmly about the Federals' actions: "I consider that the position of Chancellorsville was not a good one; it was flat country, and had no local military advantages. . . . For a commander who felt that he was forced to retire, that was the best position and the only one for the time being. But I have no doubt that we ought to have held our advanced position, and still kept pushing on and attempt[ed] to make a junction with General Sedgwick."[26]

The Union army wanted to fight, and the troops that had fought on May 1 had mostly engaged well. From soldiers in the ranks to generals commanding the corps, the Federals puzzled, griped, or fumed about the orders to fall back, especially into the low-visibility woods. Still, the fighters trusted Hooker and believed he had a plan for the battle that would result in victory. They obeyed and settled in to dig earthworks and ready for the next orders.

Hooker seemed satisfied and wrote his belief in a circular order: "The major-general commanding trusts that a suspension in the attack to-day will embolden the enemy to attack him."[27] He repeated that hope in other correspondence. To Gen. Couch, Hooker said, "It is all right. . . . I have got Lee

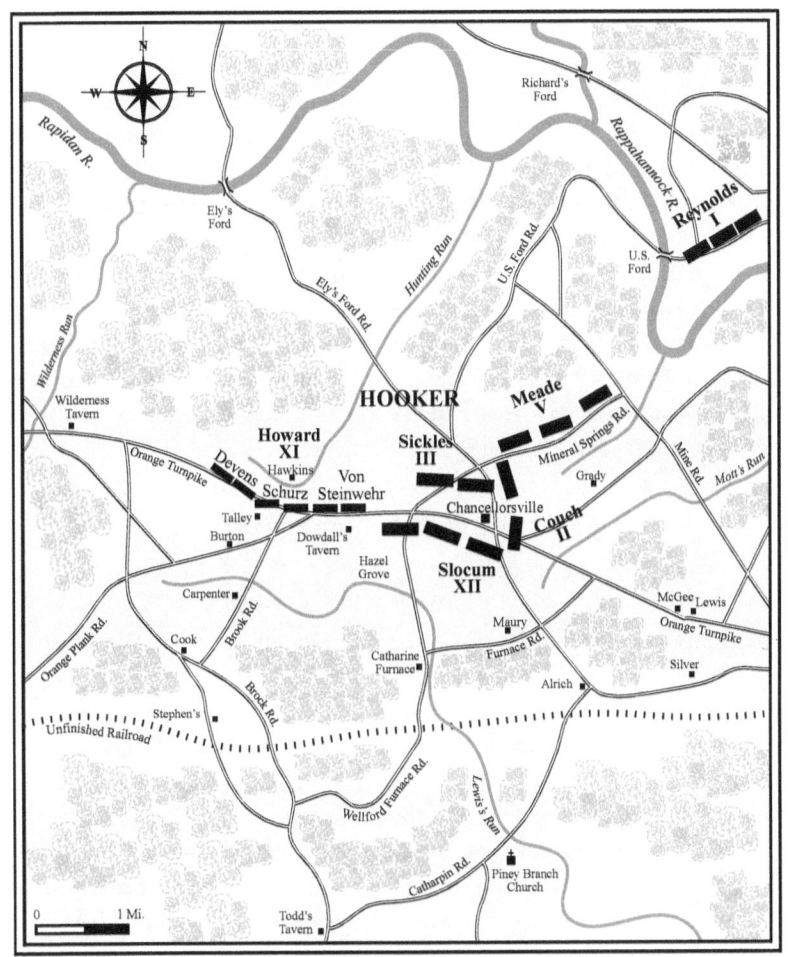

Hooker's Defensive Positions

just where I want him; he must fight me on my own ground."²⁸ Despite his optimism, Hooker had issued his orders and handed the tactical and topographical advantage to the Confederates. He would make more decisions and send more directives during the next days, but he had moved into a reactionary mode. After this critical decision to pull back and set up a defensive position, Hooker would not regain the advantage of the initiative for the duration of the campaign. He would instead be forced to respond to Confederate actions and movements.

In the ranks of Sykes's US Regulars, Lieut. Stanley Abbot had survived his first battle. He stated, "I am well and satisfied that I shall be made strong enough to do my duty faithful. I find it very hard to be brave without allowing evil thoughts of hatred and anger to master me. . . . It drives the devil into my heart to hear those screaming demons rush at us through the smoke!"²⁹ Abbott, like some of the generals, had been angry on May 1, 1863, but they would all face more screeching Confederates before Hooker got out of the Wilderness. Even as the Union soldiers dug trenches and set up the defensive position to fight on Hooker's ground, two Confederate generals pored over maps. The initiative had been handed to them, and a chance to attack lay open on the right side of Hooker's curving line.

Lee Allows Jackson to Initiate a Flank Attack

Situation

Did Hooker really want to fight? Why had he pulled back? Why had he handed the initiative to the Confederates? These questions troubled generals in blue and gray in the night hours of May 1–2, 1863. Hunched near a map illuminated by the flickering firelight, fifty-six-year-old Gen. Robert E. Lee, leader of the Confederate Army of Northern Virginia, pondered his options. His Second Corps commander and the senior battlefield commander for the opening phase of the combat sat nearby. Lieut. Gen. Thomas J. "Stonewall" Jackson wanted an opportunity to strike, but neither general felt confident as to how and where. The sound of arriving horsemen came from the shadows of the temporary headquarters site. Perhaps cavalryman Maj. Gen. J. E. B. Stuart had sent word or brought information that could inform the mighty decision of that night.

Gen. Lee had arrived near the Chancellorsville battle by midday on May 1. His presence on this battlefield signaled his firm belief that Union Gen. Sedgwick would delay near Fredericksburg and the fight would occur on the edge of the Virginia Wilderness. Jackson had already sent the Confederate di-

May 1, 1863

This 1866 photograph shows some of the tangled trees and underbrush of the region known as the Wilderness. The Battle of Chancellorsville (1863) and the Battle of the Wilderness (1864) were both fought in this region of central Virginia. Library of Congress.

visions along the roads, pushing back the Federals, who then surprisingly gave up strong high-ground positions and retreated deeper into the Wilderness and near the Chancellorsville Crossroads. Stuart and his cavalry watched and fought on the Confederate left flank, getting into a brief and intense artillery duel near Catharine Furnace. The old iron furnace sat nearly a mile and a half from the location of the generals' evening council. It offered a potential stepping-stone toward the strengthening Union lines forming around the woods encircling the Chancellorsville clearing and gripping high ground near the Fairview plantation.

While Lee, Jackson, and Stuart were not closely familiar with this part of Virginia, they fought and maneuvered in home-state territory. Small farms dotted clearings in the Wilderness, while more prosperous farms occupied larger tracts of land along some of the major roads. Many of the civilians supported the Confederacy and knew the trail systems that did not appear

Maj. Gen. James Ewell Brown "Jeb" Stuart (Confederate) was a successful and flamboyant cavalry commander. Library of Congress.

on the war maps. The Wilderness region had once been mined for gold and iron, and furnaces still billowed smoke on peaceful days, turning the iron ore into usable pig iron for the Confederate war effort. This longtime industry had shaped the landscape that these armies endured; the early metal smelting had led to the deforestation of the region, followed by the emergence of dense second-growth forest that now tangled across seventy-seven acres and formed the Wilderness. Perhaps roads unknown to the generals and their enemies could provide a tactical route toward a place of attack.

Stuart's arrival united a Confederate leadership triumvirate in one place. Lee, Jackson, and Stuart had been operating together for just less than a year, but they had developed a level of professional trust reflected in their military plans and battles. Each knew his place in the chain of command and operated well: Lee made final decisions. Jackson carried out bold orders—sometimes ones that he proposed—and Lee approved. Stuart gathered information through his cavalrymen or spy network and then directed advance or flank positions. The Second Manassas Campaign, Maryland Campaign, and Loudoun Valley Campaign in 1862 had been the officers' most successful team actions. Chancellorsville offered an unprecedented opportunity, and Stuart had just discovered it.

Joining Lee and Jackson, Stuart explained that the Union's entire right flank lay unprotected west of Chancellorsville. The majority of Hooker's cavalry had been sent on a raid toward Richmond, as decided in his original campaign strategy; now Hooker operated with few scouts and without cavalry pickets to screen his infantry. Jackson watched as Lee traced the movement that would have to be executed to shift infantry to that exposed position. "How can we get at these people?" Lee asked.[30] Stonewall interpreted Lee's question as a willingness to choose a flank attack, but the details would have to be discovered and discussed before the commander would make his final decision.

Jackson summoned staff officers, particularly those who knew the area and knew local civilians. Chaplain Beverly Tucker Lacy offered some insight, then suggested talking with the Wellford family. Jackson sought a secretive route through the Wilderness: a way to conceal thousands of marching troops. With suggestions from Charles Wellford and map sketches by topographical engineer Jedidiah Hotchkiss, Jackson was armed with information to aid Lee's decision.

Jackson's proposal involved marching troops at least ten miles in a winding route that avoided the main roads until clear of the Union army. Seemingly satisfied with the information about the proposed route and the concept of the flank attack, Lee asked Jackson, "What do you propose to make this movement with?" Jackson responded, "With my whole corps."[31] Lee verbally confirmed that Jackson had asked Lee to divide the army again and would leave about fourteen thousand troops behind, taking the rest on the flanking march. Lee weighed his choices.

During the night of May 1–2, Lee and Jackson plotted their next move after Hooker pulled into a defensive position around the Chancellorsville Crossroads. Library of Congress.

Options

Lee took Stuart's information about the exposed Union flank and considered it alongside the additional details about the routes through the Wilderness. The opportunity seemed promising, but should he divide his troops again to allow Jackson to carry out a surprise attack? As Lee pondered the situation, he had three options. First, he could keep the Confederate troops massed around Chancellorsville and seek another attack option that would not require him to separate his force again. Second, he could allow Jackson to carry out the flank attack. Third, Lee could order a retreat out of the Union's trap.

Option 1: Allow Jackson to Carry Out the Flank Attack

The first option was bold: Jackson wanted to take his entire corps and strike at the exposed Union right flank. That meant secretively moving fifteen infantry brigades through difficult terrain. It also meant leaving Lee with seven brigades and reduced artillery and cavalry support to confront Hooker's corps. If the Union generals realized the divided state of Lee's army during this plan's operations, they could strike, isolate, and piecemeal defeat the Confederates.

Lee could also order a variation of this option. He could allow Jackson to carry out the flank attack, but he could reduce the number of troops. Jackson wanted to take his entire corps, totaling approximately 29,400 soldiers and 108 cannon.[32] This proposal would leave Lee with a total of 14,900 men (infantry, artillerymen, and cavalry) and 24 cannon—a relatively small force to face Hooker's corps. Lee could order Jackson to leave part of his corps and more equally divide the troops on the flank attack and the troops staying to occupy Hooker's attention.

If Lee chose the flank attack option in any form, he had to have confidence in his subordinate and his enemy. Lee's trust in Jackson's abilities was strong, and except for the Seven Days Battles, Stonewall had a consistent record of accomplishing swift marches. Armed with the local guides and screened by Stuart's cavalry, Jackson had some odds in his favor. For this plan to succeed, Lee also had to gamble that Hooker would not make a sudden move or launch a probing attack that Stuart's cavalry could not beat back. Lee could see the boldness in Hooker's original movements, but had the Union boaster lost his nerve, and how long would he be willing to sit in the Wilderness?

Option 2: Hold Position and Seek Another Attack Opportunity That Would Not Divide Confederate Forces

A second option could keep Jackson's, Anderson's, and McLaws's Divisions in a united front against the Union position forming around Chancellorsville.

This course of action would continue the battle engagement and likely keep Hooker in place, leaving Lee more troops and options if he had to reinforce Early's Division still confronting Sedgwick near Fredericksburg. Lee had already split his army twice: once when sending Longstreet to Suffolk, and again when leaving Early along the Rappahannock.

However, the strength of the Union position directly to the Confederates' front created a deadly challenge. Lee knew that "a direct attack upon the enemy would be attended with great difficulty and loss, in view of the strength of his position and his superiority of numbers."[33]

Option 3: Retreat from the Union Trap

Lee's third option was to retreat, and it loomed in his mind. Despite Hooker's strange withdrawal into the Wilderness, he still had a formidable plan, and Lee had placed his already divided army between two elements of the Union forces. On May 2, 1863, Lee sent a message to Pres. Jefferson Davis apprising him of the situation and concluding: "It is plain that if the enemy is too strong for me here, I shall have to fall back, and Fredericksburg must be abandoned. If successful here, Fredericksburg will be saved and our communications retained. I may be forced back to the Orange and Alexandria or the Virginia Central [rail]road, but in either case I will be in position to contest the enemy's advance upon Richmond."[34]

If Lee retreated, one question remained: If his soldiers were badly beaten in an attack, would enough Confederates be able to leave the field and reposition elsewhere? Lee noted that reinforcements from Lieut. Gen. Longstreet would likely not be available for this battle, but they might be useful if he had to fall back.[35]

Decision

Lee and Jackson had parted several times in the night, each trying to rest, then rising to consult with new guides and messengers about the situation. In the early morning hours, the generals discussed the plans again. Around 5:00 a.m. on May 2, 1863, Lee was satisfied and made his decision.[36] He gave Jackson permission to make the surprise flank attack with the entire Second Corps of the Army of Northern Virginia, screened by Stuart's cavalry. Lee would remain in the current position with Anderson's and McLaws's Divisions to distract Hooker, and he would stay in communication with Early's force at Fredericksburg.

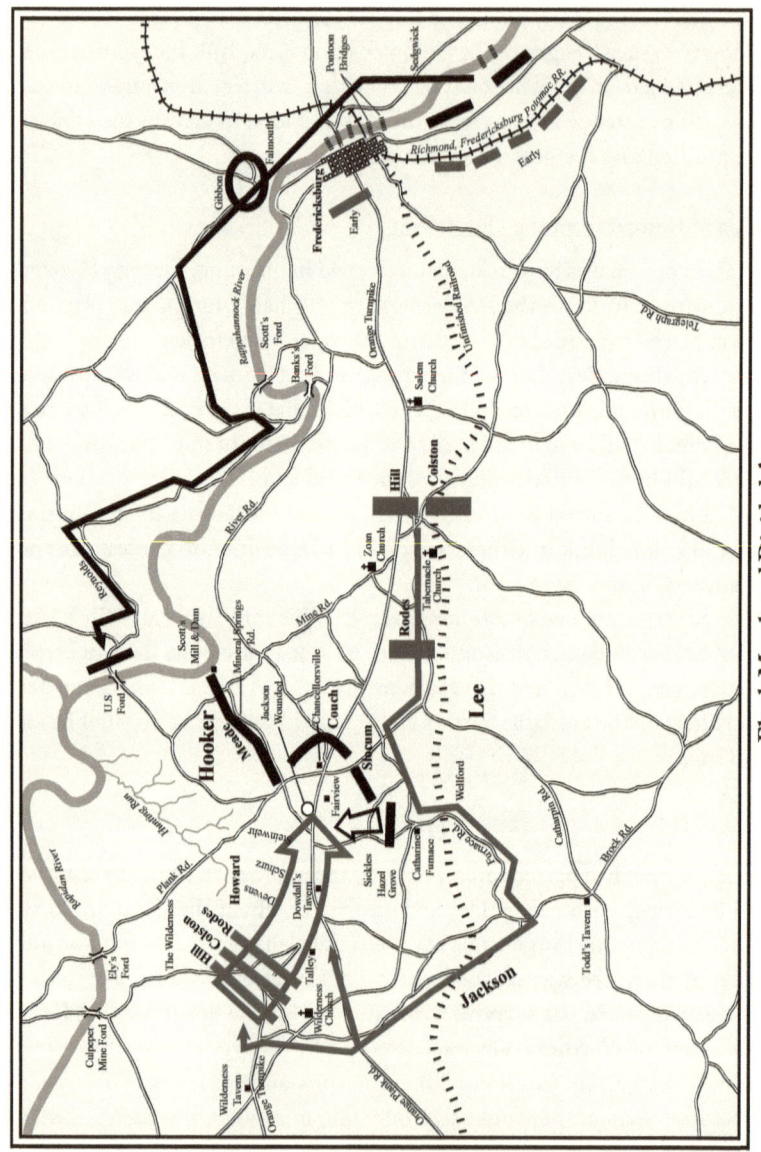

Flank March and Divided Army

Results/Impact

"My troops will move at once, sir!" Jackson responded to Lee's permission and orders.[37] In reality, while the vanguard started shortly after, it would take hours to get the entire Second Corps moving on its secretive march along the narrow track through the dense woods. Lee's decision sent more than twenty-nine thousand soldiers toward the unprotected flank of the Union army. He gambled that Sedgwick would not move and that Hooker would remain on the defense.

The decision made in the night of May 1–2, 1863, turned into action as dawn broke the darkness and light filtered through the trees beyond Chancellorsville. If Hooker did not want to fight, Lee would send the battle to him, holding and using the military initiative.

Lee and Jackson met one last time before Stonewall joined his marching column. No one heard their conversation. No one seemed to notice that Jackson was wearing his uniform, coat, and a rubber raincoat on a day that would be hot enough to make him perspire.[38] No one recalled until after the battle that when Lee had been pondering his decision in the darkness, Jackson's sword—leaned against a nearby tree—slid to the ground with a clatter.[39] Jackson would carry out Lee's verdict, and by sunset Hooker would be fighting for survival. But by midnight, so would Stonewall. Lee's decision gained tactical advantage, and the consequences of the events would shake both the Union and Confederate armies.

CHAPTER 3

THE BATTLE'S SURPRISES

MAY 2, 1863

The second day of the Battle of Chancellorsville started with both Union and Confederate armies seeing the repercussions of the critical decisions made on May 1. The rebels had fought offensively, and the Union army had fallen back into a defensive posture around the Chancellorsville Crossroads. Confederate generals Lee and Jackson decided to seize the military initiative and begin a lengthy march to attack the Union army's exposed right flank. These choices put the advantages of the movement on the Confederate side, leaving the Union army in a passive position.

On May 2, 1863, three critical decisions were made. Maj. Gen. Hooker interpreted the observed Confederate movements as a retreat. In the darkness after a successful flank attack, Lieut. Gen. Jackson pursued the idea of cutting a Union retreat route along the Rappahannock River. Gen. Lee—facing a chain of command crisis in the Confederate Second Corps—selected a new commander to help him fight to reunite the divided army. The fighting and the critical decisions on this day responded to observable reports and to unexpected situations.

The Battle's Surprises

Hooker Decides the Confederates Are Retreating

Situation

Loyalty was at stake. The German American troops who formed part of the Union Eleventh Corps believed that on a personal level. Prejudice stood against them in much of American society, and many were fighting for their new homeland and seeking to be acknowledged as patriotic citizens. As the soldiers cheered Gen. Hooker on the morning of May 2, 1863, they exhibited a type of loyalty to their commanding general. Would he return that loyalty? Would ethnic prejudices influence the military reports from the men in the ranks and officers of the corps? Would their observations and fears of an attack on that day be given less weight in the shuffle of reports because the Eleventh was not a favored corps?

Within the Union lines on May 2, 1863, Maj. Gen. Joseph Hooker rode west to inspect the position of the Eleventh Corps. Soldiers cheered when they saw him, and even with the army in the defensive posture, its morale remained strongly in Hooker's favor. Joining Maj. Gen. Oliver O. Howard, Hooker looked over the troops forming his right flank and made some suggestions to improve the position.[1] In a written message, he advised preparing trenches and advancing pickets.[2] Though Hooker hoped to entice Lee to attack his strong defensive works, he did not seem to anticipate an attack coming from the south or west toward the Eleventh Corps, which he had already recognized as one of his weakest and least experienced units.

The previous evening Hooker had sent orders for the First Corps, under Maj. Gen. John F. Reynolds, to leave Sedgwick's command, march northwest, cross the river, and join the main army.[3] He hoped to use this force to connect the right of the Eleventh Corps with the Rappahannock River and cover the important fords in his rear, thus securing a retreat route. Communication delays, a tardy start from Reynolds, and the distance to be marched prevented the First Corps from effectively reaching Hooker's line on May 2, but he had summoned the troops. Hooker had also ordered Sedgwick to attack and move toward Chancellorsville. A confusing array of messages and orders made Sedgwick pause to sort out the communications, but Hooker hoped that he would attack the Confederate troops positioned near Fredericksburg, which would add a new threat for Lee.[4]

However, seeming to be satisfied with the Eleventh Corps and its commander, Hooker headed east and back to his headquarters at the Chancellor House at the crossroads. He followed up with an order at 9:30 a.m. in which he noted, "[The right of the Eleventh Corps] does not appear to be strong enough. No artificial defenses worth naming have been thrown up, and there appears to be a scarcity of troops at that point, and not, in the general's opinion, as favorably posted as might be."[5] Hooker assumed the Eleventh Corps would carry out his orders regarding earthworks and pickets toward the west.

Maj. Gen. Oliver O. Howard led the Eleventh Corps for the first time during the Chancellorsville Campaign, dealing with suspicious and disgruntled soldiers. The soldiers lacked experience and victories. Almost one-third of the twenty-three regiments within the corps had not been in combat. The other two-thirds had never been victorious in battle.[6] Many of the regiments forming the brigades and divisions of the Eleventh Corps were recruited from the German American community, and many of these soldiers had taken personal offense when Howard replaced their hero Maj. Gen. Franz Sigel earlier in the spring. Often unsuccessful on Civil War battlefields, Sigel had a reputation in the German American community that went back to the 1848 Revolutions in Europe, and the newly immigrated citizens took pride in boasting "I fights mit Sigel." Thus far, the men serving under Howard had mocked their general, whose overly pious attitude isolated him from the common soldiers and made him an object of scorn for many in the Eleventh Corps' ranks. Despite the leadership issue, the soldiers of the Eleventh Corps were generally willing to do their duty. Many felt an obligation to support the Union cause, and others saw battlefield heroics as a way to gain respect from the prejudiced American citizenry who often looked down on German immigrants.

Maj. Gen. Oliver O. Howard (Union) commanded the Eleventh Corps of the Army of the Potomac and was better known in 1863 for his piety than for his battlefield successes. Library of Congress.

The Eleventh Corps had arrived at its current position on May 1. Troops had prepared some trenches and rifle pits, most facing to the south, and settled into camps. The men enjoyed the more open ground created by the Hawkins and Tally Farms, though they were still surrounded by the dense Wilderness. Maj. Gen. Carl Schurz, commanding the Third Division, later noted,

> The position was . . . a good one to move from if the army had followed up the offensive, which, no doubt, had originally been contemplated. As a defensive position it presented a front only moderately strong to resist a parallel attack coming from the south. I say moderately strong, as the line, especially on our right, was very thin, and we had no general reserve. . . . Our right wing stood completely in the air, with nothing to lean upon . . . and with no reliable cavalry to make reconnaissance, and that, too, in a forest thick enough not to permit any view to the front, flank, or rear, but not thick enough to prevent the approach of the enemy troops.[7]

By late morning on May 2, colonels and junior officers along the Eleventh Corps' south-facing line noticed troop movement. The Wilderness concealed the details, but along the roads and through forest gaps, Union soldiers could see Confederates. For example, Col. Adin Underwood watched from a hill through an opening and spotted "a column of moving troops," observing it "from time to time for hours."[8] Regimental commanders passed the word up the chain of command: Confederates were moving. Another Union soldier noted, "The movement became generally known all along the line of the Corps and everybody looked for, and impatiently awaited orders to contract the extended line of the Corps, with a suitable now absolutely necessary change of front, and other measures of defense."[9]

Farther to the east, the Third Corps also noted Confederate movement. Artillery fire was directed toward the column. Maj. Gen. Daniel Sickles wrote,

> This continuous column—infantry, artillery, trains, and ambulances—was observed for three hours moving apparently in a southerly direction toward Orange Court-House, on the Orange and Alexandria Railroad, or Louisa Court-House on the Virginia Central. The movement indicated a retreat on Gordonsville or an attack upon our right flank—perhaps both, for if the attack failed the retreat could be continued. The unbroken mass of forest on our right

favored the concealment of the enemy's real design. I hastened to report these movements through staff officers to the general-in-chief.[10]

Starting in the morning and continuing throughout the day, the Third Corps and the Eleventh Corps reported troop movement. Gen. Hooker had to make a decision. What were the Confederates actually doing? And should he change his army's disposition to meet a threat or begin a pursuit?

Options

Hooker had previously decided to put his army in a defensive position and hoped that Lee would attack him. The strongest part of his line wrapped around the Chancellorsville clearing, and the lines were weaker and unprotected to the west. While Hooker had ordered the First Corps to join him at Chancellorsville and complete his right flank, communication difficulties had delayed that corps' movement.

Something was happening, and Confederates were shifting to the south and west. Numerous reports from soldiers and officers pointed to that fact. Hooker needed to decide what the enemy's movement meant and prepare accordingly if he perceived it as a threat. As the situation unfolded and reports of Confederate movements continued to arrive, Hooker had four options for how to proceed. He could interpret or confirm a Confederate retreat. He could simply strengthen the Eleventh Corps' position, factoring in that the First Corps might not arrive as quickly as he hoped. In addition, he could send cavalry to intentionally probe, delay, or divert the Confederate movement. Finally, Hooker could press a major and coordinated attack near Catharine's Furnace or along the Orange Turnpike. With the exception of the first one, all choices had varying levels of risk and engagement with the Confederates. These options involved different levels of aggression and passivity in these choices.

Option 1: Interpret Reports of the Movement as a Confederate Retreat

The first and potentially the most passive choice allowed Hooker to interpret the enemy's movement as a retreat. The observed Confederate movement of troops, cannon, and wagons moving toward the south and west somewhat supported this option. If Lee wanted to disengage from the battle around Chancellorsville, he might retreat in that direction, which would place him near railroad lines and potential supply bases farther south in central Virginia.

If Hooker determined the rebels were withdrawing, he could use several variables in his decision and response. He could simply wait and see what

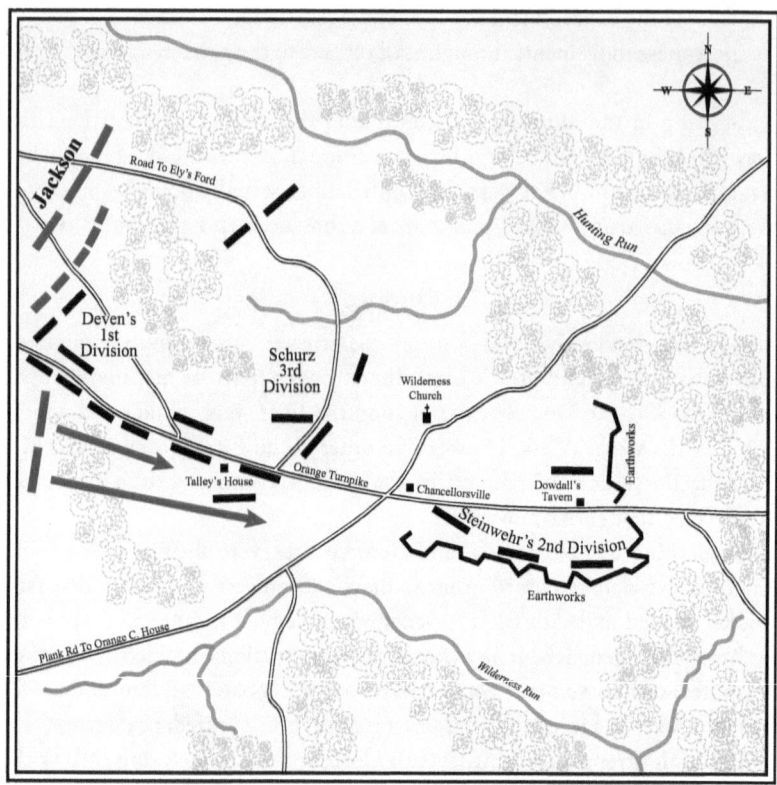

Eleventh Corps Position

happened, continuing to leave the initiative with Lee. Hooker could also send a strike force to engage the presumably retreating Confederates. Furthermore, he could organize a full-scale army pursuit to pressure the Confederates, trying to regain the offensive and fight a battle somewhere beyond the Wilderness; if Lee was leaving the Wilderness and Hooker followed him into open ground, Union cavalry raiding toward Richmond might be able to assist. Either way, interpreting the rebels' movement as a retreat opened additional considerations.

Option 2: Strengthen the Defensive Lines of the Eleventh Corps

If Hooker doubted the Confederate movement as a retreat, he would have to consider where his enemy would be moving to attack. A march toward the south and west could indicate an attempted strike on the Union's right flank.

Hooker knew this was a weaker part of his line, and he could determine that Lee would prefer to attack a less fortified area.

Part of the inherent weakness of the Eleventh Corps' line was in the topography and the way the position faced. Many of the regiments faced to the south and paralleled the Orange Turnpike. There were few helpful topographical features in the area, which was a mix of woods and farm fields. If Hooker suspected the reports pointed to a Confederate attack, the Eleventh Corps' line essentially faced the wrong way and was more vulnerable. Around midmorning after his inspection of the line, Hooker had ordered the corps to strengthen its position toward the west and build stronger fortifications and artillery positions. Since he had recognized this potential weakness, Hooker could follow up to ensure his orders were carried out or provide more troops or direction to Howard.

Option 3: Send Cavalry to Intentionally Probe the Confederate Movement

A third option could provide more information to help Hooker confirm or determine what the Confederates were doing. He could send cavalry to formally scout the enemy's movement.

Hooker had limited available cavalry; he had sent most of them with Gen. Stoneman on the raid toward Richmond as part of his original campaign plan. Other horsemen were guarding the river fords. However, one regiment had skills and was available: the Eighth Pennsylvania Cavalry. The unit had fought well during the early action on May 1. Sending the Eighth to follow and probe the Confederate march could place the Federals in direct contact with the Confederates. The cavalry might be able gather more details, allowing Hooker to decide based on more accurate intelligence information than he had.

Option 4: Press an Attack near the Catharine Furnace or Orange Turnpike

In another option, Hooker could order a large-scale offensive near the Catharine Furnace or along the Orange Turnpike east of Chancellorsville. Confederate troops had been observed moving past the iron furnace in front of the Third Corps. Union infantry and artillery had already engaged some of the soldiers, and a regiment of Georgia infantry had turned to fight while other rebels continued marching. Hooker could order a strong coordinated attack at this point. Escalating the clash into a larger-scale combat might disrupt the Confederates' movement or provide more information to confirm

The Battle's Surprises

The lack of cavalry—like this photographed cavalry officer—hampered the Union army's ability to scout, protect its lines of march, and probe the enemy's movements. Library of Congress.

whether they were really retreating. Another option would be attacking the Confederate lines in the vicinity of the Orange Turnpike, in front of the Union Second Corps. Skirmishing occurred through this area during the day, but a significant attack might throw Lee off balance. The observation of the Confederate march or retreat theoretically meant that the remaining troops were weak and probably not easily reinforced. An attack would move Union troops out of their defensive positions, but it could potentially regain the high ground or hasten the Confederate retreat.

Whether Hooker chose an attack point near the Catharine Furnace or along the Orange Turnpike, the concept of an assault could force Lee to react. If a swift Union attack happened, particularly along the turnpike and followed by Sedgwick's ordered advance, Hooker might defeat a portion of Lee's army before it could escape or before marching troops could return.

Decision

Hooker received reports about the Confederate movement throughout May 2, 1863. Satisfied with what he had seen of the improvements to the Union defensive line during his morning ride, the general returned to his headquarters. He was dismissive of the continual reports of enemy forces opposite the Union right flank, and he decided to not seek additional information or launch an attack. Hooker interpreted the reports of the Confederate movement as a rebel retreat and did not issue orders for a full-scale pursuit.

Results/Impact

Hooker's decision to interpret the Confederate movement as a retreat left him and his army sitting blindly. Failing to order a closer investigation of the enemy's marching column, Hooker kept himself and his generals on the defensive, without even knowing whether they needed to prepare a stronger defense. Hooker had already handed the offensive initiative to Lee on May 1, but on May 2, he gave up the opportunity for gathering additional information and intelligence. This choice left Hooker's army vulnerable to a surprise flank attack.

For soldiers and officers in the Eleventh Corps, the lack of direction and dismissive attitude from their unit and army headquarters proved frustrating. They could see something happening, and they struggled to understand why they were not ordered to reposition or prepare. Luther Mesnard in the Fifty-Fifth Ohio wrote, "Was up near corps head quarter and could see through a glass the rebel army moving southward and rumors were ripe that Lee's army was falling back, was retreating toward Richmond. About two o'clock when some of our boys came in from the skirmish or picket line, there were rumors that the rebs were massing on our right. I myself hear one of the men say that he could hear artillery rattle or rumble as it moved over the roads, could hear the commands of the rebel officers as the troop moved into position."[11]

Was it another instance of pushing aside reports because of ethnic prejudice? Was it simply carelessness? Did Hooker actually know something beyond what the soldiers on the right flank observed? Tension grew within the ranks, and some soldiers nervously waited. Others settled into their evening routines. Howard had defied orders and allowed the supply wagons to bring fresh provisions into the camps and military lines. The sun dipped toward the horizon. Maybe the day would end without incident. Or maybe enemy soldiers crouched in the dense woods, ready to attack and add to the Eleventh Corps' infamous record, crushing those blue-clad soldiers' hopes for a better reputation.

Jackson Plans to Cut Off the Federals from US Ford

Situation

Staff officers waited. Generals and colonels watched. The Confederate battle line had been assembled, stretching nearly two miles and ready to sweep down on the exposed flank of the Union Eleventh Corps. Lieut. Gen. Thomas J. Jackson and more than twenty-eight thousand troops had accomplished a twelve-mile march and overcome difficulties along the trek. Now, everyone waited for the word to advance. One of the staff officers who had significantly contributed to the success of the march was Capt. James Keith Boswell, chief topographical engineer for the Confederate Second Corps.

Twenty-four-year-old Boswell had been trained as a civil engineer and had constructed railroads in Missouri and Alabama prior to the war. When the war began, he returned to his native state, Virginia, and offered his services in its defense. At first, James Keith Boswell served on Gen. Magruder's staff, but Gen. Thomas J. Jackson specifically requested his transfer, and Boswell arrived in Winchester, Virginia, during the last week of February 1862. A fellow soldier described him as "an excellent, good-natured, honest Presbyterian" adding, "[He is] well off, has a sweetheart in Fauquier [County] where the Yankees are, and he talks much about her."[12] Boswell became an integral part of Jackson's staff and part of the younger clique of officers at Second Corps Headquarters, and his knowledge, creativity, and steadfastness to duty led to important roles in Jackson's campaigns.

The previous evening Boswell had been one of the staff officers scouting and working with local civilians to find a route for Jackson's march.[13] The information he gathered had helped confirm the details that led Lee to allow Jackson to divide the army and make the long march. As the Confederate infantry marched, they followed local roads that narrowed the columns and stretched the troops over miles. Cavalry reports and more work from the scouts and engineers guided the advancing soldiers farther west and north, avoiding Union troops along Orange Plank Road and directing the column to Orange Turnpike. Boswell moved along the lines "constantly seeking for information, regardless of danger all along the enemy's front."[14] It was a testament to Lee's bold decisions, Jackson's willingness to seize the unexpected, the soldiers' hard marching, and the scouts' and staff officers' work that the battle line waited.

Despite the logistical and planning success, there had been delays, and only a couple of hours of daylight remained by the time the Confederates were ready to strike. At 5:15 p.m., Jackson turned to division commander Maj. Gen. Robert Rodes and inquired whether he was ready to attack. "You can go forward, then," Jackson ordered.[15] Two signal shots were fired from the horse artillery along the turnpike, and a chorus of bugle calls sounded along the battle line in the woods. The flank attack at Chancellorsville began.

Confederate infantry burst into the clearings where nearly twelve thousand Eleventh Corps soldiers relaxed and prepared dinner. With many of

May 2, 1863

Alfred Waud sketched this scene showing soldiers of the Eleventh Corps retreating and reinforcements rushing west to fight back against Jackson's flank attack. Library of Congress.

the trenches facing south, these Union soldiers had limited options to face the attack coming from the west. Moreover, rolling terrain gave them little opportunity to make a significant stand. Panicked men in blue sprinted to the east, while others seized their rifles and made isolated stands against the Confederates. Some Union regiments rallied and formed the Buschbeck Line, fighting back until enemy artillery blasted their position.

The Confederate attack had been initially successful. However, the woods, the rolling terrain, and the Union resistance broke Jackson's battle line into an uneven and disorderly collection of soldiers. Riding along the Orange Turnpike, Jackson urged men and officers to "press on." He wanted to keep driving the Union troops, giving them little time to re-form, and he knew his men were racing the setting sun. As the battle unfolded and unraveled rapidly, Jackson would have to be make decisions quickly to keep and press the advantages.

Jackson's troops were tired. The rear of his marching column had been delayed and was late in arriving. Darkness came, but Union troops were still retreating toward the Chancellorsville Crossroads. Jackson summoned and dispatched staff officers to get information to inform his decisions.

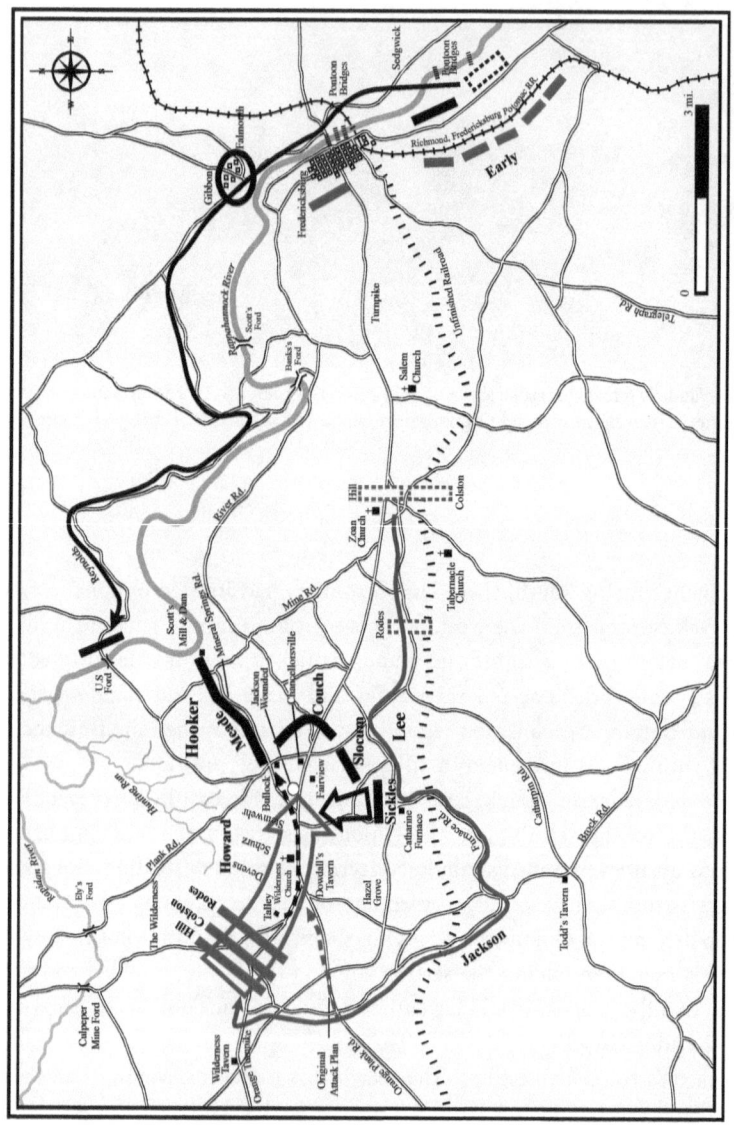

Jackson's Operations, May 2

May 2, 1863

Options

Jackson and his corps had pushed the Eleventh Corps about three miles, but the Wilderness and darkness fought against them. Disorganized and still separated from Lee and the rest of the army, Jackson had to make decisions based on the evolving battle. He had three options. First, he could halt his corps and reorganize for a dawn assault. Second, he could push his troops to fight on through the night advancing along the Orange Turnpike. Finally, Jackson could see a new attack objective, diverting from the advance due east along the turnpike to strike in a northeasterly direction toward the fords on the Rappahannock.

Option 1: Halt, Straighten the Battle Line, and Prepare for a Morning Assault

The complicated but conservative option would be to pause the advance, reorganize the battle line, and let the Confederate soldiers get ready for an early morning attack on the Union line. After pushing the Eleventh Corps for three miles, Jackson's troops approached the area where other Union corps were already positioned and had been shifting to meet the Confederates with infantry, artillery, and trenches.

Two particular difficulties would threaten this option. First, it would be challenging to realign the battle line in the darkness within the dense woods. If the line could not be re-formed before dawn, there could not be an early attack. Second, Confederates would be vulnerable if the Union recognized this difficulty and launched a counterattack.

Option 2: Fight through the Night, Continuing to Advance along the Orange Turnpike

This option would essentially renew the attack in the same manner and direction the rebels had been attacking before the troops were halted by the obstructions. The Confederate line in disarray would continue to advance disjointedly, with soldiers fighting as they met resistance and pressing forward to the east along the Orange Turnpike.

This plan's advantages included moving closer to Lee's position and to reuniting the divided Confederate army, and attempting to keep Union troops off balance and perhaps unable to set up a strong defense facing west. The disadvantage was that the uneven Confederate lines would only get worse with each step of the advance as the wooded terrain and Union resistance continued. The men in Jackson's Second Corps could find themselves in a bad situation if they came up against a solid Union defense line.

Option 3: Seek a New Point of Attack and Target the Fords on the Rappahannock River

With the Eleventh Corps' hasty retreat likely causing a panic farther back in the Union rear positions, Hooker might seek to withdraw. His decisions on the previous day had seemed to indicate an unwillingness to continue offensive operations, and his faulty defensive alignments gave the Confederates an opportunity for making the flank attack. If Hooker chose to retreat, could his escape route be cut off or at least threatened? United States Ford, often called US Ford, sat barely five miles from the Chancellorsville Crossroads, a natural crossing point on the Rappahannock River. The primary advantage of US Ford was that it would allow the Union army to retreat northward across the river without having to cross both the Rapidan and the Rappahannock Rivers.

The advantage to moving Confederate troops north and toward the river was that soldiers could possibly get into position to threaten or block a Union retreat route. The disadvantages were numerous. First, moving troops toward the river took them farther away from the rest of Lee's army, and if the Union generals realized the Confederates' divided strength and position, they could launch heavy counterattack. Second, the position of the Union's reserves needed to be identified. Without this information, rebels could move so deep into Federal lines that they could be surrounded, turning the thus-far-successful flank attack into a disaster. Third, getting the Confederate Second Corps—or part of it—organized, faced in a new direction in the dense woods and limited roads, and able to make a quick march would be logistically challenging, if not impossible. Fourth, this maneuver would expand and rewrite Lee's orders and the agreed-on plan, taking much initiative and moving the corps in an opposite direction from reuniting the Confederate army.

Decision

Lieut. Gen. Thomas J. Jackson decided to head north to cut off or threaten the Union retreat. Aware of the need for a decisive Confederate victory, Jackson explored a possibility that could either firmly trap Hooker's army with no escape route or force Union troops to fight a battle in which the Confederates held an advantage.

Results/Impact

Deciding to explore forested routes and positions to the north and toward US Ford, Jackson deployed his staff and more local scouts into the darkness. As he met division or brigade commanders, he urged them to organize their lines and keep pressing forward. Both actions were to keep Union troops nervous and prevent them from digging more trenches. Jackson had been in the battle area throughout the late afternoon and early evening, complimenting artillerymen on their skill, directing officers, and observing the attack near the front. His anxiousness and decision kept him close to the front line as darkness settled.

Meeting Maj. Gen. A. P. Hill and his staff on the turnpike, Jackson quizzed the officer, anxious to know when he would advance and whether he was familiar with the land between Chancellorsville and US Ford. Hill admitted his lack of knowledge and asked for a guide. Turning to his topographical engineer, Capt. Boswell, Jackson ordered him to accompany Hill, then finished giving advance orders for continuing the attack.[16]

The fighting had lulled as troops from Hill's Division approached the front and positioned themselves to receive orders and continue the battle. Seeming unwilling to wait for other staff officers or scouts to return with reports, Jackson wanted to ascertain whether Union troops in his immediate front were entrenching. That information would contribute to his decision whether to pursue a maneuver toward the river or alter his choice with new information. Jackson and a small group of officers rode beyond the Confederate line along Mountain Road, which paralleled the Orange Turnpike. After pausing and listening to the sounds of Federals building trenches and barricades, Jackson

Jackson's decision to scout ahead of his lines resulted in friendly fire and a command vacancy for the Confederate Second Corps during a critical point of the fighting around Chancellorsville. Library of Congress.

turned back, riding west and toward the Eighteenth North Carolina infantry. Shots rang out, and Jackson was wounded.

Friendly fire blazed along the battle line, hitting Jackson's group and also bringing Hill's staff under fire. Jackson—the "famous" casualty of the night—was not the only one from Second Corps Headquarters to fall that evening. In the same volleys that felled Stonewall, James Keith Boswell, the chief of engineers, took three bullets. One wounded his leg. The other two struck him full in the chest, tearing through his engineering sketchbook in his breast pocket, penetrating his flesh, killing him instantly.[17] Boswell's life ended on a dark battle night along a lonely turnpike, and even his memory would eventually be overshadowed by another casualty falling at the same time.

The friendly fire brought a sudden halt to Jackson's decision to pursue a maneuver toward the river. Jackson's wounding removed him from the battle at a critical time. With Jackson shot, his corps disunited in the darkness, and Union troops preparing stronger defensive works around the Chancellorsville Crossroads, the Confederate soldiers would await orders from the next general in the chain of command—or whomever else Lee chose to take command.

Lee Puts J. E. B. Stuart in Command of the Second Corps

Situation

Lieut. Gen. Stonewall Jackson lay in an ambulance, probably near Dowdall's Tavern. The officer was wounded by friendly fire as he tried to return to Confederate lines after a scouting ride, and his decisions and battle plans unraveled in the darkness while doctors rallied to try to slow his blood loss and save his life. Earlier in the day—May 2, 1863—the Confederate Second Corps had completed a lengthy march that concluded with soldiers poised to strike the right flank of Hooker's army. Shortly after 5:00 p.m., Jackson ordered his battle lines forward, smashing into the Union Eleventh Corps and forcing a Federal retreat. Ordered on by Jackson and the division commanders, Confederate soldiers continued to advance, driving Union troops out of small defensive positions and back toward the Chancellorsville Crossroads. Darkness had overtaken everyone on the battlefield. Union troops used the darkness to prepare western-facing entrenchments, and the Confederate battle line was disjointed, paused by the dense woods and weariness.

Capt. Richard E. Wilbourn, a signal officer on Jackson's staff, had been with Stonewall when the friendly fire from the North Carolinians erupted. Wilbourn caught and halted Jackson's panicked horse and helped to lift the general to the ground. Finding Jackson's left arm broken and another shot in his right hand, the captain worked with other officers to get Jackson away from the fighting and toward a field hospital. Wilbourn had witnessed Maj. Gen. A. P. Hill interact with Jackson just moments before Hill was wounded. The Confederates' chain of command was in jeopardy, and their battle situation was tenuous.

With Jackson finally in an ambulance and heading for a field hospital, Maj. Alexander S. Pendleton, who essentially acted as Jackson's chief of staff at Chancellorsville though not officially holding that position, pulled Wilbourn aside to speak to him. Wilbourn recalled subsequent events as follows:

> [Pendleton said to me,] "Capt W., Gen. Hill is slightly wounded in the leg and Gen. Rodes is in command & requests me to send for Gen. Lee & ask him to come here. I wish you would go to Gen. Lee with this intelligence and send for Gen. Stuart. There are a plenty here to take care of Gen. J & you have done all you could do."
>
> I asked Capt. Randolph of the couriers to go for Gen. Stuart and he started for Gen. Stuart. I reached Gen. Lee about an hour before day and found him laying on the ground [a]sleep but as soon as I spoke to Maj. Taylor, he asked who it was & when told, he told me to come & take a seat by him & give him all the news. After telling of the fight & victory, I told him Gen. J. was wounded—describing the wound—then he said, "thank God it is no worse, God be praised that he is yet alive." He then asked me some questions about the fight.[18]

Maj. Gen. A. P. Hill (Confederate) was next in line for command of the Second Corps, but he was also wounded during the night of May 2, 1863. Library of Congress.

The Battle's Surprises

Brig. Gen. Robert Rodes (Confederate) led a division for the first time during the Battle of Chancellorsville; he did not feel confident to take command of the Second Corps. Public domain.

Lee faced a chain of command situation with the Second Corps. That force was still separated from him and the two divisions under Lee's immediate command, and the Union army sat between the two elements. Jackson, commander of the Second Corps, was wounded. The next senior commander, Maj. Gen. A. P. Hill, had been slightly wounded and seemed reluctant to take charge of the battlefield situation. Moving further down the chain of command, Brig. Gen. Robert Rodes came next; Rodes had asked for Lee to come to the Second Corps. Meanwhile, Maj. Pendleton—an experienced and long-trusted staff officer—had asked Lee to allow Maj. Gen. J. E. B. Stuart to command the Second Corps.

That corps was in an exposed and separated position that could endanger the command and the entire Confederate army. Lee had to make a decision for leadership and provide guiding orders that would set the objectives for the coming day.

Options

To choose a new commander for the Second Corps, Lee had several options. Some specific requests had come from officers of the corps, but with two senior leaders wounded, he needed to decide who would provide the needed leadership. First, Lee could keep Rodes in command. Second, Lee could appoint a

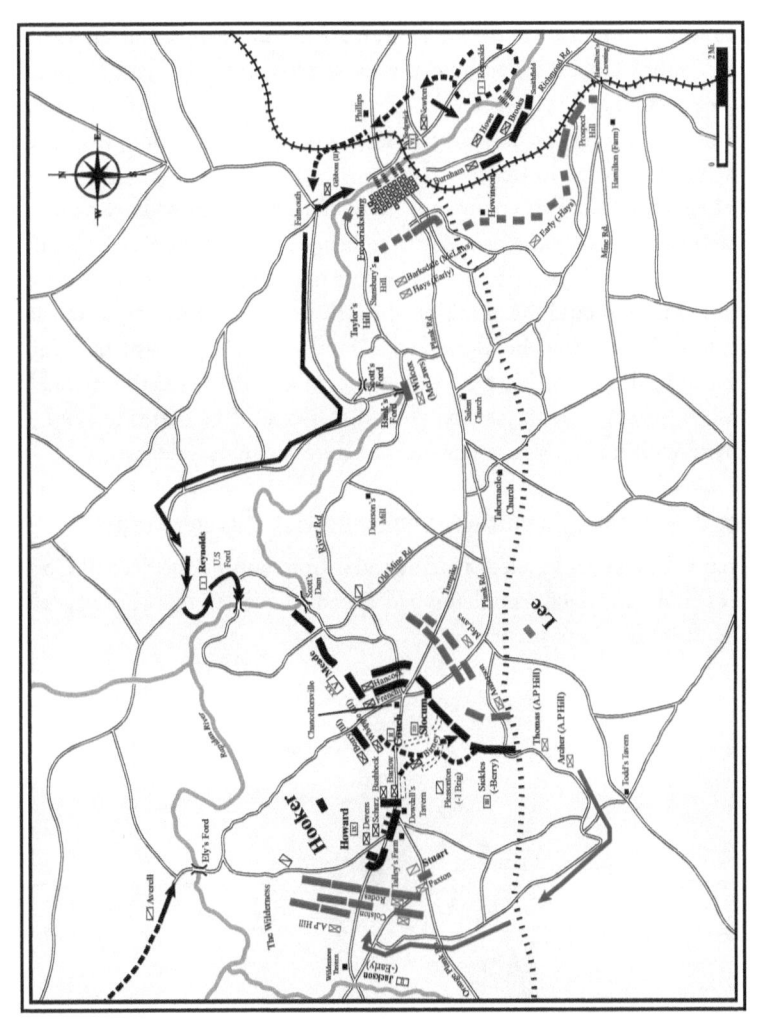

Position of Lee's Army Night of May 2–3

commander from outside the Second Corps chain of command—as Pendleton was requesting. Third, Lee could personally take command of the corps.

Option 1: Keep Rodes in Command

Thirty-four-year-old Robert E. Rodes had graduated from Virginia Military Institute and taught at that school briefly before pursuing civil engineering in the Deep South prior to the Civil War. At the Battle of Chancellorsville, Rodes commanded a division officially for the first time. He had previously led at regimental and brigade levels. Inexperienced with the corps command and knowing that the Second Corps was in a dangerous position, Rodes had sent a communication to Lee.

If Lee kept Rodes in command, he would need to provide clear directions and objectives for the next day of fighting. Lee was not closely familiar with Rodes or how he would perform at this high level of authority. Keeping Rodes in charge would mean taking the risk that he had the drive and initiative to either reunite the Confederate forces or strike toward the Union rear. Keeping Rodes in his post would potentially maintain the morale of the troops; however, with Jackson wounded, would it be better to keep the command within the corps rather than sending for an outsider?

Option 2: Appoint a Commander from Outside the Second Corps

Alternatively, Lee could select a commander from outside the Second Corps' chain of command. Maj. Pendleton had already requested this option, asking for J. E. B. Stuart in particular.

Stuart took command of the Second Corps on May 3, 1863, following requests from that corps' officers and directions from Lee. Library of Congress.

Maj. Gen. Stuart commanded the Army of Northern Virginia's Cavalry Corps. Sending him to lead infantry was an interesting proposal. To Stuart's advantage, he was already in the vicinity of the Second Corps and knew the overall situation of the previous march and flank attack. He was also an experienced division commander, but he had been without a command since Gen. Fitzhugh Lee ably led the cavalry brigade on the field at Chancellorsville. Stuart was a popular commander in the Army of Northern Virginia and recognized for his dash and victorious exploits with the cavalry. Moreover, the major general would already have access to information about the general situation and Union disposition. He would have to sort out the more precise situation of the Second Corps' battle lines in the woods and darkness, but Jackson's still-active staff officers and brigade commanders could assist with that. A risk would be Stuart's lack of experience with infantry command; he was a cavalry commander. However, Stuart had been West Point–trained and knew general principles of infantry combat.

Lee could also consider sending either Gen. Anderson or Gen. McLaws to the Second Corps from their divisional commands. These options had multiple risks. Neither general had led at the corps level or had shown particular talent for it in the past. Neither general had been involved in the planning for the Second Corps' march and attack, and they would be almost entirely unfamiliar with the situation west of Chancellorsville. Also, Anderson and McLaws had been overseeing the skirmishing on the east and south side of the Union army's Chancellorsville lines, and they would be needed to keep pressure on those points while the Second Corps resumed fighting again from the west on May 3.

Option 3: Lee Takes Command of the Second Corps

Finally, as Rodes had requested, Lee could go to the Second Corps and either advise Rodes in person or take direct command of those troops. A benefit to this idea was the ability to issue direct orders to the part of the Confederate army on the offensive. However, Lee would have to travel through the Wilderness on a circuitous route through no-man's-land to get to the Second Corps, since it was still divided from the rest of the Confederate army. Going to the corps would also remove Lee from his central position, which allowed him to monitor the happenings on Anderson's and McLaws's lines while receiving messages from Early at Fredericksburg. Additionally, if Lee took charge of the Second Corps, he would be splitting his focus as army commander and tactical corps commander. Previously in the campaign, Lee had had to make critical decisions about strategy and tactics for the entire army. Leaving his central location and command headquarters would put him in the wrong place and limit his role.

Decision

Weighing the options to keep Rodes, send an "outside" commander, or go personally to the Second Corps, Lee made his decision. He ordered Stuart to take command of the Second Corps.

Results/Impact

Messengers from the Second Corps and from Lee's headquarters hurried to find Gen. Stuart. He came from Ely's Ford, took charge, and immediately started consulting with the infantry command's officers to understand the situation and what lay ahead of Jackson's Command on the battlefield.

An order from Lee to Stuart, penned at 3:00 a.m. on May 3, 1863, provided Lee's direction for the battle's objectives:

> It is necessary that the glorious victory thus far achieved be prosecuted with the utmost vigor, and the enemy given no time to rally. As soon, therefore, as it is possible, they must be pressed, so that we can unite the two wings of the army.
>
> Endeavor, therefore to dispossess them of Chancellorsville, which will permit the union of the whole army.
>
> I shall myself *proceed* to join you as soon as I can make arrangements on this side, but let nothing delay the completion of the plan of driving the enemy from his rear and from his positions.
>
> I shall give orders that *every* effort be made on this side at daylight to aid in the junction.[19]

Every sentence in Lee's orders directed Stuart to coordinate an attack that would move the Second Corps closer to Chancellorsville and reunite the Confederate army. Jackson's decision to explore and move toward the Rappahannock River became obsolete and was risky from the beginning. Now, Lee wanted to put the two wings of his divided army back together and drive an attack to break the Union lines around the Chancellorsville Crossroads.

Already assessing the situation and talking with the Second Corps' officers and staff, Stuart recognized that a piece of high ground stood ahead of the stalled Confederate line on its right. This land was also part of the area separating the parts of the Confederate divisions. Called Hazel Grove, this prominence could be a key artillery platform, and Stuart prioritized it as an objective for the initial attack on May 3.[20]

Shortly after sunrise, Stuart launched the attacks toward the Union trenches. He rode along the infantry lines, calling for the troops to "charge and remember Jackson!" The day unfolded, and the most intense fighting of the Battle of Chancellorsville exploded. Lee's decision to place Stuart in command gave the Second Corps an energetic and inspiring leader who had a basic understanding of the situation. However, with Stuart in command, the Second Corps would suffer long-term losses through his frontal assault tactics; these would cripple the regimental and brigade structure and fighting numbers of the Confederates.

CHAPTER 4
BATTLE TO THE EAST
MAY 3, 1863

The third day of significant fighting during the Chancellorsville Campaign saw battles at Chancellorsville, Fredericksburg, and Salem Church. Lee successfully reunited his forces around Chancellorsville and pushed Hooker, forcing Union troops to withdraw from the positions they had held at the start of the day. However, Lee faced a new threat coming from the east. This chapter focuses on the critical decisions connected to the fighting at Fredericksburg and Salem Church, both east of Chancellorsville; the following chapter will examine the critical decisions made at or near the Chancellorsville Crossroads. The outcomes of these critical decisions at each location affect the battles at all the other places. Up to the morning of May 3, the Union force commanded by Maj. Gen. John Sedgwick near Fredericksburg had not posed a significant combat threat, but as Hooker's troops got pummeled by attacks in the Virginia Wilderness, Hooker started to rely on Sedgwick to come to his aid. Meanwhile, Lee would need to reunite his forces around Chancellorsville and then decide how to meet Sedgwick's new aggression.

On May 3, 1863, on the eastern side of the Chancellorsville Campaign, three critical decisions were made. In the Sunken Road beneath Marye's Heights at Fredericksburg, Col. Thomas Griffin decided to allow a flag of truce. Union troops under artillery and small arms fire decided to stage a rushing charge to capture the heights. To face the new offensive threat,

Gen. Lee decided to divide his army again, sending reinforcements to Salem Church in an effort to stall Sedgwick. The fighting near Fredericksburg and at Salem Church and the critical decisions created unexpected results that impacted the fighting around Chancellorsville.

Griffin Grants a Temporary Truce

Situation

Twenty-three-year-old artillery captain Dudley Pendleton accompanied Confederate Brig. Gen. William Barksdale, observing the scene below Marye's Heights and overlooking the sloping nine hundred yards of open ground that lay between the high ground and the town of Fredericksburg. The young captain served on the staff of the chief of artillery for the Army of Northern Virginia and carefully noted the effect of the artillery duel on May 3, 1863, probably after two Union attacks on the position. Approaching Brompton House—one of the structures on the series of hills called Marye's Heights—Pendleton noted,

> Not an inch of the surface of the bricks on the front of the house exposed to this fire was free from the mark of a Minie ball. Bushels of flattened ones were to be seen on the ground, while the woodwork was torn to pieces by them, independently of the destruction wrought by cannon. The level between the house and railroad cut was covered with the dead and dying. . . . General Barksdale's troops held the line until the advance on Chancellorsville. He was upon this hill at the time that Sedgwick's troops came in sight. It happened that he had no attendant, all of his staff being temporarily absent with orders. I said to him: "General, those troops are Yankees." He said: "Oh, no! It is impossible!" Presently, recognizing the uniforms, he exclaimed: "My God! who will save my regiments down there?"[1]

Barksdale's concerned question as he realized his predicament could have been echoed by most of the Confederate soldiers on the high ground immediately west of Fredericksburg. The question might even have been echoed by Gen. Lee at Chancellorsville. If these Confederate regiments could not hold their positions, he would find a Union force closing on his rear. The situation near Fredericksburg directly influenced the fighting around Chancellorsville, and one key decision led to the unfolding disaster on the Fredericksburg front.

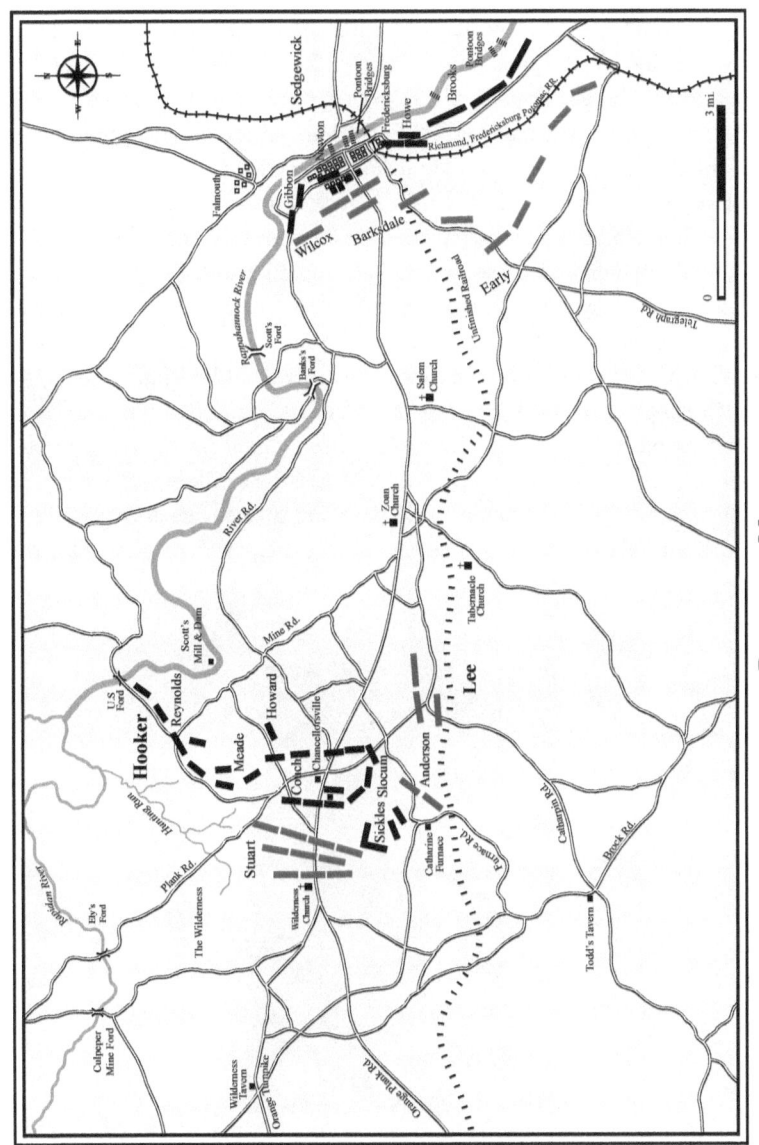

Positions on May 3

Four days earlier, when Lee and Jackson took the majority of their available troops west to fight Hooker in the Wilderness, Maj. Gen. Jubal Early commanded approximately twelve thousand Confederates who had stayed near Fredericksburg to watch Maj. Gen. John Sedgwick and his nearly twenty-seven thousand Federals. May 1 passed with relative quiet for Early. On May 2, a messenger informed the major general that Lee wanted him to leave some of the artillery and one brigade of infantry near Fredericksburg and bring the rest of his force to Chancellorsville.[2] Early doubted the orders at first, but if Lee wanted more troops to crush Hooker and intended to deal with Sedgwick later, Early would obey. He left Hays's Brigade and the Twenty-First Mississippi Regiment in place and got the other infantry units on the road, marching west. Then another messenger arrived with clarification: Lee wanted reinforcements, but only if Early could leave Fredericksburg safely. Lee left it to Early's discretion.[3] The confusion annoyed Early—the general whose temper and swearing had earned him the nickname Lee's Bad Old Man.

Surprisingly, Sedgwick had not moved quickly and had not seemed to realize that most of the Confederates had been absent for hours. However, enough Union movement had occurred to worry the artillerymen and infantrymen who had been left behind, and they sent messengers asking Early to return. Barksdale and his brigade—the last in the march column—got the

Maj. Gen. Jubal Early (Confederate) commanded a division and had been left near Fredericksburg to block the roads toward Chancellorsville and Richmond. Library of Congress.

news before Early, and Barksdale turned back, intending to reoccupy and hold the high ground at Marye's Heights. Early agreed, sent word to Lee, and brought the rest of the Confederates back too.

After this miscommunication and marching misadventure, Early's Confederates retook their defensive position. They used the high ground of Lee's Hill (a new name for the position where Lee had watched the First Battle of Fredericksburg) and the hills forming Marye's Heights to block access along the Orange Turnpike and the Unfinished Railroad, which both led west toward Chancellorsville. The high ground also covered the Telegraph Road, the most direct route south toward Richmond. Early's line was stretched thin. His own brigades—Smith's, Gordon's, Hoke's, and part of Hays's—covered nearly six miles of terrain, essentially the Confederate line from the First Battle of Fredericksburg. Barksdale's Brigade from McLaws's Division covered Marye's Heights and had some additional support from Hays.

During the night of May 2–3, Barksdale received a message from his Mississippians near the town and the river: the Yankees were building a new set of pontoon bridges. Sedgwick had already crossed downstream, and most of his troops were still on the southern side of the river, so more Union troops must be coming and assembling in the town. Barksdale had about 1,500 men under his immediate command to hold the high ground that particularly

Maj. Gen. John Sedgwick (Union) led the Sixth Corps of the Army of the Potomac and commanded the Union troops poised near Fredericksburg while Hooker had the main force near Chancellorsville. Library of Congress.

Brig. Gen. William Barksdale's brigade covered Marye's Heights and the infamous Sunken Road on May 3, 1863. Library of Congress.

covered the best routes to Chancellorsville and Richmond.[4] A few artillery batteries were positioned on the heights, but they did not possess the same powerful cross fire that had brought division after division to a standstill in the previous battle.[5]

Barksdale described what happened next:

> The battle commenced at daylight. A furious cannonade was opened from the enemy's batteries in town and along both banks of the river. Two assaults were made upon Marye's heights, but both were signally repulsed. . . . With a line as extended as this, and in consideration of the small number of troops at my disposal, and the uncertainty as to the point against which the enemy would hurl the immense force he had massed in town, I deemed it proper that the regiments should remain as they then were, and await the happening of events.[6]

But Barksdale did not know about a situation one of his regimental commanders faced. Below where Capt. Pendleton and Gen. Barksdale watched, the Eighteenth Mississippi Regiment held the infamous Sunken Road. Months before, Confederate strength eventually had eventually grown to three entire brigades occupying that position, but now it fell to this one regiment to shoulder the bulk of the defense. The men had fought well and had already repulsed the two morning attacks. Dead and wounded Yankees lay in front of their position. Barksdale had some right to assume that if there was a significant change in his front at a regimental level, that unit's commander would notify him.

The Eighteenth Mississippi's colonel, Thomas M. Griffin, noticed his enemy signaling: the Federals wanted a temporary truce. The forty-seven-year-old regimental commander had joined the unit when it formed in 1861 and had been elected colonel in December of that year. Wounded in July 1862, Griffin had been absent from the regiment through February 1863, returning in time for the spring fighting.[7] Now his regiment had beaten back Union attacks, and the battle seemed to lull. Barksdale, though not with Griffin at the time, later summarized the situation in his own battle report: "Upon pretext of taking care of their wounded, the enemy asked a flag of truce after the second assault on Marye's Hill."[8] Perhaps it seemed like a simple and humanitarian choice, but the decision in front of Griffin regarding the flag of truce would have far-reaching implications for him, his brigade commander, and the Army of Northern Virginia.

Options

Griffin had to decide how to respond to the Union's flag of truce request. He knew the Confederate line was thin, and at some level, he knew the Confederates had been struggling with communications that had created the previous day's fiasco. Observing Union soldiers signaling and wanting permission to aid their wounded in the open field, Griffin had several options.

First, he could simply ignore the parley. Second, he could pass the decision up the chain of command and let Gen. Barksdale know about the request. Third, he could decide the request affected only his immediate front and grant the truce on his own.

Option 1: Ignore the Request for a Temporary Truce

A request for a flag of truce did not have to be acknowledged or granted in Civil War precedents. Typically, commanders allowed for a truce after a battle had ended in order to gather the wounded and bury the dead. Sometimes regiments would hold their fire during lulls in a battle, often in an unspoken truce, allowing a few soldiers to rescue wounded comrades. If Col. Griffin ignored the request—and thus denied it—he would not be violating rules of war. He could always grant the request later in the day if the pause in the battle turned lengthy or the fighting seemed to end.

Option 2: Inform General Barksdale and Let Him Approve or Deny the Request

Probably the simplest option for Col. Griffin would be to send a messenger to Gen. Barksdale and ask him to grant or deny the temporary truce. Barksdale might make a quick decision, or he might visit the Eighteenth Mississippi's position and evaluate the situation. How close were the wounded Union soldiers to Confederate lines? How near would the compassionate rescuers get to the Confederate position, and what would they be able to observe of the rebel dispositions and troop strength? Sending the decision to Barksdale would take the pressure off of Griffin and possibly allow both officers to evaluate the circumstances together if the general was willing to consider it.

Option 3: Allow the Truce

The truce seemed like a simple request, and Col. Griffin could reasonably grant it himself. The battle seemed to have lulled, and his regiment covered the entire Sunken Road position. Seeking Barksdale's approval might be seen as avoiding a decision that could be handled at the regimental level. If Griffin allowed the truce, he should inform Gen. Barksdale of his decision and seek to inform other Confederate infantry and artillery units so that they could respect the pause to recover the wounded.

With a clear line of sight over the open ground to Griffin's front, the risk of allowing a handful of Union soldiers to approach and remove their wounded seemed low. Depending on how close the Union rescuers came, there could be some danger that they would observe the Confederate position. However, it was not a secret that rebels held the Sunken Road, and Griffin did not intend to make any major changes to his regiment's position.

Decision

Col. Griffin granted the request for a temporary truce. It seemed like a right and kind gesture with little danger to his regiment if a few Union soldiers approached through the open field and helped their wounded friends. Perhaps Griffin's own experience with a battlefield wound the previous summer influenced his decision. While making his choice, the colonel did not consult with or inform his commanding general about the situation. Whether he consciously cut Barksdale out of the choice or merely neglected to inform him is unclear, but Barksdale did not receive the information about the truce.[9]

May 3, 1863

Results/Impact

Under the flag of truce, some Union soldiers advanced toward the Eighteenth Mississippi and the Sunken Road. Some regimental officers ordered their men to "keep down" in the Sunken Road and stay hidden.[10]

Whether the Confederates realized it or not, the Union soldiers looked at the line in the Sunken Road. The Mississippians were approximately a yard apart across the position, certainly not a formidable mass of troops. One Confederate complained with hindsight, "The bearer of the flag was, as we were subsequently informed, a officer of high rank in the disguise of a subaltern—a shrewd, Keen, observant fellow who made his eyes do their full duty."[11] Confederates never quite determined in their postbattle memories whether the flag of truce had been a deceptive trick or had started as a genuine relief mission and turned into an opportunistic scouting mission. A soldier in the Twenty-First Mississippi in Barksdale's Brigade recounted,

> They then sent a flag of truce requesting permission to get off their wounded and bury their dead. Unfortunately for us, Gen. Griffin of 18th Miss Regt., granted it and under cover of this, they came up close to our works and discovered what small force we had here and all the time the flag of truce was flying, they were arranging their plans to flank us both right and left and attack us with an over whelming force in front. And in five minutes after the flag of truce was taken down They made the attack. And in less time almost than I can describe it they had flanked us both right and left, and as they had an over whelming force of at least twenty to one coming down upon us in front, so that they had us almost entirely surrounded we were compelled to get out the best way we could. We fought as long as we could fight and as long as there was any use in fighting.[12]

Whatever the motive, the information gained during the flag of truce that Col. Griffin granted ultimately revealed the Confederates' lack of numerical strength to the enemy, handing the Federals an informational and tactical advantage. (Primary sources lack clarity about the timing of the Union attack after the truce period, leading to debate that the idea for the attack might have already been underway, and that the information was just helpful confirmation obtained somewhat accidentally.) Whatever the timing and original motives, Union soldiers would move swiftly with their new knowledge and other observations they had made in their first two assaults. When Barksdale and other officers looked out over the open fields and saw the next Union strike heading for the Sunken Road and Marye's Heights, "the distance from town to the points assailed was so short, the attack so suddenly made, the difficulty of removing troops from one part of the line to another was so great, that it was utterly impossible" for reinforcements to be sent to Griffin.[13]

Barksdale's lines broke, and Union soldiers captured Marye's Heights. Among the Confederate prisoners stood Col. Griffin. Barksdale still praised the colonel as "brave and gallant" in his officer report, but he pointed to Griffin's "flag of truce without consulting me" as the decision that led to the disaster. Other attacks along Early's line pushed his whole Confederate force into retreat. Unless they could make a stand somewhere between Marye's Heights and Zoan Church Ridge, the Confederate troops at Chancellorsville must fight their own battle while thousands of Union soldiers—encouraged by their victory at Fredericksburg—marched toward their rear.

Sedgwick's Troops Move Forward

Situation

Maj. Gen. John Sedgwick, a career officer in the United States Army, found himself trying to manage his commanding general's long-distance expectations. The forty-nine-year-old Sedgwick had exhibited good intentions and slow, steady deliberation in his actions. He was not likely to execute surprise flank marches, but he could be the proverbial anvil while Hooker pretended to be the hammer in the original double-envelopment plan of the campaign. However, by May 2, 1863, Hooker's orders to Sedgwick—transported the long way around through Stafford County and via chief of staff Maj. Gen. Butterfield at the central headquarters—called for Uncle John to become the strike force while Hooker attempted to focus Lee's attention at the Chancellorsville Crossroads. The roles had been reversed.

Since April 28, Sedgwick had been maneuvering thousands of troops on both sides of the Rappahannock River near Fredericksburg. As the days passed, the Third Corps and the First Corps were pulled from his control and sent to join Hooker at Chancellorsville. By the night of May 2, 1863, Hooker wanted Sedgwick to take the approximately twenty-seven thousand soldiers still under his command (mostly the Sixth Corps and a division of the Second Corps) and launch a night attack against the Confederate position on the high ground. Union signal officers and balloonists had observed some of Early's marching debacle, when he had started most of his infantry toward Chancellorsville only to march back again. They had counted the cannon on the high ground and had a good idea that the Confederate force was small, and the position thinly defended.[14]

May 3, 1863

Sedgwick was a beloved army general to his staff and troops in the ranks. Once the attack at Fredericksburg succeeded, he moved west with surprising speed, threatening the rear of Lee's army at Chancellorsville. Library of Congress.

Correspondence was sent between Sedgwick and Butterfield, and between Butterfield and Hooker during the night of May 2–3, 1863, as they tried to clear confusion and confirm plans. One message that Sedgwick received about 11:00 p.m. attempted to lay out his new objectives, though it was not clear to Hooker whether Sedgwick was still on the Fredericksburg side of the river: "The major general commanding directs that you cross the Rappahannock at Fredericksburg on the receipt of this order, and at once take up your line of march on the Chancellorsville road until you connect with him. You will attack and destroy any force you may fall in with on the road. . . . You will probably fall upon the rear of the forces commanded by General Lee, and between you and the major-general commanding he expects to use him up."[15]

Sedgwick ordered Gen. John Gibbon, commander of the Second Division of the Second Corps, to lay new pontoon bridges at Fredericksburg and cross the Rappahannock River directly into the town. Meanwhile, Sedgwick would move the Sixth Corps upstream from its previous crossing point and use the Bowling Green Road to march into Fredericksburg and join Gibbon.[16] For veteran soldiers in Gibbon's division, their route across the river, through town, and toward Marye's Heights seemed like reliving a nightmare; barely five months earlier they had attacked that high ground in the repeated failed assaults during the First Battle of Fredericksburg. Losses had been heavy, the outcome futile, and the scene of Union bodies carpeting the open field still lingered in these men's minds. Many of the Sixth Corps soldiers had been present at that first battle, but not engaged in the fight for Marye's Heights, though they had seen the sights and knew some of the stories.

The Second Battle of Fredericksburg opened on May 3, 1863, with artillery. Then Sedgwick formed his attack lines. Two attack columns and a line of battle would rush toward Marye's Heights, while other troops would head for Lee's Hill farther south. The right attack column would use William Street and try to seize the portion of Marye's Heights that lay along that route. The left attack column would use Hanover Street, which also crossed perpendicularly over Marye's Heights. Meanwhile, the line of battle would advance directly against the infamous Sunken Road.[17] Sedgwick's force outnumbered the Confederate defenders, and if the Federals could capture the high ground, they could secure the roads leading west toward Chancellorsville.

Two Union attacks surged toward the high ground, paused, and fell back under the Confederates' fire. The Sixty-First Pennsylvania Infantry—one of the lead regiments in the right attack column—came under heavy fire. Abraham Titus Brewer's history of the regiment states, "The enemy ran out artillery and fired grape and canister down the road taking the column in flank and slaughtering many brave men who were helpless and uncertain which way to go, and the rebel infantry poured in a deadly fire from the rifle pits."[18]

The columns and the battle line stalled after their second charge, with men taking cover where they could find it. In front of the Sunken Road, some Union soldiers put up a flag of truce, and they went forward to rescue some wounded comrades when the Confederates responded favorably. In or close to town, Sedgwick did not have direct control of the situation, and other generals were also silent or absent. But within the Union ranks, men noticed opportunities, and they began to consider their options and calculate the risks.

Most critical decisions are made by colonels or generals, but in some cases, the common soldier and his regimental line officers will make collective decisions in the absence of additional direction and leadership. Those choices can impact the battle in critical and significant ways.

Options

The Union soldiers in the two columns and battle line had fallen back and now considered their situation. Many had taken cover or withdrawn toward the millrace that cut across the battlefield, not far from the outskirts of town. They had already been under heavy fire twice in the attempt to take the high ground, and thus far in this lull, no generals had appeared to rally them. The

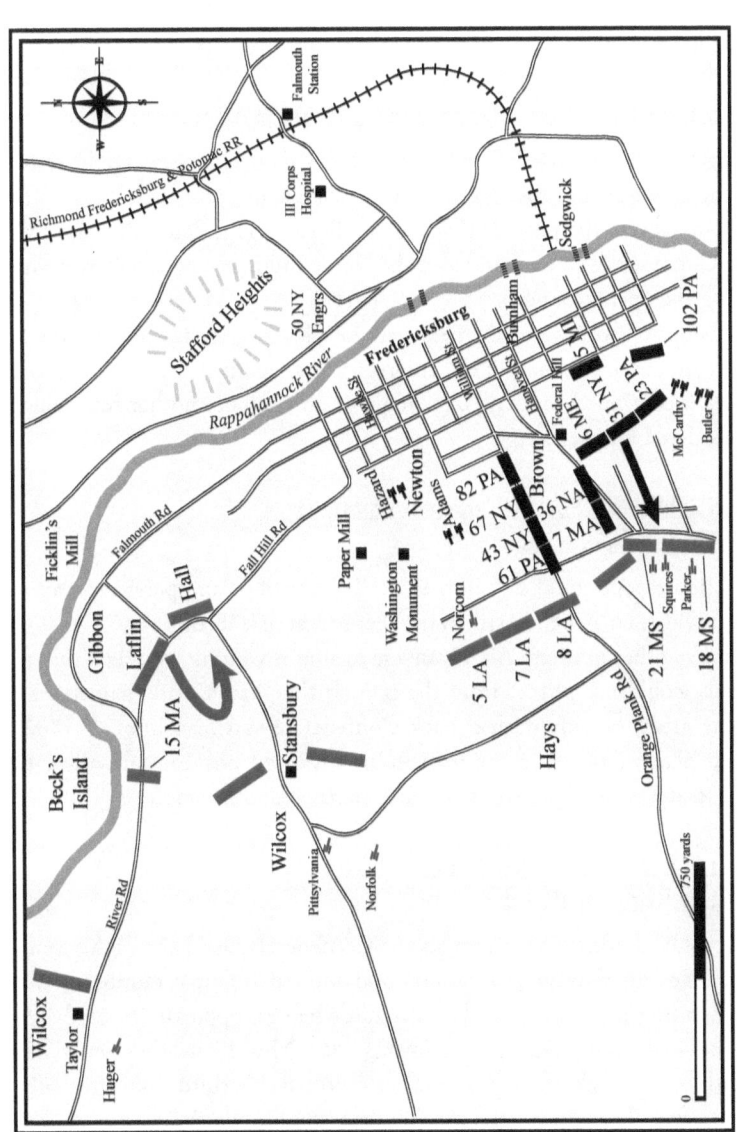

soldiers collectively had three options. First, they could retreat and take cover in the town, giving up the advanced position. Second, they could simply wait for new orders from officers higher in the chain of command. Third, they could begin to realize the opportunity in front of them and attack with only regimental orders.

Option 1: Retreat Closer to Town and Give Up the Advanced Position

Two attacks and no battlefield success. The Union regiments could retreat closer to town or into town, forcing the generals to order them back to the assaults or revise the plan. Perhaps an artillery barrage could damage some of the Confederate cannon and give the Union infantry a better chance while crossing the open ground.

This option would put the next decisions back on Sedgwick and his division commanders. Most likely, the regiments would still have to attack if Sedgwick continued carrying out Hooker's orders, but another route might be considered for the charge.

Option 2: Wait for Specific Orders from Higher in the Chain of Command

The Union troops could stay in their stalled positions and passively wait for orders. Did their generals still want them to attack in this way? Or was it time to try other options? An advantage to simply waiting would be that the Federals would not retreat from the ground they had already gained—and in some areas, already pushed back Confederate skirmish lines. However, waiting here would leave the men in an advanced position and allow the Confederates time to prepare to repulse another Union assault.

Option 3: Realize the Opportunity and Attack with Only Regimental Orders

Union soldiers noticed that though the Confederates held the high ground, they had comparatively few cannon and limited infantry numbers. With overwhelming numbers, the Union soldiers had an opportunity on May 3, 1863, that had not existed on December 13, 1862. Most likely, they would have to continue to attack. Perhaps it was better to attack a third time after only a limited pause that might catch the Confederates off guard.

The regimental officers knew the orders for the attack formations and knew that they were supposed to take the heights and open the roads toward Chancellorsville. If they ordered a third assault without waiting for more specific directions, they would still be following their original objective.

May 3, 1863

Decision

Within the ranks of the Union regiments in front of Marye's Heights, the same idea took hold. Do not delay; attack again. Their retreats early that morning or the memories of the attacks here in December 1862 were not enough to keep these troops from advancing. Union soldiers and their regimental officers decided to strike again, and strike without stopping.

Results/Impact

Col. Thomas Allen paced in front of his men in the Fifth Wisconsin Infantry. Ahead of his regiment, Marye's Heights rose. "When the signal forward is given," he told them, "you will start at the double quick. You will not fire a gun and you will not stop until you get the order to halt. You will never get that order."[19] In his 1890 history of the regiment, Nelson V. Hutchinson described how the Seventh Massachusetts, along with the Thirty-Sixth New York, formed the left attack column again:

> Just as we got in motion, the rebel batteries all along the Heights opened with shell. . . . On the column moved in mass by fours . . .

The Sunken Road at Marye's Heights was an important position in the First Battle of Fredericksburg (1862) and the Second Battle of Fredericksburg (1863). This photograph was taken after the Union assault on the position during the Chancellorsville Campaign, and it shows casualties and debris of war left behind as the fighting shifted farther west toward Salem Church. Library of Congress.

shell and cannister cutting through it until we had got within a hundred feet of the stone wall, when Barksdale's brigade of Mississippians poured in a terrific volley from right and left, and checked us for about five minutes. The road or gulch, was filled with the dead, wounded, and dying . . . but still we lunge forward, the brave. . . . On we stagger, men falling around us like leaves in autumn. Soon out of the confusion rings the clarion shout of Lieut.-Col. Harlow, "Forward, forward, boys!" and led by that gallant officer, ably seconded by his brave comrades, the old Seventh struggled through and over the stone wall, bleeding at every step.[20]

All across the Union front, regiments reached the Sunken Road—some directly, some shifting to the left and coming up on the flank. Along William Street and Hanover Street, the Union columns were opening the roadways, pushing the Confederates back. Some soldiers stabbed and parried with bayonets in the Sunken Road. Others paused and took Confederates prisoner, including Col. Griffin of the Eighteenth Mississippi and many of his Sunken Road defenders. The majority of the Union survivors raced up the steep slopes of Marye's Heights and confronted the artillery at the top, capturing some of the cannon. For the first time in Fredericksburg's battle history, Union flags in Union hands fluttered and streamed at the top of the horrific heights.

To the Union left of Marye's Heights, other US brigades assaulted Lee's Hill, driving off more Confederate defenders and clearing the Telegraph Road and Unfinished Railroad Cut. Gen. Early and his Confederates retreated. Nearly ten miles to the west lay the unprotected rear of Lee's army.

The decision of the common soldiers and regimental officers to try one more time and to charge without stopping opened the way for Sedgwick to carry out his orders and march his troops on toward Chancellorsville. This choice resulted in one of the rare Union victories during the Chancellorsville Campaign. It also provided a sliver of opportunity for Hooker's plan to threaten the Confederates from two directions to successfully trap Lee's multidivided army.

Hooker had ordered Sedgwick to adapt and reverse roles, moving from a distraction force to an attack force. An opportunity for success lay ahead of Sedgwick predominantly due to his soldiers' ability to adapt to a role reversal in the decision process. Officers and even soldiers in the ranks gave the orders for the third assault on the Confederates' high ground, and the "movements were gallantly executed under a most destructive fire."[21]

May 3, 1863

Lee Divides His Army Again

Situation

Shortly after noon on May 3, 1863, two horsemen galloped west toward Chancellorsville. Both had set off separately to carry the news to Gen. Robert E. Lee that Marye's Heights had been captured by the Yankees and Sedgwick's entire force could march nearly unopposed toward Lee's rear. It remained to be seen whether Gen. Early would be able to rally and re-form his troops somewhere between Marye's Heights and Zoan Church Ridge.

Lieut. Andrew Pitzer, the first messenger to ride toward the Confederate army commander, spurred his horse hard. He was one of Early's staff officers, but he rode off on his own accord to bring the news of the retreat and impending threat. When he reached Lee, Pitzer reported and gasped out the news. Lee accepted the ill-timed information with calm stoicism. A short time later, the second messenger arrived. This chaplain from Barksdale's Brigade had his faith in Confederate victory shaken by what he had witnessed near Fredericksburg, and his anxiety revealed itself in his words and actions. Nothing seemed to shake Lee's calmness. "Thank you very much," he interrupted, gently putting off the chaplain and his now repeating news, "but both you and your horse are overheated. Take him to that shady tree yonder and rest a little. I'll call you as soon as we are through."[22] Sedgwick might be heading toward Chancellorsville, but Lee had to deal with Hooker first and gain some assurance that officer was unlikely to leave his trenches.

While Gen. Early tried to hold Marye's Heights and Lee's Hill near Fredericksburg on the morning of May 3, Lee had been fighting to gain important terrain around Chancellorsville and to reunite the main Confederate force. On the previous night, Gen. Stonewall Jackson had been wounded, and Maj. Gen. J. E. B. Stuart had taken temporary command of the Second Corps. Jackson's surprise flank attack on the Union Eleventh Corps and night pursuit had been moderately successful, but they had stalled with the Second Corps still separated from Lee and the divisions of Anderson and McLaws. If Hooker realized the exact positions of the divided rebels and acted quickly, one wing of the Confederate army could be pinned in place, and another wing could possibly be destroyed without an easy way for either wing to reinforce the other. Lee had to reunite the army and gave Stuart orders to that effect.

Stuart particularly targeted a platform of high ground called Hazel Grove that was situated on the right on the Second Corps' line. If the troops could take this position, the Confederate lines could reunite more easily and gain a significant artillery platform to bombard Hooker's lines and headquarters in the clearing of the Chancellorsville Crossroads. The infantry under Stuart's

Command was stacked in formations, and his tactics for the morning of May 3 called for repeated and costly infantry charges. By late morning, the Union lines around Chancellorsville were collapsing. Anderson and McLaws began to advance their brigades from the south and east. Lee rode forward with the advancing Confederates, and one of his aides-de-camp later remembered the scene:

> The troops were pressing forward with all the ardour [sic] and enthusiasm of combat. The white smoke of musketry fringed the front line of battle, while the artillery . . . shook the earth with its *thunder*, and filled the air with the wild shrieks of shells that plunged into the masses of the retreated foe. . . . Chancellor House and the woods surrounding it were wrapped in flames. In the midst of this awful scene, General Lee . . . rode to the front of his advancing battalions. His presence was the signal for one of those outbursts of enthusiasm which none can appreciate who have not witnessed them. The fierce soldiers with their faces blackened with the smoke of battle, the wounded crawling with feeble limbs from the fury of the devouring flames, all seemed possessed with a common impulse. One long, unbroken cheer . . . rose high above the roar of battle.

Confederate troops cheered Lee as he rode victoriously into the Chancellorsville Crossroads on May 3, 1863, as imagined in this circa 1900 illustration. Library of Congress.

... As I looked upon him ... I thought that it must have been from such a scene that men in ancient days rose to the dignity of gods.[23]

The troops and staff officers considered the scene as the Chancellorsville Crossroads came into Confederate possession a victorious moment. At some level, it was: Fighting Joe Hooker was retreating, and the Confederate army around Chancellorsville had reunited. But more strategy and tactics would need to be planned, and the battle had not really ended.

Even as he paused near the crossroads and heard his soldiers cheering, Lee faced a new decision. How would he confront Sedgwick and the thousands of Union troops already marching west toward his rear? He had the reports and the news. Hooker was retreating. Now, he had to decide how to fight, trick, or evade Sedgwick. The Union Sixth Corps could not be allowed to reinforce Hooker, as that might give fresh boldness to the currently confused commander. But where to position troops to prevent the threat of a Union "reunion"? And how to ultimately defeat Hooker and gain a decisive battlefield victory that truly meant something for the Confederacy? These questions weighed on Lee as he turned to the next critical decision.

Options

Lee had three viable options regarding the situation on the afternoon of May 3, 1863. First, he could turn a portion of the Confederate army to the east and set up a defensive position, forcing Sedgwick to attack if he continued the advance. Second, Lee could continue to focus on attacking Hooker. Third, he could divide the Confederate force, devoting even more resources against Sedgwick than needed in the first option, and then pursue offensive movements against Sedgwick.

Option 1: Set Up a Defensive Line along Zoan Church Ridge and Let Sedgwick Attack

Returning some Confederate troops to Zoan Church Ridge while the majority of them remained at Chancellorsville would enable Lee to hold both portions of his force within a couple of miles of each other, able to quickly offer support if needed. This option confronted Sedgwick's advance with a defensive stand. With enough time, the ridge could be a strong position facing east with artillery and entrenched infantry. The Confederate army would sit like a wedge between Hooker and Sedgwick, using terrain to its advance. If Sedgwick attempted to move men toward the River Road, Confederates could shift north from Zoan Church Ridge to block them.

A risk with this option was letting the two Union elements get so close to each other. Would Hooker be tempted to try an offensive strike? Lee knew that his troops had not yet fought all the Union corps with Hooker. What would happen if the Fifth Corps and the First Corps went on the offense and simultaneously attacked while Sedgwick attacked at the ridge? Depending on how motivated Hooker and Sedgwick were to unite their forces, the Confederates could be in a desperate situation.

Option 2: Continue to Focus on Attacking Hooker's Corps

Lee had been moderately unconcerned about Sedgwick up to this point in the campaign. Lee had left Early with twelve thousand troops to watch Sedgwick, and that Union general had obligingly done little of note for five days. How quickly would Sedgwick move on the road to Chancellorsville? And how good were his roundabout communications with Hooker? Lee had known Sedgwick before this war, when they had both been United States Army officers. Based on his previous knowledge of Sedgwick's habits and character, Lee had judged that he would not move quickly, and that opinion had proved correct until now.

Lee could have Early continue to monitor and delay Sedgwick while concentrating his efforts and most troops on attacking Hooker again. Pressing the offensive on Hooker might prevent him from building a new defensive line, either forcing an unarguable Union defeat, or at the very least compelling Hooker to recross the Rappahannock River.

Option 3: Divide the Confederate Force, Sending a Portion
to join Early and Fight Sedgwick

Lee could order elements of his army to leave the Chancellorsville area, march east, unite with Early, and try an offensive movement to delay or defeat Sedgwick. An offensive movement against Sedgwick might throw him off balance and alter his enthusiasm for getting to Chancellorsville and Hooker. Reinforcements and a sharp battle might be enough to make Sedgwick overly cautious, perhaps retreating toward Fredericksburg or toward a ford on the Rappahannock River.

Lee had divided the Confederate army almost daily during the Chancellorsville operations. It was always risky. Anderson's or McLaws's Divisions were the closest Confederate troops to Sedgwick and could most easily turn and go east; they had fought hard around Chancellorsville, but they had not made the flank march or suffered the staggering losses that the divisions under Jackson and Stuart had. If troops needed to turn east, march a half-dozen miles or so, and fight, units from those divisions would be the best choices.

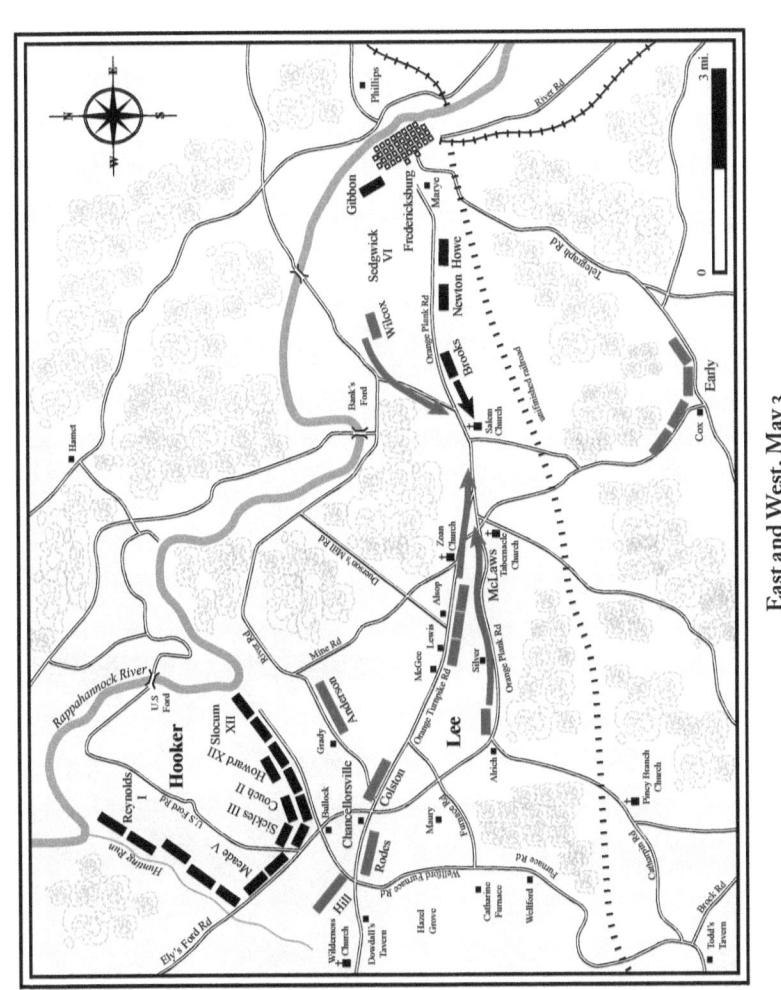

East and West, May 3

Decision

Lee decided to divide his army. First, to help pin and threaten Hooker, he sent Brig. Gen. Raleigh Colston with his division of the Second Corps toward US Ford Road. Then, to face Sedgwick, Lee selected McLaws's Division to head east and join the Confederates resisting the Union advance.

Results/Impact

Various Confederate units had been trying to delay Sedgwick's advance. Enthused by their success on the high ground near Fredericksburg, the Union troops pressed west. It was annoying to have to stop, deploy, and push small Confederate units off high points of the rolling terrain, but the Federals had kept moving steadily until they approached Salem Church.

That brick sanctuary stood on a notable piece of high ground that Brig. Gen. Cadmus Wilcox had selected as the appropriate place to make a solid stand. Wilcox and his brigade had been holding the far left of the Confederate line near Fredericksburg, but they had fallen back toward the west when the rest of their comrades had retreated south. Now, his brigade blocked the road to Chancellorsville.

Union artillery had just opened fire on Wilcox's position as McLaws's Division arrived. Ordered east to fight Sedgwick, McLaws approved of Wilcox's concept and brought his brigades into the battle line on either side of Wilcox's

Salem Church sits on a ridge between Fredericksburg and Chancellorsville, a good defensive position for Confederates forming to confront Sedgwick's advancing Union troops. National Park Service.

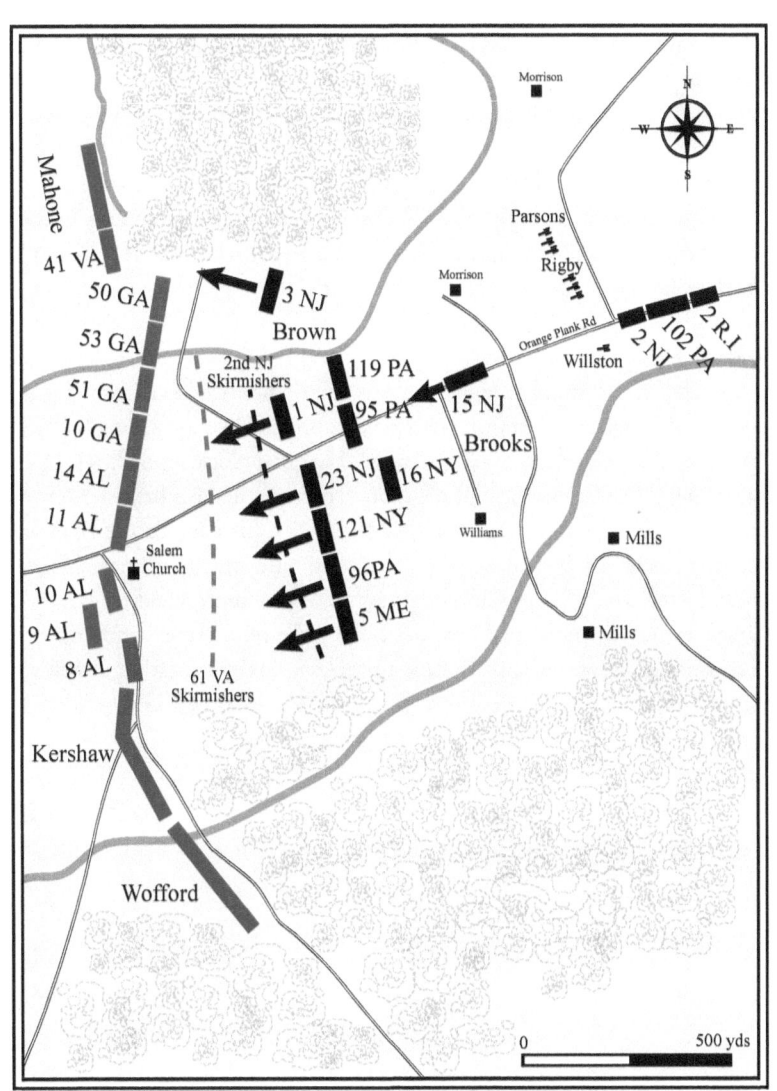

Salem Church

men. The Confederates used the reverse slope of the ridge to protect the reinforcements and get them up to the fighting lines in an orderly manner. The timely arrival of brigades under McLaws—Mahone's, Semmes's, Kershaw's, and Wofford's—turned the fighting at Salem Church from a delaying action into a full battle.

By nightfall, the Confederate line held at Salem Church, and Union troops had begun to feel depressed and discouraged at their lack of triumph. In the darkness, Lee sent messages to McLaws and to Early. The latter had managed to re-form most of his men, and Lee envisioned an opportunity for another flank attack: Early smashing into Sedgwick's left flank as he fought at Salem Church. Obligingly, Hooker and his generals stayed quietly in their new position north of Chancellorsville, and Lee felt confident they could be held stationary a little while longer. Hooker's inactivity encouraged Lee to send Anderson's Division to join McLaws and Early, and Lee then joined those three divisions in person.

On May 4, the combined forces of McLaws, Anderson, and Early steadily pushed Sedgwick's men toward the Rappahannock River. A strong Confederate detachment also reoccupied Marye's Heights, blocking Sedgwick's retreat through Fredericksburg. The Union general turned his brigades toward Bank's Ford on the Rappahannock, settling with his back to the river and Confederates in his front. Lee was dissatisfied with his subordinates' failure to destroy the Sixth Corps, but Sedgwick had been neutralized for now. Dividing his army yet again had paid off, buying the rebels time and temporary safety. Perhaps he would now be able to make a final devastating attack and destroy Hooker's army. Perhaps on May 5, there would be anxious riders on galloping horses with threatening news from the east.

CHAPTER 5

A FATEFUL DAY

MAY 3, 1863

The third day of combat saw action in three separate areas: the Chancellorsville Crossroads, Fredericksburg, and Salem Church. The fighting at each place directly affected the decision and results of the engagements at all the other locations. While the Confederates kept the advantage of offense around Chancellorsville, they had to employ defensive operations to slow Maj. Gen. Sedgwick's advancing troops from the east. Union generals had advantages in all locations, and with hindsight, they had a strong opportunity to crush General Lee's divided Confederates.

On May 3, 1863, three critical decisions made near the Chancellorsville Crossroads influenced the campaign and battle. Hooker failed to recognize the importance of a piece of high ground and handed the Confederates a significant topographical platform for artillery. After Hooker suffered a painful and frightening injury, he refused to relinquish command, and his officers and doctors declined to declare him medically unfit. The Union army was thus left with an unresponsive commander and chain of command as the enemy began to break through its defensive lines. Then, after a day of difficulty and underused artillery operations, Hooker decided to return his chief of artillery, Brig. Gen. Henry Hunt, to active command. The fighting and the critical decisions on this third day of battle continued to give new chances to the Confederates and forced the Union army around Chancellorsville into retreat and command difficulties.

Hooker Orders Sickles to Abandon Hazel Grove

Situation

Maj. Gen. Daniel Sickles wanted to be a hero. Commander of the Union's Third Corps at Chancellorsville and a faithful, social friend with General Hooker during the winter of 1862, Sickles just needed the right moment to write his military saga. As darkness settled across the battleground woods and the Confederate flank attack slowed, the Third Corps seemed to be in the right place at the right time. Would this be the decisive night or day?

Sickles already had plenty of notoriety for his actions before the war—shooting and killing his wife's lover in broad daylight and then getting acquitted after pleading temporary insanity. With his ability to reason miraculously restored by the verdict, the officer continued his political angling and longtime cronyism within the political machine of New York, Tammany Hall. Aspiring politicians like Sickles often saw the Civil War as their chance to publicly parade their patriotism and possibly bring home a visible reminder of their courage with a physical wound or some captured military trophies. Sickles quickly

Maj. Gen. Daniel Sickles (Union) commanded the Third Corps of the Army of the Potomac and was ordered to re-form his lines on May 3, 1863, giving up strong defensive ground near Hazel Grove. Library of Congress.

volunteered to save the Union, and by September 1861, he had been appointed brigadier general. He was confirmed as a major general in March 1863. Though noted for his bravery in battle, Sickles's scandalous reputation preceded him, and he had a habit of getting into conflicts with his peers and superiors.[1] He was also a crony of Hooker and an instigator of rumored scandals, and he received command of the Third Corps of the Army of the Potomac.

That corps had arrived promptly and taken position around Chancellorsville. By the morning of May 2, 1863, the Third Corps faced south and sat at the heart of the Union lines. To the left curved the lines of the Twelfth Corps and the Second Corps. Out to the right, the Eleventh Corps had lounged and waited during the day on the second.

To his credit, Sickles had been active on May 2, noting the Confederates moving along his front near Catharine Furnace and sending word to Hooker. Sickles did more, though; he "hastened to report these movements through staff officers to the general-in-chief [Hooker], and communicate the substance of them in the same manner to Major-General Howard . . . and also to Major-General Slocum, inviting their cooperation."[2] Receiving permission, Sickles began to push his troops south, exploring the Confederate movement and finding strong resistance. He brought in artillery and cavalry and positioned two of his three divisions to pressure the rebels. The Federals would be ready in case Hooker agreed to order Slocum's Twelfth Corps or Howard's Eleventh Corps to join in a coordinated attack against the presumably retreating enemy.[3]

The Eleventh Corps' collapse and retreat took Sickles by surprise. Even so, he rode toward the challenge, positioning artillery and some cavalry units to cover the gap between his division remaining in place along the main battle line and his forces advancing south. The Confederate flank attack against the Eleventh Corps had sent that force into confusion, with fugitives fleeing into the lines and trenches of the other corps and spreading wild rumors. In the darkness ending May 2 and starting May 3, Union generals grappled with the changes that had occurred in a matter of hours and the confusion in the dark Wilderness woods.

Sickles recalled the brigades of his corps that had advanced to challenge the "retreating" Confederates, and then he made preparations for a night attack. Realizing he could form on the right flank of the broken Confederate lines meshed in the Wilderness on the south side of the Orange Turnpike, Sickles hoped an attack could confuse the enemy and regain some ground. "The night was very clear and still; the moon, nearly full, threw enough light into the woods to facilitate the advance, and against a terrific fire of musketry and artillery . . . the advance was successfully executed," he later penned in his official report. Sickles took an overly optimistic view of his operation.[4] The advance did not successfully connect with the rest of the Union lines, and the position put Sickles's divisions in a position protruding from the rest of the Federal lines encircling the Chancellorsville Crossroads.[5] In the morning, Hooker wanted to get his corps into a strong, unified position.

Part of the topography that Sickles held included Hazel Grove, a piece of high ground that was a "beautiful position for artillery, an open grassy ridge, some 400 yards long, extending N.E. [northeast] and S.W. [southwest]." This position overlooked an "extensive clearing" that reached toward Fairview and beyond to the Chancellorsville Crossroads.[6] As seen on a map without topography lines, abandoning Hazel Grove would pull Sickles into a position conforming with the rest of the Union line. However, withdrawing from this high ground could hand the Confederates an artillery platform and also give them a vital link to reuniting their divided forces.

The previous day had not gone well for Hooker, and the approved advance of Sickles's divisions had created some threat to the Union position and slow realignment to face the Confederate attack coming from the west. In the morning of May 3, 1863, the commanding general needed to decide whether to keep Sickles and the Third Corps where they were or reposition them elsewhere.

Options

Hooker had three possible options. First, he could allow Sickles to hold a defensive position, using the high ground to advantage and staying in the protruding position. Second, he could focus on mitigating a possible salient threat to his overall position and order Sickles into the encircling line. Third, Hooker could use the foothold that the Third Corps had established as a position to take offensive action, fighting the divided Confederate forces.

Option 1: Keep Sickles Defensively on the High Ground

While Sickles's night attack had not been successful, he still had a strong position with a significant number of troops. On and around the high ground at Hazel Grove, Birney's and Whipple's divisions from the Third Corps waited, supported by a brigade loaned from the Eleventh Corps the previous day. Thirty-eight artillery pieces were available for combat at this location.[7] Given the strength of the topography and this force, the Federals could hold Hazel Grove defensively.

Keeping Sickles at Hazel Grove could force the Confederates to attack a strong position. If they tried to bypass Hazel Grove to the north and head

May 3, 1863

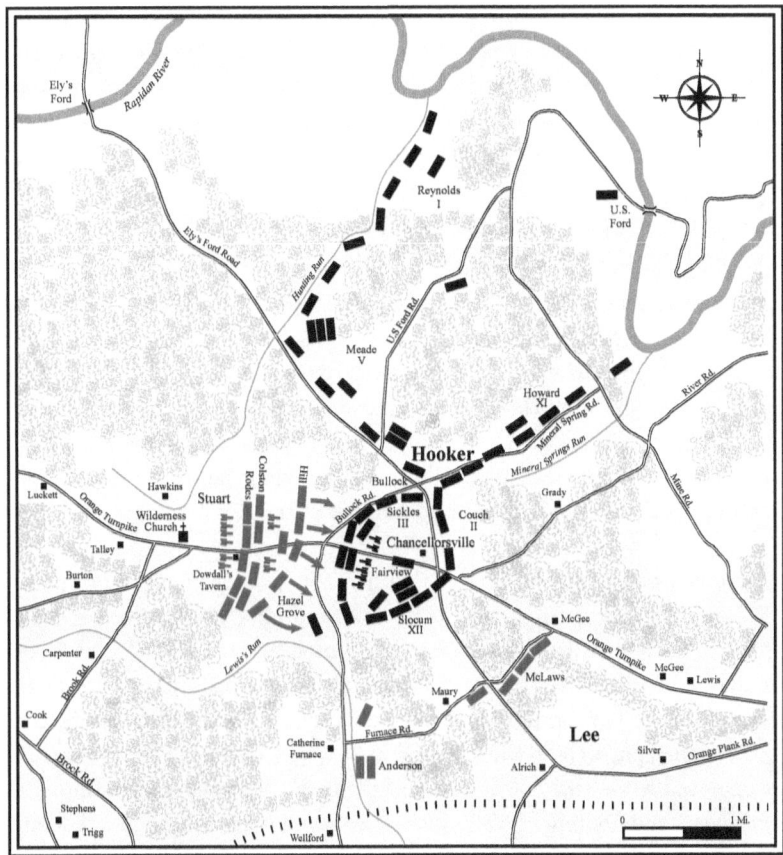

Hazel Grove

for the Chancellorsville Crossroads, they would still encounter resistance from the positioned soldiers astride the Orange Turnpike. Also, Hazel Grove would create flank and rear artillery fire as the rebels approached the clearing. Meanwhile, the Union infantry could take defensive positions, building northwest-facing trenches to confront the right flank of Stuart's wing.

Option 2: Order Sickles to Withdraw into the Main Union Line

Another option would require Sickles to give up the strong topography at Hazel Grove and fall back into the encircling position with the rest of the Union corps. This plan appeared the least risky since it would pull an advanced corps back into the main line and avoid leaving troops in a possibly exposed position between elements of the divided Confederate force around Chancellorsville. However, if Hooker drew Sickles back, the Confederates could obtain Hazel Grove and make it an artillery position that could fire on the main Union line and into the crossroads clearing.

Option 3: Use Sickles's Advanced Position as a starting point for counterattacks on the Divided Confederates

Hooker was aware that the Confederate troops fighting him at Chancellorsville were divided. He also hoped that Sedgwick would be able to break through the rebel defenders near Fredericksburg and come in on the rear of Lee's multidivided army. Hooker could act offensively to prevent or at least delay the reunification of the Confederate Second Corps to the west and the two divisions at the southeast. Hazel Grove sat between the Confederate forces, and the Union already had a strong number of infantrymen and artillery in place.

Hooker had a corps in reserve that had not yet been engaged in the battle. Sending elements from the Fifth Corps and First Corps to be part of an offensive movement or to strengthen the Union line to and at Hazel Grove could be an option. The First Corps was covering the roads to the fords on the Rappahannock but did not seem to be threatened. The Fifth Corps held an unthreatened position on the morning of May 3, and some of its troops could be deployed while still holding part of the corps as a reserve. Sending reinforcements and holding Hazel Grove or even counterattacking Confederates from this position could take advantage of the division of the Confederate force and the troops' confusing night.

Decision

Hooker had been informed of the topographical importance of Hazel Grove. It also seems that he rode toward that position early in the morning of May 3. There, Hooker ordered Sickles to abandon Hazel Grove and take his infantry, artillery, and the supporting cavalry into the main Union line, establishing a position in the open clearing near Fairview.

Results/Impact

This critical decision would change the course of the battle. Sickles promptly obeyed Hooker's orders to withdraw to Fairview. However, some of Sickles's troops were attacked as they retreated. Once they reached the position near Fairview, the Third Corps infantry fought and "drove the enemy back upon himself with incalculable slaughter."[8] The Union soldiers faced attack after attack from the Confederate Second Corps while rebel artillery set up a cross fire.

Rejoicing in the artillery platform at Hazel Grove, Confederate artillerists positioned approximately thirty cannon on that high ground and entered into counterbattery duels with the Third Corps guns now at Fairview. Meanwhile, about twenty Confederate cannon along the Orange Turnpike near Dowdall's Tavern took advantage of what open areas they could utilize and set up a cross fire toward the Union position.[9] As the morning hours passed, the Third Corps artillery had not been resupplied with ammunition and was forced with withdraw closer to the Chancellor House.[10]

According to later testimony before the Joint Committee on the Conduct of the War, Gen. Sickles declared that Hooker "had determined to occupy a line somewhat less extended than he had held on the previous day. The disorganization of the eleventh corps had practically left him with one corps less for Sunday's operations than before."[11] However, Sickles was more willing to blame the Eleventh Corps than to deeply consider the topographical position he had given up at Hazel Grove or criticize his friend, the commanding general.

The decision to retreat from Hazel Grove stacked Union soldiers in the defensive position, handed the Confederates an offensive artillery position, and opened the door for Lee and Stuart to more easily reunite their forces. The choice emphasized army preservation instead of bold battle plans. It pinned Union hopes on the prospect of Sedgwick's force marching west toward Chancellorsville to rescue Hooker's entrenched army.

This critical decision might arguably have influenced more than the Battle of Chancellorsville. During the Battle of Gettysburg, two months later, on July 2, 1863, Daniel Sickles disobeyed direct orders to stay in a defensive line position and instead advanced to claim a strong piece of high ground in his front. Historians have speculated that memories of Confederate artillery on the high ground of Hazel Grove pounding his infantry lines influenced his Gettysburg insubordination.

Pulling back the Third Corps might have strengthened the Union line near Chancellorsville. However, other circumstances and decisions resulted in a lack of support and ineffective handling of the early morning retreat and re-forming of the Union defense. Hooker's control of the battle continued to spiral, and the lack of artillery ammunition resupply that affected the Third Corps was directly tied to other critical decisions of May 3, 1863.

Union Officers Do Not Replace Hooker after His Injury

Situation

The large brick house at the Chancellorsville Crossroads had withstood artillery rounds on May 2, 1863, but the intensity of the fire grew as the Confederates positioned cannon on the high ground at Hazel Grove nearly a mile distant. After ushering the civilians who either lived or took refuge in the Chancellor House into the cellar, the occupying Yankees had found multiple uses for the dwelling at the center of it all. General Hooker had made the house his headquarters since his arrival at the crossroads; it was the central point for orderlies, generals, and staff officers. A few doctors had used the place as a temporary field hospital since May 1, but it was too exposed to become one of the corps' medical sites. By the morning of May 3, a pile of amputated limbs lay outside the sitting room window, dead men had been placed in a nearby row for burial, and cries of agony echoed from the rooms.[12]

Dr. Jonathan Letterman, medical director of the Army of the Potomac, came and went from this headquarters, overseeing the large field hospitals established in the rear. He also oversaw the comparatively swift ambulance evacuation over pontoon bridges to remove the transportable wounded from the combat area. Letterman had reformed and transformed the medical system for the Union army in 1862, creating an organized ambulance and evacuation system, firing incompetent surgeons, and assembling medical teams

Dr. Jonathan Letterman (Union) was the medical director for the Army of the Potomac; he had transformed medical care for Union soldiers in 1862, and at Chancellorsville he took care of wounded officers. Library of Congress.

that had the most skilled doctors, assistants, and administrators in their proper places. In addition to overseeing this vast logistical operation to save as many lives as possible, a medical director could be summoned to look after the commanding general or other high-ranking officers if they were injured.

At midmorning on May 3, 1863, as Confederate attacks repeatedly struck the Union lines and pushed the repositioned Third Corps to the limits of its strength and ammunition, Letterman witnessed an incident that would create a moment of critical decision. He later wrote about it in his memoirs:

> The headquarters of General Hooker were much exposed to the fire of the enemy. On the 3d of May a round shot struck the stone steps of the portico, upon which the Commanding General stood, watching the progress of the battle, knocked down a solid wooden pillar, which struck him, and felled him to the floor. Being within a few feet of him at the time of the accident, I saw him fall, and was instantly with him, and had him taken to his room; he was very much stunned by the blow, although no bones were broken. The rumor spread rapidly that General Hooker was killed, and to dispel that idea, he appeared to the troops, though scarcely able to sit upon his horse. The effect of this blow and fall, lasted for some hours.[13]

Bystanders and staff officers were confused. Hooker "was knocked senseless . . . and from his appearance and the character of the blow, they supposed at the time that the injury would result fatally."[14] In the midst of the stunning blow and the medical examination, someone sent word to Maj. Gen. Darius Couch, who reported, "About 9:45 a.m. I was called to the Chandler house to briefly take command of the army, simply acting as executive officer to General Hooker in fulfilling his instructions, which were to draw in the front and make some new dispositions."[15] (Couch might have meant the Chancellor House, or he might have been referring to the Bullock House, where Hooker was eventually moved.)

Officers noted Hooker's disposition following his injury. For example, around 11 a.m. Brig. Gen. Birney, commanding a division of the Third Corps, described meeting Hooker on horseback near the Chancellor House: "[He] rode up to me and said he was suffering a great deal from the concussion. . . . He seemed to suffer a great deal from the accident; so I judged from his manner."[16] Birney also recalled the general being quieter and more subdued in manner than usual.[17] Later in the day, officers found Hooker lying down in a tent; Gen. Meade, commander of the Fifth Corps, was running interference and saying that Hooker was not available.[18]

At 1:30 p.m., chief of staff Gen. Daniel Butterfield, positioned on the north side of the Rappahannock between Hooker and Sedgwick, telegraphed Pres. Lincoln in Washington, DC. Butterfield had been communicating fairly regularly with government officials throughout the campaign, but now he had to carefully relate what he had heard while downplaying possible results of the injury: "General Hooker slightly, but not severely, wounded. He has preferred thus far that nothing should be reported, and does not know of this, but I cannot refrain from saying this much to you. You may expect his dispatch in a few hours, which will give the result."[19]

Hooker seems to have gone through several phases of incapacity following the head injury. While the limited medical details about his condition are open to study and speculation, the impact of the blow to his head and the resulting pronounced concussion created a command dilemma for the Union. Was Hooker capable of leading, especially as Confederate attacks began to heavily press and overrun Union defenses? If he was not able to command—even temporarily—who should assume the role and direct the corps?

Options

Medical personnel, senior corps commanders, and staff officers needed to make a critical decision. Was Hooker capable of the decisions and duties of a commander? Hooker himself could be involved in this decision if and when he was conscious. First, the general could recognize the extent of his injury and turn full command over to his next senior officer, Maj. Gen. Darius Couch. Second, the medical director or assigned attending doctor could declare Hooker physically unfit for duty, resulting in the leadership role going to the next senior officer. Third, everyone could observe Hooker and allow him to stay in command while rallying around him to try to pick up the reins in the moments he was unable to actively lead.

Option 1: Hooker Turns Over Command to a Senior Officer

The blow to Hooker's head was serious. He regained consciousness and hurried to mount a horse to be a visible figure, but throughout the rest of the day, he sought rest. In addition, his demeanor seemed significantly altered. Hooker could remove himself from command, even temporarily, and give full authority to his next senior officer in the field, Maj. Gen. Darius Couch, commander of the Second Corps.

To its advantage, this option would have one person making command decisions at key moments as the entire Union position around Chancellorsville faced heavy attacks. Someone needed to be in charge, making decisions, and overseeing orders for supplies, positioning, and overall tactics. However,

May 3, 1863

Maj. Gen. Darius Couch (Union) commanded the Second Corps of the Army of the Potomac and would be the senior ranking officer to step into army leadership if Hooker was unable to command. Library of Congress.

a disadvantage of this option was the man who would be next to command. Couch, as described by one of his division commanders, was "a person naturally very cautious about making a decision,"[20] and Hooker might be understandably reluctant to give him full authority. Hooker could bypass the usual chain of command and order another senior general to take control of the army, dealing with any pushback from Couch beyond the day of battle. Maj. Gen. George G. Meade from the Fifth Corps could be a possible option further down the chain of command.

Option 2: Officers and Medical Experts Declare Hooker
Unfit for Command

If Hooker did not recognize the severity of his injury, officers and doctors might need to step in. Dr. Letterman or another assigned attending physician could express concern about Hooker's concussion and the effects it was clearly producing on his mental awareness and physical capabilities. They might convince the general to fully turn over command—even temporarily. If they judged the situation severe enough, they might declare him medically unfit. Staff officers or general officers could urge a better medical analysis and decision.

The danger with this option would be accusation of mutiny. The campaign was not going well, and staff and general officers knew it. It was far from lost, but in the days prior to May 3, Hooker had made decisions that his corps commanders had not supported. The Army of the Potomac always had a political faction with both national and army politics at work. If staff or corps commanders pushed for Hooker to be declared medically incapable, they could risk repercussions if their concerns proved groundless.

Option 3: Hooker Stays in Command, but Officers Knowingly Step In When He Is Incapacitated

Another option was to essentially do nothing but try to salvage the situation. If Hooker did not remove himself, and if there was no feeling that he needed to be declared unfit, then staff officers and corps commanders would have to work with and around him. In the moments when Hooker was upright and all right, he was in command. When he retired to lie down or could not make immediate decisions, surrounding officers would run interference or make the choices themselves.

This possibility would create a disjointed chain of command and a fluid situation without strong, decisive leadership. To this plan's advantage, it would not change commanders in the middle of the battle and risk morale plummeting. The disadvantage would be that the Union position around Chancellorsville was under intense attack without clear direction from a commander.

Decision

The officers and doctors around General Hooker left him in command and without recorded challenge to his leadership. Hooker retained his position, sometimes active and on horseback and other times lying down and unable to quickly respond to information or make decisions.

Results/Impact

In testimony before the Joint Committee on the Conduct of the War, Brig. Gen. Birney from the Third Corps explained, "I think that if on Sunday morning we had been properly supported—that is, if the troops that were there had been brought up, the enemy could have been defeated then. I regard not doing this a great mistake." When asked why this action had not been taken, Birney replied, "I have understood that it was owing to the accident to General Hooker early in the morning."[21]

All along the Union lines encircling Chancellorsville—the Second, Twelfth, and Third Corps—men were dying in order to hold their trenches against determined and repeated Confederate attacks. Ammunition ran low. Artillerymen retreated, leaving infantry unsupported. By midday the Union lines were on the point of collapse.

Hooker, Couch, and Meade sent orders at various times through the day, leading to confusion in the chain of command and concern from the generals receiving these messages. Gen. Sickles later testified that from midmorning until midafternoon he received no communications from Hooker, but Meade had sent orders. What was happening at headquarters? Hooker appeared and rode in view of the troops at some points but seemed completely absent at other times.

By midafternoon, Union troops had retreated and a new defensive line was forming. Anchored by the Fifth Corps, the retreating Second, Twelfth, and Third Corps came into a new position north of the Chancellorsville clearing and crossroads and closer to the river. Here, Hooker rode among his troops. But Gen.Sickles noted that all was not well: "He [Hooker] was then . . . in a condition, from his injury, that forbade his reassuming command; he was evidently suffering great agony, and I suppose nothing but the highest sense of duty could have prompted him to resume command under such circumstance. He was mounted on his horse, and was perfectly clear in all respects as to orders and everything, but was evidently suffering great bodily pain."[22] Sickles did not realize that Hooker had not actually given up his post. However, he didn't hesitate to comment on the effects of Hooker's non-response to the request for reinforcements in the morning of May 3. Sickles said that if thousands of reinforcing soldiers had been deployed on the orders of a commanding general, the Union lines around Chancellorsville might have held.

Because Hooker managed to put on a show of command, he was not easy to remove from the position even though his physical capability on May 3 was doubtful. His dedication and courage were commendable. However, the fact that he remained a lame-duck commander while his troops battled for survival contributed to the Union retreat from the Chancellorsville position. It also placed heavy responsibility on corps and division commanders to get their infantry and artillery out of the original location and into the fallback lines without clear directions or a sense of stability from headquarters.

Hooker Brings Hunt from the Rear

Situation

On May 3, 1863, as Gen. Hooker lay in a tent along the Ely's Ford Road trying to recover from his head injury, Col. Charles S. Wainwright, chief of artillery for the First Corps, arrived and needed to speak with him. A sentry held Wainwright back, and Gen. Meade tried to run interference, but Hooker spotted the artillery officer and insisted he could come inside. In his diary, Wainwright recorded the conversation:

> General Hooker. "Well, Wainright, how is the artillery getting on?"
> Self. "As badly as it well can. Batteries are being ordered in every direction, blocking up the roads; and no one seems to know where to go. Where is General Hunt?"
> General Hooker. "What is the matter?"
> Self. "As near as I can understand, every division commander wants his own batteries, and battery commanders will obey no one else's orders. It is just the condition I told you of and wanted to provide against, by giving artillery officers of rank actual command, so that they could order any battery. The ammunition trains, too."
> General Hooker. "Well, we have no time to talk now. You take hold and make it right."
> Self. "Where is *General* Hunt?"[23]

Wainwright and other Union artillery officers on the Chancellorsville Battlefield desperately wanted the leadership, guidance, and orders from Gen. Henry J. Hunt. Chief of artillery for the Army of the Potomac since September 1862, Hunt had begun his long career with cannon in the Mexican-American War. He was also one of the authors of *Instructions for Field Artillery*, which taught and influenced Northern artillery tactics during the Civil War.[24] Artillerists respected Hunt, and knew he would help ensure good battery placement and support the logistics for ammunition resupply. However, General Hooker had chosen to ignore Hunt's skills during the reorganization of the army during the early months of 1863.

Shortly after Hooker took command, Hunt approached him and asked for clarification of his position and duties. Hooker informed Hunt that he "would not have command of the artillery." "I would have the administrative duties of the arm," Hunt recalled, which "consists in seeing it supplied with horses, men, and ammunition; that it is properly instructed and properly equipped; that the ammunition is of proper quality; that the officers are fitted for their duties, &c. The command would involve the command of the troops, with the right to issue orders outside of those relating to its internal economy and administration."[25] Hooker then proceeded to remove overall command of the artillery batteries from Hunt and assigned them to infantry division commanders. Left with administrative duties and with his cannon and cannoneers under the command of infantry generals, Hunt asked what

Brig. Gen. Henry J. Hunt (Union) had effectively commanded and supplied Union artillery at the 1862 Battles of Antietam and Fredericksburg. Hooker's decision to place Hunt in a limited role during Chancellorsville resulted in artillery confusion. Library of Congress.

Hooker wanted him to do during a battle. Hooker declared that he expected Hunt "'to be about' and see that the artillery was properly used and to give such orders in his name as . . . necessary."[26]

The chief of artillery protested the irregularity of this new arrangement and suggested that it could be disastrous for artillery effectiveness in the next battle. Hooker made no major alterations and then neglected to inform Hunt of the initial departures for the campaign. "It was only by accident," Hunt explained, "that I learned that the batteries so left behind were afterward ordered to rejoin their corps. As soon as the battle commenced on Friday morning, I began to receive demands from corps commanders for more artillery, which I was unable to comply with, except partially, and at the risk of deranging the plans of other corps commanders."[27]

Corps commanders tried to rely on Hunt to send more artillery and oversee their ammunition resupply as he had done at the Battles of Antietam and Fredericksburg. However, Hooker had ordered Hunt "to Banks' Ford, to take command there, and was absent at that place until the night of the 3rd from general headquarters."[28] Hunt remained at Banks' Ford from May 1 to May 3 to oversee the placement of artillery covering the fords and crossing points on the upper Rappahannock River. He did not know how artillery was placed at Chancellorsville or Fredericksburg, and he was not privy to most of the artillery and supply communications.

On the Chancellorsville Battlefield, chiefs of artillery within the Union corps were highly frustrated. Were they in command of the artillery, or were the infantry generals? Infantry commanders got artillery in bad positions or neglected to set up the ammunition resupply for the positioned batteries. After the smooth deployment and command of Union artillery at Antietam and Fredericksburg, it did not take the artillery officers at Chancellorsville long to figure out that Hunt's absence and the new divisional authority were disastrous.

When Col. Wainwright arrived at General Hooker's tent and repeatedly asked, "Where is General Hunt?" it was both a practical question and a veiled criticism of the commanding general. Hooker had broken a system that had worked well at two previous battles, reduced his army's chief of artillery to administrative work and watching river fords, and let officers who did not understand artillery give orders affecting the cannon and the gunners.

Artillery batteries had run out of ammunition and been forced to retreat, contributing in part to the overall Federal retreat from the defensive lines around Chancellorsville. The roads through the Wilderness were traffic logged, and in the new defensive lines, artillery struggled to find their positions or get their needed ammunition. The corps-level artillery officers had tried to remedy the situation, and battery commanders had protested bad positions. Yet all of them lacked the authority and rank to override the infantry officers' poor decisions.

Options

Cannons and ammunition would add strength to the new Union position, and Hooker had a few options for fixing the artillery debacle by the evening of May 3, 1863. First, he could summon Hunt to headquarters and put him in active command. Second, he could increase the power of the chiefs of artillery to oversee their batteries. Third, Hooker could order Hunt to send more ammunition and let the battery commanders and infantry generals figure out how to best use the resupplied artillery.

Option 1: Order Hunt to Headquarters and Put Him
in Active Command of the Artillery

Bringing Hunt from Banks' Ford to headquarters and ordering him to take active command of the artillery in the field offered an easy solution to the

May 3, 1863

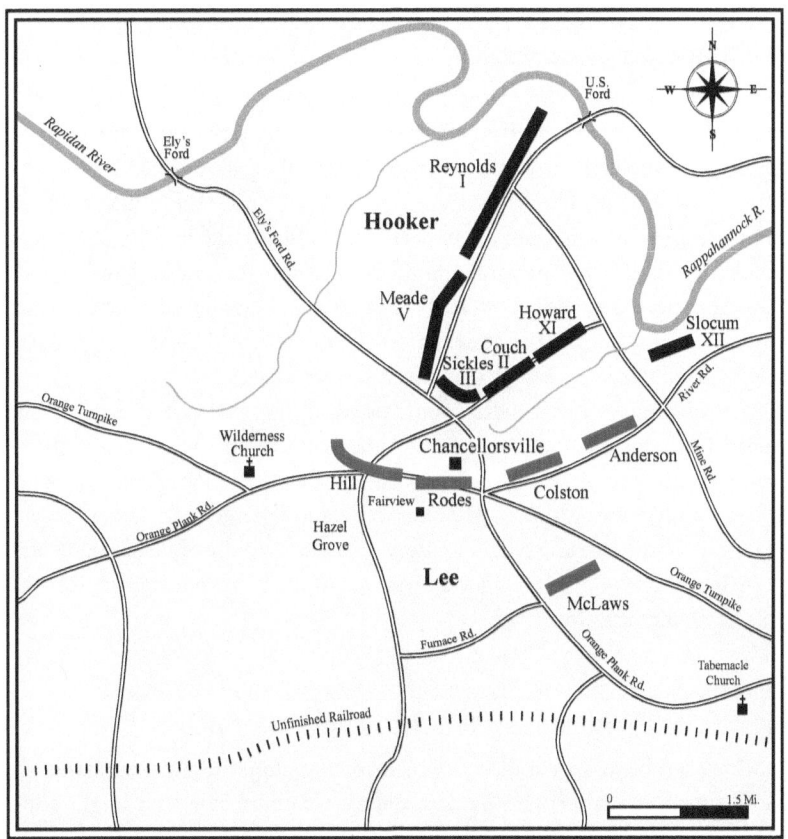

Retreating from Chancellorsville

problem. This decision would push Hunt into a battlefield situation he knew little about, but it would remove the unraveling situation from Hooker's immediate responsibility. From previous battles and campaigns, Hunt had a reputation for getting problems sorted and fixed. Thus the artillerists wanted him back in active command. The disadvantage for this option stemmed from forcing Hooker to admit that he had made a mistake with his artillery operations and logistics. Even if he did not admit his error verbally or in writing, ordering Hunt back into command after dismissing his skills would speak loudly of Hooker's miscalculations.

Option 2: Give the Corps-Level Chiefs of Artillery More Power to Place and Supply the Batteries

Part of the problems within the Army of the Potomac's artillery came from the rank of artillery commanders. Captains led batteries, and chiefs of artillery were typically at the corps level—all of them outranked by infantry generals who, under Hooker's arrangements, could order the artillery officers to poor positions or neglect to support them. During the middle of a battle, Hooker could not fix the rank and chain of command issues. But he could give more power to the corps chiefs of artillery for the duration of the campaign; he could return the assigned artillery chiefs to their direct oversight roles and inform the infantry generals of this change.

An advantage of this choice would be restoring artillery to the command of artillerymen. However, the disadvantages were numerous, especially for making this type of change in the middle of a battle. Power struggles between infantry and artillery commanders could emerge if the situation was not clear. Also, several skilled artillery colonels had already been moved up in their authority during the day on May 3, but their best efforts had not been able to fix the situations.

Option 3: Order Hunt to Fix the Supply Situation but Continue to Leave the Deployment Positions to the Infantry Generals

Hooker's problem was multifaceted, involving supplies and command authority for the artillery on the battlefield. A compromise that might allow Hooker to save face with his previous organizational choices would have Hunt fix the ammunition supply situation while leaving the artillery command situation on the battlefield untouched. In this scenario, the infantry division commanders could still order the artillery batteries where to deploy, but in theory, the ammunition would be available. This option still left the situation without an overall commander, but it could be a get-by solution allowing Hooker to save face for a few more days and then reorganize the artillery command chain after the battle ended.

Decision

In the night of May 3, 1863, Hooker sent orders to Hunt to report to headquarters within the new defensive position. The chief of artillery wrote, "On my arrival at general headquarters, at 10 p.m. of May 3, I was directed by you [Hooker] to take charge of all the artillery."[29]

May 3, 1863

Union artillery dominated many battlefields, but not Chancellorsville. (Photograph shows Union guns, but was not taken at Chancellorsville.) Library of Congress.

Results/Impact

Hunt returned to active command but inherited a tangle of cannon in an army forced to retreat and still sitting defensively in the Wilderness. He met with Col. Wainwright, who had been trying his best to take charge and provide organization, but had not been able to fully coordinate across all the corps. Hunt later reported, "Colonel Wainwright informed me that he had made the best practicable arrangement for the lines of defense, but that in the general confusion, from the want of a commander of the artillery, the batteries of the corps had become separated and mixed with each other."[30]

In the darkness, Hunt acted promptly, tracking down the majority of the batteries in the Union position. He examined their locations and condition, "giving instructions as were required." Next, he located the artillery guns set up in a defensive position closer to United States Ford, the likely escape route if the army was forced to retreat. Here, Hunt worked with the artillery officers to set up a better position and ensured that the ammunition was replenished.[31]

Other events on May 4–5 dictated the limited role of the artillery for the rest of the action at Chancellorsville. However, Hunt's expertise and experience in active command had been recognized and restored. Hunt also oversaw the final withdrawal of the Union artillery and the safety of that important military asset. In the aftermath of Chancellorsville, he was allowed to reorganize the artillery into brigades for each corps with a central artillery reserve under his own direction; this change would impact the Battle of Gettysburg and the solid Union artillery performance there.

The question "Where is General Hunt?" had been answered at Chancellorsville, but other questions lingered for both armies as May 3 ended and May 4 dawned. Where was Sedgwick? Could the Union armies withstand another attack? Would the Confederate troops fight another day after their costly victory at the crossroads?

CHAPTER 6

FINAL MOVES

MAY 4–6, 1863

In the final days of the Battle of Chancellorsville, the Union forces remained divided. Sedgwick's wing had crossed to the north bank of the Rappahannock, and Hooker's isolated forces to the west sought refuge in a salient on the south bank, protecting a route of retreat across US Ford. While the Confederates were still divided, the wing that had confronted Sedgwick then scrambled west, hoping to resume the fight with Hooker. Lee had the benefit of moving more freely south of the Rappahannock, with the threat of Sedgwick defused, while maintaining the initiative. Insufficient intelligence and weary troops, however, would blur his advantages. Hooker looked for ways out of his failing campaign, and in doing so he managed to ignite tensions and create a toxic atmosphere where soldiers at every level of the army identified scapegoats and pointed out blame.

During the night of May 4, Maj. Gen. Hooker made the critical decision to retreat, overriding most of his corps commanders. The fighting and choices during this period built off previous critical decisions with the Union army and also laid the groundwork for the next campaigns and battles in 1863.

Hooker Retreats

Situation

"Lay in the trenches send out skirmishers[;] warm," Edward F. Hopkins noted in his daily diary on May 4, 1863.[1] A soldier in the 149th New York Infantry in the Third Brigade, Second Division of the Union Twelfth Corps, Hopkins had been through some intense fighting, and he and his regimental comrades had fought on the three previous days of battle. Just the day before, he wrote, "[The enemy had] turn[ed] our right 149th Rgt fight bravely Lay under a raking fire from two batteries for one hour several of our Rgt wounded shell & balls fly all around, forces all fall back except the 149th. 149th break on the right Rgt all pass our Co & we hold the enemy in check fall back slowly."[2] In Hopkins's company, eleven men fell wounded, and Confederates briefly captured the regiment's colonel, who was quickly rescued by a counterattack. By nightfall on May 3, the 149th had fallen back an estimated three miles behind the new entrenched line. As day broke on May 4, the unit returned to skirmishing and occupying trenches. Just thirty-two men reported present for duty, but as Hopkins noted, his regiment kept busy: "Change our position farther to the left and commence throwing up masked batteries and entrenchments Change our position again in the night & commence another work about 11 o'clock work all night."[3]

Hopkins's diary entries reflect the lull in the battle along some parts of the Union line. Skirmishing and entrenching occupied the soldiers, and many looked at the reduced sizes of their companies and regiments, beginning to realize the cost of this battle. On the whole, though, morale stayed strong among the troops on both sides. The generals had decisions to make about the situation. Both armies were still divided. Both Union forces—Hooker's and Sedgwick's—had backed themselves into entrenched corners against the Rappahannock River with protected access to fords and pontoon bridges.

The morning of May 4, 1863, found the Union corps with Hooker snugly encapsulated behind strong earthworks. A curving salient line of Federal earthworks used part of Ely's Ford Road and Mineral Spring Road (a continuation of Bullock Road) as guiding points, and United States Ford and the Rappahannock River were in the fortifications' rear. Slocum's Twelfth Corps held the left of the line. Howard's Eleventh Corps, Couch's Second Corps, Sickles's Third Corps, Meade's Fifth Corps, and Reynolds's First Corps anchored the right of the line. Approximately 75,500 Union troops in total were with Hooker in this new position.[4] Nearly 25,000 Confederates from Jackson's Corps, still temporarily commanded by Stuart, held Hooker at bay.[5]

For Hooker and his assembled corps near United States Ford, the day passed in relative quiet. Skirmishing occurred at points of the line, and sharpshooters added to the casualty numbers, but no large-scale movements or attacks developed. Union reconnaissance missions convinced Hooker that there was no opportunity to successfully attack the Confederates in his front.[6]

Meanwhile, about seven miles to the southeast (as the crow flies), Major General Sedgwick had regrouped after the Battle of Salem Church on May 3, 1863, and occupied a similar salient position with the river and Banks' Ford to his rear. He had approximately twenty thousand troops and faced twenty-five thousand Confederates. Sedgwick waited to see whether he would be sent reinforcements, and whether he should maintain his position and a foothold on the south side of the Rappahannock.[7]

By 9:45 a.m. on May 4, Sedgwick sent word to Hooker: "The enemy are pressing me. I am taking position to cross the river whenever necessary."[8] He was setting up an escape and waiting for directions. Correspondence throughout the day ordered Sedgwick to maintain a position on the south side of the Rappahannock River through the evening of May 5.[9] However, Confederate attacks through the morning and midday resulted in a "sharp fight," and Sedgwick became concerned about his ability to maintain a position for a longer period. He began writing about holding until dark on May 4 and then getting across the river. The major general kept fighting and contracting his lines toward the river and the pontoon bridges throughout the afternoon and evening. Meanwhile, he and Hooker continued to exchange correspondence. At one point in the day, Hooker declared Sedgwick was "separated from him so far" that he could not give him advice or clear orders.[10]

In the last hour of May 4, Hooker "called the corps commanders together, not as a council of war, but to ascertain how they felt."[11] Major Gens. Reynolds, Couch, Sickles, Meade, and Howard attended the meeting; Slocum arrived late. Chief of staff General Butterfield and chief engineer Brig. Gen. Gouverneur K. Warren were also present. Hooker later explained the midnight scene:

> I showed them my instructions, stated our circumstances, as clearly as I could, and explained to them the only means that was left, in my judgment, for extricating myself. . . . After stating to the corps commanders, the condition of affairs, and what measures I proposed to take if we advanced, I said I would withdraw for a time and let them confer among themselves, and come in again when they had determined their opinions upon the subject. When I returned, I called upon them individually for their opinions. General

Meade stated that he was for an advance, for the reason that he did not believe we could recross the river in the presence of the enemy. General Reynolds had thrown himself on a bed, being very tired that night from hard work, and had gone to sleep, saying, before he did so, that his opinion would be the same as General Meade's. General Howard voted for an advance, assigning as a reason that he felt as though the army had been placed in the position in which it was by the conduct of his corps, and he had to vote for an advance under any circumstances. His opinion was received for what it was worth. General Couch and General Sickles were of the opinion that the army should re-cross the river.[12]

Now the stage was set for Hooker to make or confirm his decision. Would he follow the majority counsel of his generals, or would he decide to retreat?

Options

Hooker weighed the circumstances and the opinions of the assembled officers. His choice would define or at least reshape the campaign, and it would also confirm his trust in his corps commanders or potentially undermine their confidence in his leadership. He had several options for proceeding. First, Hooker could go with the majority opinion to stay on the south side of the river and fight. Second, Hooker could follow the minority opinion, withdrawing both his force and Sedgwick's. Third, forging a compromise solution, Hooker could withdraw across United States Ford, march east on the safer side of the river, and try to recross to reinforce Sedgwick.

Option 1: Take the Majority Opinion and Stay to Fight

Meade, Reynolds, Howard, and Slocum (late arriving) agreed that the army should stay and fight. The generals had differing preferences for the tactics and differing reasons for their conclusion. Meade and Howard were the most vocal advocates of an attack. Reynolds fell asleep but had previously made it clear he would support whatever Meade preached, and Slocum apparently arrived in time to have a brief say.

If Hooker decided to stay and fight, he could still remain on the defensive and try to provoke a Confederate assault. Or he could create a plan with the several options to break out and fight toward Sedgwick, battling Confederate resisters along the way. The morale of the army remained strong despite the retreat on May 3, and there were multiple choices for fighting forward.

A few options could possibly unite the Union forces. Hooker could attack out of his new position, break through the much smaller Confederate force in his front, and turn east along the turnpike, approaching the rear of the enemy threatening Sedgwick. Alternatively, after a breakout, Hooker could take the Mine Road toward Zoan Church or the River Road directly toward Banks' Ford. Any of these plans would require multiple hours to get reinforcements to Sedgwick. Withdrawing Sedgwick and bringing his troops to join the rest of Hooker's force would allow the Confederates to reunite and give them the opportunity for a total force to attack or maneuver against Hooker.

Option 2: Take the Minority Opinion and Retreat

Hooker could take the advice of the two generals who suggested a retreat. Couch wanted to fall back because he claimed there was not enough information to do otherwise. (In later years, Couch would try to revise his statements for historical memory, declaring that his lack of confidence in Hooker influenced his vote.)[13] Sickles turned on his crony, using abusive language and blaming Hooker for a failing campaign and advocating for a retreat to avoid political trouble.

The lack of information was a worthy consideration, and political pressures were real. However, a retreat would be calling off the campaign without trying to strike back, without taking advantage of the still-divided Confederate force.

Option 3: Compromise by Retreating and Recrossing to Fight Again

Hooker might have been surprised by the majority vote to stay and fight, and he could blend this idea with a retreat. He could start by falling back with just one portion of his army and then marching that force to another point to either reinforce the other wing or open a new attack point. Hooker could order Sedgwick's force to retreat across the river, then march west, cross the river at US Ford, and reinforce Hooker's wing; then approximately ninety-five thousand troops could battle Stuart near Chancellorsville. Or Hooker could take his main army across the river and march to Banks' Ford, reinforce Sedgwick, and throw the combined force against Lee's three divisions.

Decision

After the discussions, Hooker decided to retreat and get the army back to safety on the north side of the Rappahannock River. An intact army could fight another day and at another place.

Results/Impact

Edward Hopkins and his comrades in the 149th New York Infantry dug trenches while the generals voiced their opinions, and Hooker made his decision. The common soldier expected to stay and fight, but the newly dug earthworks would be abandoned as result of the orders after the generals' meeting. Confusion swept through many men in the ranks. They wanted to fight and did not feel defeated. Anger rose in some regiments as they realized what Hooker had decided. Hooker's choice effectively ended the Chancellorsville Campaign. Retreating halted the idea of continued fighting—either defensively or offensively.

By 1:00 a.m. on May 5, 1863, Hooker and Butterfield started sending orders to begin the retreat. Sedgwick was directed to get back across the river at Banks' Ford. Pontoon bridges were confirmed or ordered into place at Banks' and United States Fords, while artillery would cover positions in case the Confederates attempted to attack during the withdrawal.

Sedgwick completed his crossing by 5:00 a.m. on May 5. His soldiers were "much exhausted," but as they reached the northern bank of the river, he received orders countermanding the directive to withdraw. Weary with the confusion he had experienced over the last few days, Sedgwick replied simply, "The dispatch countermanding my movement over the river was received after the troops had crossed."[14] Remaining Union troops at Fredericksburg also recrossed the river, and pontoon bridges swung free from the southern bank.

At Hooker's position, the crossing was completed by the morning of May 6. The general telegraphed Pres. Lincoln at 4:30 p.m. on the sixth, replying to several previous telegraphs from the Executive Mansion offering encouragement and hopes of continuing the campaign, especially since so few Union corps had been heavily engaged. Hooker briefly stated, "I saw no way of giving the enemy a general battle with the prospect of success which I desire. Not to exceed three corps, all told, of my troops have been engaged. For the whole to go in, there is a better place nearer at hand."[15]

Hooker confirmed the orders that took his army back across the river. He would later claim that most of the generals had not spoken against the plan to withdraw, and that some had supported the retreat. Politics and historical memory added their shadows to the night Hooker decided to retreat. Across the battle lines, Lee was surprised by Hooker's disappearance and angered even as newspapers began to pronounce Chancellorsville a strong Confederate victory.

CHAPTER 7
AFTERMATH AND CONCLUSIONS

The Army of the Potomac retreated, leaving victory to the Army of Northern Virginia. The Confederates had opened the 1863 campaign season with a success at Chancellorsville that gave them both military and morale momentum that Lee planned to exploit. However, neither commander had accomplished his objective, and neither side had won a crushing final victory. The outcomes of the sixteen critical decisions led to the end result that would have far-reaching effects following the battle. Loss and victory affected the commanders, their generals, the soldiers in the ranks, the politicians, and the nation—North and South—in wrenching ways that would lay the groundwork for the future campaigns and critical decisions.

At Confederate headquarters, Gen. Robert E. Lee had a battlefield victory, but he was upset. The ending of the battle especially irritated him. He passed into historical memory like a god of war on May 3, 1863, as he entered the Chancellorsville Crossroads clearing, but he acted like a man obsessed with an unreachable goal from May 4 to May 6. Lee needed a crushing victory that would decisively defeat Hooker and the Army of the Potomac. It was not enough to force the Union troops back to the north side of the river to accomplish Lee's strategic aims.

By 10:00 a.m. on the morning of May 4, Lee had arrived on the Salem Church / Banks' Ford battlefield. Confederates skirmished with Sedgwick's force, but no strong attack seemed to be planned or underway. The commanding general was visibly angry, probably about lost time or the lack of information about the Union position.¹ Then Lee disappeared, probably seeking information about the Union force and placement around Banks' Ford and Fredericksburg. Though the Confederates fought enough to hasten Sedgwick's retreat, no decisive, overwhelming assault crushed this isolated part of the Union army. The Confederates knew that Sedgwick was crossing the river in the night of May 4–5, but they again offered no major opposition.

With Sedgwick gone, Lee had turned his attention to Hooker and the entrenched salient position near United States Ford. Stuart and divisions from the Second Corps still eyed Hooker's new line and kept him in place. Lee sent Early back to Fredericksburg to take possession of the high ground and town, then shifted the other Confederate divisions back to the west to join Stuart. The rebel commander wanted to attack Hooker's line on May 5 and sent staff officers to scout for routes and artillery positions.

Col. Edward Porter Alexander, commanding part of the artillery reserve, scouted Hooker's line and did not like what he observed. The position was well defended against artillery enfilading fire and other advantageous opportunities for Confederate cannon, which would make it difficult for the attacking infantry to have supporting firepower. Alexander noted, "When I saw how the enemy had been throwing up dirt & strengthening himself; & reflected how easy it was in that Wilderness thicket to make a line impregnable by abattis in front, it made me very unhappy to think of seeing our infantry sent to charge such a tremendous force in those intrenchments."²

Marching Anderson's and McLaws's troops back toward Chancellorsville took time. The weather was uncooperative for the Confederates, and the soldiers were tired from the previous marches and fighting. Unable to get the troops positioned on May 5, Lee delayed his longed-for attack on Hooker's lines until the next day.³ Longstreet's absent corps was beginning to return to Richmond and lower central Virginia, but it had not yet reached the Chancellorsville Battlefield to be able to support an attack on May 5 or 6.

Early on May 6, Lee sent a message to Pres. Davis updating him on the situation as he understood it: "General Hooker did not recross the Rappahannock after his defeat on Sunday, but retreated to a strong position in front of the United States Ford, where he is now fortifying himself, with a view, I presume, of holding a position this side of the Rappahannock. I understand from prisoners that he is awaiting reinforcements."⁴

Lee's army had already suffered heavy losses as a result of the frontal assaults against an entrenched enemy. The Confederate general praised his soldiers for "attacking largely superior numbers in strongly intrenched positions" because "their heroic courage overcame every obstacle of nature and art, and achieved a triumph most honorable."⁵ Casualties had been particularly high on May 3, when Stuart's tactics drove regiments repeatedly against strong Union trenches. The weak Federal artillery deployment and lack of ammunition for those cannon contributed to the success of the hammering Confederates that day. Days of combat had decimated the rebels; some units had lost one-third of their men, while others had lost a majority of their line officers.[6]

The preparations for the Confederate infantry attack were ready by the morning of May 6, and the skirmishers went forward ahead of the main battle lines. Gen. Stuart reported, "Our skirmishers found the enemy's works abandoned, and, pressing forward to the river, captured many prisoners. The enemy had another work 2 miles in rear of the other, which was also abandoned."[7]

Among those officers, like Col. Alexander, who had concerns about the strong Union position, and among the soldiers who saw the intimidating network of earthworks they had been ordered to attack, prevailed. These Confederates would live another day. "The campaign was over! There was to be no bloody assault of those strong intrenchments!" Alexander penned decades later, still remembering the feeling when he understood what had been averted.[8]

However, Lee did not share the sigh of relief. Fury bubbled inside him but did not burst. Officers who were pleased that the Union army had disappeared met with cold reprimands. Gen. William Dorsey Pender arrived at the commander's headquarters with the news that the skirmishers had found abandoned lines and campsites. Lee scolded him, "This is the way that you young men are always doing. You have again let these people get away. I can only tell you what to do, and if you do not do it[,] it will not be done."[9] Despite all the risks Lee had taken and opportunities he had exploited, he had not secured a crushing defeat of the Union army. The flank attack, the capture of the Chancellorsville Crossroads, the pinning of Sedgwick's force against the river, and Hooker's last defensive lines—all these points of battle had forced the Union army to act, but they did not cut off, surround, or slaughter the enemy force to a degree that it would break. Lee had won a victory at Chancellorsville through his daring and leadership decisions. Unfortunately, it was not the victory he needed, and it had taken irreplaceable officers and men from his ranks.

While Lee fumed and then saw the newspapers laud his battlefield victory, Major General Hooker had a different experience. By the morning of May 6, 1863, the Union soldiers destined to leave the south bank of the Rappahannock River had retreated toward the camps in Stafford from which they had departed. The pontoon bridges swung away from the southern bank at United States Ford. The dead, wounded, and prisoners in blue remained behind. The survivors trudged back toward where their marches had started, their old winter camps.

The Army of the Potomac did not return defeated in spirit; rather, a sense of pent-up frustration and even anger simmered in the ranks. The soldiers wanted a fair fight with all corps engaged, maneuvering, and winning. They did not want advances, pauses, and strategic withdrawals in the dense Wilderness that limited their movements and often brought the battle to the regimental level and seemingly unsupported skirmishes and combat. The common soldiers quickly began looking for someone to blame for the Chancellorsville debacle. Perhaps surprisingly, they generally did not blame Hooker and still expressed a willingness to have him as an army commander. Instead, the overall pattern of blame targeted politicians, particular generals—usually Howard or Sedgwick—and corps besides the troops' own.

For example, Carl Wickesberg of the Twenty-Sixth Wisconsin Infantry (Eleventh Corps) wrote the following to his parents and siblings: "It was all General Howard's fault. General Schurtz was going to give us some cannons to help us. But that coward, I cannot call him by any other name, said he was going to try it first with what we have here. He is a Yankee, and that is why he wanted to have us slaughtered, because most of us are Germans."[10] Stephen Pingree from the Fourth Vermont Infantry (Sixth Corps) declared to his cousin, "We have been checked—but we are not whipped. I do not regard the result of this affair as a substantial defeat, in any sense. I still have faith in Gen. Hooker. Had the German troops—11th Corps, behaved like men—all might have been well."[11] Warren Person from the Sixty-Fourth New York Infantry (Second Corps) explained to his mother, "It was evident Hooker's Grand Army was on a magnificent skedaddle. Sedgwick's corps had been driven back from Fredericksburg and Hooker was forced to retreat. Otherwise we could have held our own."[12]

Like the soldiers in the ranks, Gen. Hooker started looking for someone to blame for the problems that lead to the defeat at Chancellorsville. Animosity grew at headquarters; Hooker eyed his corps commanders and found them untrustworthy, and they scowled back in his direction. Certainly, the general had dealt with some difficult corps commanders during the Chancellorsville Campaign, but he had frequently been unclear, unhelpful, or absent. The Army of the Potomac's fighting men in the ranks had been forged during the winter of 1862–63, but the officers, especially at the corps level, were still wanting.

Pres. Lincoln arrived at Hooker's headquarters in Stafford on May 7, and Hooker and the other generals hastened to tell their sides of the story. Couch and Slocum instigated a backdoor coup against Hooker. Other detractors did not go that far, but they had lists with examples of the general's negative leadership and poor critical decisions for which they held him accountable. Some officers recognized that Hooker had suffered a severe injury on May 3, 1863, which might have impaired his reasoning—and it is likely that injury had more effect than nineteenth-century medical practices could detect or understand. Other officers spread stories that Hooker had been drunk during the campaign, and still others rallied to his cause and said that he had been abstinent during the military operations. Finally, some corps commanders blasted Hooker for a lack of character and resolve.[13]

Despite his defeat, Hooker retained the confidence of the army, though not of many of the high-ranking officers. He had the opportunity to destroy, ignore, or try to rebuild the tenuous situation with the latter men. Hooker could accept a level of responsibility for the failed campaign, admitting where he had been at fault. By setting an example, he might be able to defuse the situation slightly. Paired with a quick return to the campaign field, changes of corps commanders done promptly and simply before the next movement would reduce the time that generals had to reason, complain, or plot. However, Hooker decided to tally some of the Chancellorsville problems and look for scapegoats. He settled on corps commanders as his prime targets, particularly Gens. Stoneman, Howard, and Sedgwick.

In General Orders No. 49, issued on May 6, 1863, Hooker laid the groundwork to absolve himself and keep himself popular with the soldiers in the ranks. The opening paragraph read, "The major general commanding tenders to this army his congratulations on its achievements of the last seven days. If it has not accomplished all that was expected, the reasons are well known to the army. It is sufficient to say they were of a character not to be foreseen or prevented by human sagacity or resource."[14] Hooker continued, assuring the army that the retreat had happened only to avoid fighting at a disadvantage, and that the soldiers should be proud of their accomplishments. He stated, "[We have gone on] long marches, crossed rivers, [and] surprised the enemy in his intrenchments, and whenever we have fought [we] have inflicted heavier blows than we have received."[15] That was mostly true, and Hooker ended the orders with a reflection on the "loss of . . . brave companions" and the consolation of "the conviction that they . . . [fell] in the holiest cause ever submitted to the arbitrament of battle."[16]

With the niceties accomplished, Hooker started blaming his corps commanders of the Cavalry, Eleventh, and Sixth Corps. Stoneman and the cavalry had not accomplished all of Hooker's objectives in their sweeping raid toward Richmond. Though they had reached a level of success for Union cavalry operations in Virginia, they had not created as much destruction as

Hooker apparently expected; they had not damaged the railroad supplying Lee's army to the extent that Lee had to consider falling back to protect his supply lines. Howard and the Eleventh Corps were easy targets for Hooker's rage since they had been swept into a startling retreat and—in some cases—flight from the Confederates' surprise flank attack. Howard justifiably shouldered a share of blame. Yet a good portion of the fault also lay unacknowledged with Hooker, who failed to properly ascertain where the Confederates had been moving. Sedgwick had his share of problems during the Chancellorsville Campaign, but he had accomplished a strong victory at Marye's Heights, and although slow, he had moved on Lee's rear as ordered. Though Sedgwick's reputation was attacked, Hooker's scapegoating did not stick to him.[17]

Hooker's quickness to pass blame happened privately and publicly. He berated Sedgwick in a private meeting and let the press fault Howard and the German Americans of the Eleventh Corps, bringing ethnicity into the blame game. Stoneman took a medical leave to get away from the situation. Other generals not immediately targeted by Hooker chafed under the circumstances and did not gain respect for him. The commander still had the support of Pres. Lincoln, who eagerly awaited the next military move but crushed the idea of an ill-planned movement back across the Rappahannock near Fredericksburg.

The Army of the Potomac still had growing pains with leadership. Neither the corps commanders nor the commanding general had performed flawlessly. There was plenty of blame or responsibility to go around; many had contributed to the setback. However, despite the retreat and defeat, the Army of the Potomac had survived to fight another day.

John M. Cate of the Thirty-Third Massachusetts Infantry summed up the soldiers' philosophy at that point: "You ask what seems to be the idea among the troops about the war. We think that the rebels have got to give up the unequal contest, for it is impossible for them to hold out and lose as many men as they did in the late battles."[18] Hooker's and some of the corps commanders' days were numbered because of their actions at Chancellorsville and the politicking afterward, but their army readied to fight again, seeking a fair field and a chance to beat the Confederates. Victory had evaded the Union soldiers once again, but they felt they could be successful if allowed to fight under good advantage and good leadership.

When Hooker and Sedgwick retreated across the Rappahannock and the Battle of Chancellorsville ended, thousands of casualties lay on the battlefield, groaning in field hospitals, or enduring evacuations in wagon-ambulances. Officially, 17,304 Union soldiers had fallen from the ranks—dead, wounded, or missing—and Confederate casualties totaled 13,460.[19] The fighting had been ferocious, and burning woods added to the battlefield horrors. A Confederate soldier in the Stonewall Brigade later remembered the aftermath of the fighting:

> Our pioneer corps then went to work burying the dead, when I witnessed the most horrible sight my eyes ever beheld. On the left of our line, where the Louisiana Brigade had fought the last evening of the battle, and where they drove the enemy about one mile through the woods, and then in turn fell back to their own position, the scene beggars description. The dead and badly wounded from both sides were lying where they fell. The woods, taking fire that night from the shell, burnt rapidly and roasted the wounded men alive. As we went to bury them we could see where they had tried to keep the fire from them by scratching the leaves away as far as they could reach. But it availed not; they were burnt to a crisp. The only way we could tell to which army they belonged was by turning them over and examining their clothing where they lay close to the ground. There we would usually find some of their clothing that was not burned, so we could see whether they wore the blue or gray. We buried them all alike by covering them up with dirt where they lay. It was the most sickening sight I saw during the war and I wondered whether the American people were civilized or not, to butcher one another in that manner; and I came to the conclusion that we were barbarians, North and South alike.[20]

The horrors of Chancellorsville Battlefield were limited to those who witnessed them, but the results of the losses reverberated across the divided nation. "My God, what will the country say?" Abraham Lincoln reportedly groaned when he heard the casualty numbers from this Union defeat.[21] Long lists of casualties appeared in newspapers, leaving family and friends peering anxiously at the printed names. Some could turn away with a sigh of relief. Others started sobbing, and still others would simply never know the fate of their loved ones. The terrain and dense woods of Chancellorsville that had hindered the soldiers during the battle sometimes became an impenetrable veil, hiding the dead and leaving many of them unidentified. Wounded survivors at Chancellorsville who were rescued from the battlefield had varying experiences. The Union wounded "lucky" enough to be evacuated during the retreat were moved to field hospitals and then to permanent city hospitals comparatively quickly, thanks to the evacuation system designed by Dr. Jonathan Letterman. The Confederate wounded who could get to their field hospitals also received comparatively good care. However, the fates of the captured wounded—particularly those left behind during the Union retreat—were desperate. Some endured days without food, shelter, or care, nearly abandoned in an already overwhelming medical triage situation.

The common soldier in the ranks of both armies left Chancellorsville with high morale. Perhaps surprisingly, the average Union soldier in the Army of the Potomac wanted to fight again, and specifically wanted a fair fight in open ground. The retreat irritated or angered many of the troops in blue. Some vehemently denied that Chancellorsville was a Union defeat, admonishing friends at home to not believe any newspaper reports. In the Confederate army, soldiers recognized their victory and believed that 1863 could be the turning point of the war. Though they had not crushed their enemy, they felt a surge of enthusiasm that would carry through the summer campaign. However, the rebels could see the losses in the ranks, and some commented on the lost officers and comrades in their letters home.

The Confederate Army of Northern Virginia lost 23 percent of its infantry at Chancellorsville.[22] The force had reached its zenith as the divisions reunited and charged into the Chancellorsville Crossroads. But the thousands of casualties in its wake could not be easily replaced. Lee's army would not approach another battlefield with the same leadership that it had at Chancellorsville. While many would remember July 1863 and the Confederate defeat at Gettysburg as the high-water mark of the Confederacy, numerically, that point happened at Chancellorsville. The losses extended into the highest parts of the officer corps too. Lieut. Gen. Stonewall Jackson's wounding on May 2 had opened a leadership crisis that Lee temporarily plugged by sending Stuart to take command of the Second Corps. On May 10, 1863, Jackson died of pneumonia, and Lee would have to make longer-lasting decisions about army organization and commanders before his next campaign.

Every critical decision connected to Chancellorsville contributed to the final outcome: a Confederate battlefield victory. Lincoln's appointment of Hooker set the leadership climate for the campaign, and Hooker's pursuit of an offensive strategy started the military movements. Lee's decision to send the majority of Longstreet's Corps away left him with a more limited number of troops to confront Hooker, initially forcing him to adhere to defensive action.

However, Lee's decision to turn and fight on May 1, 1863, caught Hooker by surprise, setting up the opportunity for Lee to seize the initiative as Hooker pulled back into a defensive position. Lee decided to take the risk and divide his army, allowing Jackson to pursue a bold flank attack on May 2. Confident in his defensive posture, Hooker chose to ignore the reports of enemy troop movement, allowing Jackson to successfully execute his march and flank attack. Jackson's decision to pursue a night attack led to his overeager scouting mission and incapacitating wound, forcing Lee to make cavalry commander Maj. Gen. Stuart head of the Second Corps.

To the east, near Fredericksburg, the decision on May 3, 1863, to allow a temporary truce gave Union soldiers an information advantage. The Federals exploited this benefit with a sudden charge leading to the capture of Marye's Heights and the creation of a credible threat to Lee's rear. To meet the new threat, Lee divided his army again, sending troops east to confront the advancing Union force.

Meanwhile, around Chancellorsville on May 3, Hooker's decision to consolidate his lines and abandon Hazel Grove handed a positional advantage to the Confederates. Union officers left Hooker in command even though he was medically injured and unwell, thus creating a leadership crisis at the time when Union lines were under direct attack. Hooker's decision to bring Hunt from the rear to organize the artillery in the field restored confidence and put the Union army in a stronger position as its troops readied new defensive lines.

Hooker's final decision overrode the advice and preferences of the majority of his commanders, taking the army across the Rappahannock River and ending Chancellorsville as a Union battlefield defeat. Ultimately, Lee's decisions and bold risks contributed to his victory, but Hooker's decisions also played into Lee's hands, allowing Confederates to capitalize on their advantages and minimize their weaknesses.

The decisions and their results lingered in the minds of generals and soldiers as the armies departed Chancellorsville. They carried those memories into the next campaign. Lee—still seeking a crushing victory—would commit all his corps to battle when a fight started near the town of Gettysburg, Pennsylvania. Hooker—smarting from his defeat and mistrustful of his generals—played politics with Lincoln, eventually resigning in the middle of the Pennsylvania Campaign. George G. Meade took command of the Army of the Potomac, an army of soldiers anxious for a fair fight in an open field. The fields and ridges near Gettysburg had no dense, continuous woods like Chancellorsville, and Union soldiers won their victory after three days of fighting.

Looking at Chancellorsville alone misses the opportunity to see the far-reaching effects of the critical decisions. Battles do not occur in siloed circumstances. Just as the critical decisions examined at Chancellorsville affected one another, the critical decisions of one battle could reach to the next fight in the minds of the men. Approximately eight weeks after Chancellorsville and more than one hundred miles to the north, the Army of the Potomac and the Army of Northern Virginia clashed near Gettysburg, Pennsylvania.

Lee—still seeking that elusive crushing victory—would hurl his troops against the flanks and the center of the Union line. Perhaps remembering giving up the high ground at Hazel Grove, Sickles disobeyed orders by vacating his assigned position to secure high ground to his front in the Sherfy's Peach Orchard near Gettysburg. Hunt had reorganized the Federal artillery and had the logistics under control, making the Union guns a formidable and nearly ceaseless firepower when needed. Meade called his meeting of corps commanders in the night of July 2–3, but he assessed that their opinions aligned with his wishes before taking a vote. He then abided by the consensus of the other generals: stay and fight at Gettysburg. While Gettysburg was not the final battle for these two armies, it was another decisive moment in which memories and decisions were strongly influenced by the fighting at by Chancellorsville.

In May 1864—exactly one year after the closing days of the Battle of Chancellorsville—soldiers of the Union army marched into the Wilderness again as the Overland Campaign opened. Some passed through the Chancellorsville Crossroads and the old battlefield, bringing the ghosts of memory around them. John Haley of the Seventeenth Maine Infantry noted, "We moved on through the interminable forest and endless night. The winds toss the leafless branches of the trees, seeming to moan and shudder." As he looked at the burned ruins of the Chancellorsville House, he observed, "It would be a trifle singular if, surrounded as we are by soul-harrowing memories, we were not apprehensive." Haley's hope that "this campaign will positively be . . . [the] last and also that it will be decided in . . . [the Union's] favor" kept the soldiers pressing forward even as they approached the uncertainty of the dense woods and the ghosts of the critical decisions from the previous year.[23] Union and Confederate soldiers returned to Chancellorsville and marched over the skeletons of the dead as the war continued. Decisive victory had not been won in May 1863, and the American Civil War continued in the woods and fields for another two years beyond the Chancellorsville Crossroads and the Rappahannock River.

APPENDIX I

BATTLEFIELD GUIDE TO THE CRITICAL DECISIONS AT CHANCELLORSVILLE

Standing where the Battle of Chancellorsville and the Chancellorsville Campaign happened while examining the critical decisions and outcomes is a valuable learning opportunity. Battlefield preservation through the National Park Service and several nonprofit organizations has resulted in the protection of significant acreage where the fighting occurred. The preservation challenges and work continue, however. Some areas of the battlefield have been lost to urban development, especially at Second Fredericksburg and Salem Church.

This tour is designed to follow the battle's decisions chronologically, though you will complete all the Chancellorsville stops before heading east to explore Second Fredericksburg and Salem Church sites. Some locations that were involved in important action on multiple days will include interpretation for all those days to avoid backtracking or revisiting. Driving and walking instructions will help you use the national parks and publicly accessible land held by the American Battlefield Trust to explore the battlefields of the Chancellorsville Campaign where the critical decisions were made or implemented. Each stop includes orientation information, including which direction to face, what units fought near your location, the critical decision connected with the stop, and the action and results of that critical decision.

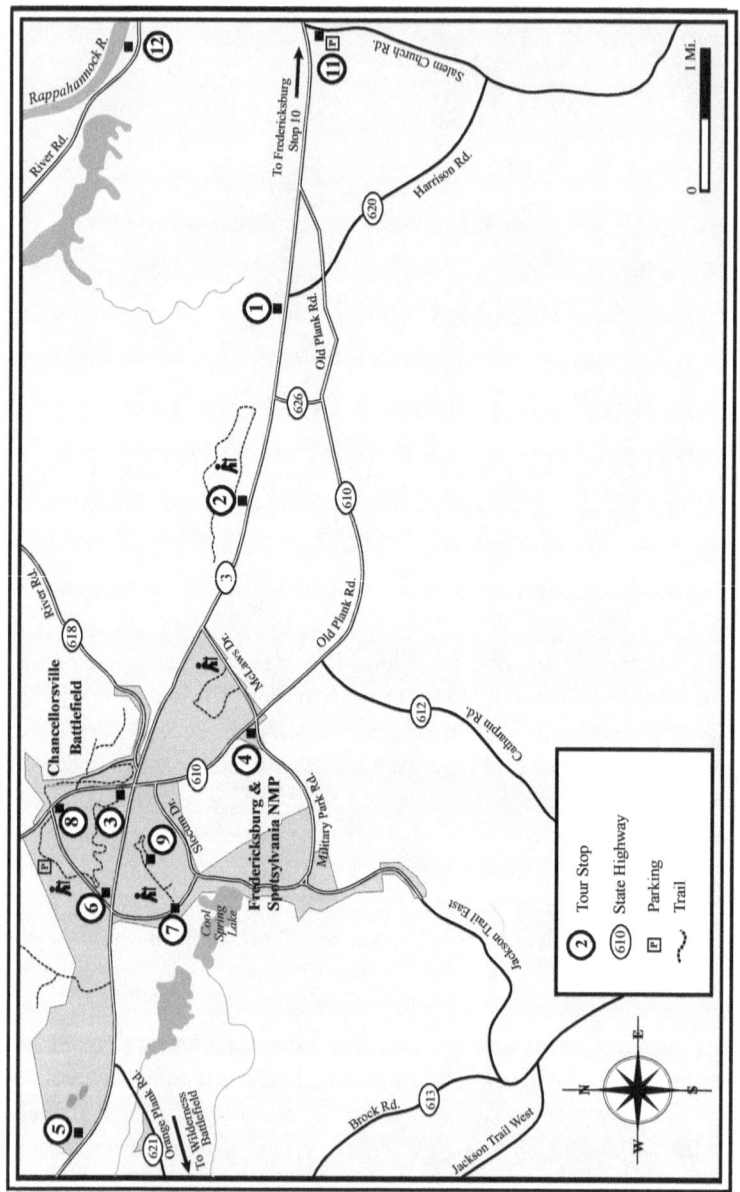

Tour Stops

Primary source material has been included for the tour stops to let the battle's participants describe what they saw in their own words. Please note that the primary source excerpts contain the soldiers' or civilians' original spellings and grammar. If you would like additional information about the sites and decisions, please refer to the decision discussion in the previous chapters.

Chancellorsville—like most Civil War operations—involved continuous movement and unfolding changes. Maps attempt to provide a stilled moment of time to help visualize those movements. The maps included throughout this book and in this battlefield tour serve as a frame of reference for those moving attacks, retreats, and marches.

Thirteen of the sixteen critical decisions examined in this book were made at sites that can be visited, or have outcomes connected to the battle landscape that are worth exploring. Three of the critical decisions were made at locations that are not preserved, not accessible, or out of the general area of the tour's focus. Alternate sites are provided at the beginning of the touring section for consideration. The main tour begins at the Chancellorsville Battlefield Visitor Center with Stop 1.

The tour includes driving on busy highways and along National Park Service roads. Left turns onto highways have been minimized in the directions. All parking areas for the tour are in clearly marked lots (there is no pulling off along the side of the road in undesignated areas). Please use caution and observe traffic signs, signals, speed limits, and other travel conventions as you explore by car and on foot. (Equestrians are not permitted on Chancellorsville, Fredericksburg, or Salem Church Battlefields.)

Alternate Site: Union Winter Camps

This site relates to:
    Critical Decision 1—Lincoln Appoints Hooker
    Critical Decision 3—Hooker Determines His Offensive Strategy

Across Stafford County, Virginia, the Union Army of the Potomac encamped during the winter of 1862–63. At his winter headquarters, Maj. Gen. Joseph Hooker made his first critical decision that would set the Chancellorsville Campaign in motion. A new general and in command of the army beginning in January 1863, Hooker had confidence and ability. He spent the winter reforming the supply system, furloughs, and morale of the Army of the Potomac, molding the demoralized soldiers into a fighting force that expected victory the next time they marched to battle.

Two critical decisions have connections to the winter camps in Stafford.

Appendix I

Reconstructed cabins at Stafford Civil War Park give visitors an idea of the close quarters of an encamped army during the winter of 1862–63.

Though Pres. Lincoln made the first critical decision from the White House and War Department in Washington, DC, his choice to remove Maj. Gen. Ambrose Burnside from command and place Hooker in charge had its results play out in the camps. Lincoln visited the Union camps in Stafford County as spring approached, meeting with Hooker and reviewing the readying troops. Putting Hooker in command brought a needed change to the Army of the Potomac and gave it a new leader going into the fighting season of 1863. During the winter months in Stafford County, Hooker formed and made his critical decision to pursue an offensive strategy. He decided to divide his forces, sending Union cavalry sweeping toward the Confederate capital at Richmond, march the majority of the army's corps west along the Rappahannock to cross and swing east on the Confederates' rear. Meanwhile, a distraction force near Fredericksburg would occupy the enemy's attention. This choice set the early movements for the campaign and put the Union forces on the offense, which would force Lee to react or retreat.

The land for the vast collection of tents, temporary structures, supplies, and people working in and around Hooker's headquarters has not been preserved. Though a road sign notes the vicinity of the headquarters, it is not safely accessible. However, Stafford Civil War Park preserves forty-one acres including two artillery positions and campsites used by divisions of the Union Eleventh Corps. The park is regularly open and accessible, featuring walking trails and interpretive signs to help visitors explore and consider the experience of the soldiers before Chancellorsville.

Stafford Civil War Park is located at 400 Mount Hope Church Road, Stafford, VA 22554. It is approximately twenty-three miles from the Chancellorsville Battlefield Visitor Center. For more visitor information, please refer to the park's website: https://www.staffordcountyva.gov/business_detail_T12_R584.php.

Alternate Site: Hamilton's Crossing

This site relates to:
   Critical Decision 2—Lee Sends Longstreet's Corps Away
   Critical Decision 4—Lee Decides to Turn and Fight

The Confederate Army of Northern Virginia spent the winter months of 1862–63 on the south side of the Rappahannock River in Spotsylvania and Caroline Counties. Hamilton's Crossing on the Richmond, Fredericksburg & Potomac Railroad served as an important supply depot, allowing the rebels to bring food and furloughing soldiers to and from Richmond, the capital of the Confederacy. Hamilton's Crossing also served as a centralized point that Gens. Lee and Jackson used at the end of April 1863 as they observed the Union movements and critical decisions.

Two critical decisions are connected to Hamilton's Crossing. Lee sent Lieut. Gen. James Longstreet and divisions of the First Corps south to Suffolk to relieve the strain of food and forage on the central Virginia region and reduce the amount of supplies brought by rail to Hamilton's Crossing. This choice reduced the number of available troops in the immediate area of operations, but it also kept the army from enduring more logistical hardships during the winter. Lee's decision to turn and fight Hooker, blocking Hooker's advance toward Fredericksburg and the Confederate rear, had its beginnings around Hamilton's Crossing as Lee and Jackson observed the situation. They knew about the distraction force crossing the Rappahannock below

Appendix I

Part of Hamilton's Crossing is preserved on National Park Service land, giving visitors an opportunity to explore an important supply position for the Confederate army during the winter of 1862–63.

Fredericksburg, and they continued receiving reports about significant movement at upriver fords and Union troops marching east. Lee's determination to turn and fight divided his available force and clearly emphasized that Hooker and the army advancing through Chancellorsville would be the first objective of military action. Accordingly, Lee sent Jackson and his corps to the west, then followed them shortly after, arriving in the afternoon of May 1, 1863.

Hamilton's Crossing had a railroad turntable in 1863 and served as a major supply point for the Confederates in their winter camps. It was located somewhat between Lee's and Jackson's headquarters. The nearby high ground at Prospect Hill and the open ground beyond allowed the generals to observe the Union troops commanded by Maj. Gen. John Sedgwick as they crossed as a diversionary force.

Today, the turntable is gone, and historians are not sure of its exact location. However, modern railroad tracks still pass through Hamilton's Crossing, and the whistle and rattle of trains echo through the historic area. Hamilton's Crossing is within Fredericksburg and Spotsylvania National Military Park and is accessible in two ways. First, park at Prospect Hill at the end of Lee Drive (6 Lee Drive, Fredericksburg, VA 22408), pass through the fence at the east side of the parking lot, and follow the worn, sloping trail down to Hamilton's Crossing; it is just over a half-mile walk, round trip. Second, park at the small lot for Hamilton's Crossing at the very end of Lee Drive Extended, and explore the flat area (Lee Hill Extended, Fredericksburg, VA 22408). Please note that you cannot drive directly between Prospect Hill and Lee Hill Extended.

The Chancellorsville Battlefield

Begin this tour at the Chancellorsville Battlefield Visitor Center (9001 Plank Road, Spotsylvania Courthouse, VA 22553). During operating hours, you can explore displays about the battlefield, watch a short film, pick up a national park map, or browse in the bookstore. You may want to see the large map located outside the visitor center (between the visitor center and the parking lot) for a beginning orientation to the battlefield.

To Tour Stop 1. Exit the Chancellorsville Battlefield Visitor Center parking lot toward Bullock Road. Turn right (north) onto Bullock Road, and proceed for 0.8 mile. At the stop sign, turn right (southeast) onto Ely's Ford Road, and drive for 0.7 mile. At the traffic light, turn left (east) onto Plank Road / Route 3. Please note that this traffic light intersection is the Chancellorsville Crossroads. You will return here later in the tour; for now, just note the location as you drive east on Plank Road and into the area of the battle on May 1, 1863.

Proceed for 3.8 miles, and at the traffic light for Harrison Road, use the left turn lane to make a U-turn. In 0.2 mile, turn right (north) into the shopping center driveway, and continue straight for 0.1 mile. To the left, there is a small parking lot and paved trail. Park in the lot, and walk up the switchback trail to the crest. As of the early 2020s, this land is preserved and maintained by Spotsylvania County, and there are several Battle of Chancellorsville interpretive signs at the site.

Tour Stop 1: Zoan Church Ridge

This site relates to:
Critical Decision 4—Lee Decides to Turn and Fight

At the crest of the trail and Zoan Church Ridge, face west—which means the shopping center and parking lot will be at your back. You are now in a Confederate position for the morning of May 1, 1863. The view at the time this tour guide was written is rather obscured and will likely remain that way; it would have been more open in 1863. However, this stop allows exploration

Appendix I

of the eastern edge of Chancellorsville fighting and will help give perspective in terms of distance to other stops on this tour. To your left is modern Route 3, which mostly follows the bed of the much narrower historic road called the Orange Turnpike. To your right, not visible and approximately 2.5 miles away, is the Rappahannock River; River Road, an alternate east–west route toward Fredericksburg, parallels the Rappahannock. You are standing on the ridge where Confederate Lieut. Gen. Thomas J. "Stonewall" Jackson put into tactical motion Lee's decision to turn and fight.

Heading east, Zoan Church Ridge is the highest topographical point between Chancellorsville and the Atlantic Ocean. Had the Union advance reached this area, Federals would have cleared the Virginia Wilderness and entered open ground to the east, which would have been advantageous to the larger Union army and its superior artillery. The terrain just west of the ridge was a mix of field and forest, especially near the north side of the turnpike, where several civilian farms had cleared the ground.

The name of the ridge comes from the Zoan Church, a frame building built on the high ground around 1853. This house of worship was the meeting place of part of the congregation that split from Salem Church to the east

The remains of low earthworks along Zoan Church Ridge are a reminder of Lee's decision to turn and fight and Jackson's orders to stop digging and advance to the west.

over the issues of prohibition and temperance.[1] The historic Zoan Church structure no longer exists, but there are two modern places of worship on the ridge.

On April 30, 1863, Confederate troops commanded by Maj. Gen. Richard Anderson set up a defensive position here, ready to continue opposing the Union advance out of the Wilderness and toward Fredericksburg. They prepared to either retreat farther east toward Fredericksburg or fight a delaying action against the advancing Union troops. One soldier in the Nineteenth Mississippi Regiment remembered arriving at Zoan Church Ridge and beginning to build earthworks in the night. The remains of some of the Confederate fortifications may be visible in the woods in front of you; they are easiest to see during the late fall or winter months, when the leaves are not as dense. Please do not climb on the earthworks, because doing so leads to erosion and destruction of the trenches.

Diary of Lieut. A. L. Peel, CSA, Adjutant, Nineteenth Mississippi, Barksdale's Brigade, McLaws's Division, Longstreet's Corps, Army of Northern Virginia

Gen Posey ordered us to hold our position 1/2 an hour then fall back to Chancellorsville hold it 1 hour and follow the Brigade towards Fredericksburg, our pickets fought. We came to the Brigade and halted near the frame church, dug rifle trenches, our pickets fought the enemy. One man from our Regt was wounded. We chopped the bushes down in front of our line. Sleep in the trenches.[2]

Reinforcements would be arriving to bolster the thin line of Confederates on the ridge. Facing a divided Union army with an active element of that force marching on his rear, Confederate Gen. Robert E. Lee had decided to divide his own army. He sent the majority of his men toward the Virginia Wilderness and Chancellorsville and left a small force to monitor the enemy troops near Fredericksburg.

The soldiers in Jackson's Corps made a night march and were ready to reinforce Anderson by morning on May 1, 1863. Jackson assessed the situation to the west and decided to take an offensive interpretation of Lee's decision. Instead of just defending Zoan Church Ridge, he would use it as a launching point to actively oppose the Union advance from the Wilderness.

Report of Maj. Gen. Richard H. Anderson, CSA, Commanding Anderson's Division, Longstreet's Corps, Army of Northern Virginia

Upon arriving at the intersection of the Old Mine and Plank roads [on April 30], I met Col. W. P. Smith, chief engineer Army of Northern Virginia, and Captain [S. R.] Johnston, of the Engineer Corps, who had been sent by the commanding general to examine the position and establish a line of intrenchments. The work of intrenching was commenced immediately after the line had been selected, and was continued with great diligence and activity throughout that day, the night following, and the early part of the next morning.

During the day there were occasional skirmishes with the enemy's cavalry, who had followed from Chancellorsville. In the afternoon, Colonel [T. H.] Owen, commanding the Third Regiment of Virginia Cavalry, joined me with his regiment, and threw out pickets to the front and upon each flank.

A little before sunrise on May 1, Major-General McLaws, having come up with his division, strengthened the force immediately in front, and secured our right flank by occupying the trenches along Mott's Run. At 8 a.m. Lieutenant-General Jackson arrived. By his orders the work on the trenches was discontinued, and the troops were put in readiness for an advance, Wilcox's and Perry's brigades, which had been left above Fredericksburg, being at the same time ordered to join their division. The advance commenced at 11 a.m.[3]

Lee had decided not to let Hooker advance without heavy opposition. Studying the situation, Jackson ordered an attack to substantially delay or deter the Union advance. Using Zoan Church Ridge as a forming point, Jackson's divisions spread across land on both sides of the turnpike and prepared to use the Orange Plank Road, an old parallel road running south of the main one. The outcome of the fighting launched from the ridge and enacted in the fields and woods to the west would trigger the next critical decision. To further explore the fighting and decisions on May 1, 1863, return to your car and drive to the next stop.

To Tour Stop 2. Exit the parking lot, and head south (right) 0.1 mile to westbound Plank Road. Turn right (west) onto Plank Road / Route 3; be aware that the right lane ends abruptly, and Plank Road becomes two lanes just beyond your exit turn. Drive west for 1.4 miles, turning right into the parking lot of Spotsylvania County Museum / First Day at Chancellorsville Battlefield. You may wish to explore the Spotsylvania County Museum, which is open during select hours. For more information, please visit https://www.spotsylvania.va.us/898/Museum.

There are several options for exploring this expansive tract of preserved land held by American Battlefield Trust. An approximately two-mile trail loops east and west across this battlefield section, with the parking roughly at the center of the loops. If time permits, walk the trail to the east (to the right, when facing the red museum building with the parking lot behind you), and then walk the trail to the west to the suggested point of exploration. If you do not wish to walk, face west and read the notes.

To reach the suggested point for the tour stop, follow the trail from the parking lot and county visitor center to the west (to the left, when standing with the parking lot behind you). The trail will slope down and eventually cross Lick Run; there is a solid bridge at this point. Continue to follow the trail up the steep slope, and when you reach the crest, continue across the little plateau, then up the next short rise to the highest point of the trail thus far. (If you reach the modern road into the housing tract, you've gone too far.) Here, turn about-face and look to the east. You are now standing on ground where Union soldiers of the Fifth Corps fought on May 1, 1863.

Tour Stop 2: First Day at Chancellorsville Battlefield

This site relates to:
Critical Decision 4—Lee Decides to Turn and Fight
Critical Decision 5—Hooker Pulls Back

Facing east, you are looking over the land where Confederates in Jackson's advance on May 1, 1863, clashed with Union cavalry and infantry reinforcements. The road to your right is modern Route 3, built over the narrow traces of the historic Orange Turnpike. Farther to the south (right), but not visible historically or now, Old Plank Road parallels the turnpike. Confederates advanced along that route as well. You might be able to spot a "pine tree" cell phone tower near the horizon to the east on the right side of Route 3; this is a good reference point for Zoan Church Ridge, which is about 1.5 miles away.

Throughout the day on May 1, the results of Lee's decision to turn and fight played out across this landscape. Advances and retreats had the combat seesawing across this rolling land, the turnpike, and territory farther south. Note the high-ground position you currently occupy, and consider the terrain advantages that Union infantry and artillery could have had here against advancing Confederates.

Appendix I

A view looking east over the First Day at Chancellorsville Battlefield, preserved by the American Battlefield Trust.

Turn to the west, and notice how the ground continues rising to make an optional artillery position. During 1863, this ground was fairly open farmland—similar to its appearance today. Beyond that western ridge, sometimes called McGee Ridge, the dense wooded Wilderness stretches for approximately a mile before the Chancellorsville clearing and crossroads.

Union Maj. Gen. George Skyes described bringing his division of the Fifth Corps troops to this battlefield on May 1, setting the stage for Maj. Gen. Hooker's critical decision to fall back and establish a defensive position at Chancellorsville.

Report of Maj. Gen. George Sykes, USA, Commanding Second Division, Fifth Corps, Army of the Potomac

A mile and a half from Chancellorsville, I found some cavalry engaged with the enemy's skirmishers. The former were giving ground, and, by their behavior, giving confidence to the enemy. My three brigades were at once deployed.... By sharp fighting, we soon recovered the lost ground, drove in the enemy's pickets, and took possession of a crest just in front of a heavy forest, and in range of some rifle-pits or breastworks on our left. Weed's battery (Company I, Fifth

Artillery) . . . crowned the crest, and opened an effective cannonade, and was supported by a part of my third brigade. . . . The enemy held the road in front with infantry and two guns, threw a considerable force in the breastworks, and for a couple of hours maneuvered to turn both my flanks. His forces were so superior to my own that he partially outflanked me both right and left. . . . The battery checked any advance by the main road, and the dispositions to secure my flanks kept the enemy quiet; but as both of these flanks rested on a dense growth of forest, and as I was completely isolated from the rest of the army, I felt that my rear could be gained by a determined movement of the enemy under cover of the forest. Griffin was far to my left, Slocum far to my right, the enemy in front and between me and both those officers. In this situation, without support, my position was critical; still, I determined to hold it as long as possible. At this period, General Warren, chief engineer Army of the Potomac, who had accompanied me, rode to the major-general commanding the army, to explain the state of affairs, and, on his return, I was directed to retire in the direction of Chancellorsville.[4]

Much to the anger or frustration of the Union generals fighting here, bringing up reinforcements to this position, or successfully holding and advancing along Orange Plank Road, Hooker's critical decision to break off the fighting and consolidate his army around the Chancellorsville Crossroads meant that Federals gave up this strong position to take lower ground in low-visibility forest. As far as primary sources suggest, Hooker did not view this part of the battlefield, instead relying on reports and wavering in his decision and its execution. If this is correct, he did not see the terrain advantage that that this open high ground might afford if held and reinforced.

To explore the Chancellorsville Crossroads and this decision further, please return to your vehicle, and follow the directions to Tour Stop 3. Take as much time as you wish to further hike the First Day at Chancellorsville Battlefield. You can walk farther west, following the trail and exploring McGee Ridge for more terrain consideration too.

To Tour Stop 3. Exit the First Day at Chancellorsville Battlefield parking lot, and turn right (west) onto Plank Road / Route 3. Continue for 2.2 miles. At the traffic light intersection, turn right (north) onto Ely's Ford Road. In approximately 400 feet, turn left into the parking lot for the Chancellorsville House Site.

Walk along the paved path, and face the foundation ruins of the Chancellorsville House; you are facing south. The traffic signal should be to your front left.

Tour Stop 3: The Chancellorsville Crossroads

This site relates to:
    Critical Decision 5—Hooker Pulls Back
    Critical Decision 7—Hooker Decides the Confederates
        are Retreating
    Critical Decision 14—Union Officers Do Not Replace Hooker
        after His Injury

The heart of the Union defensive lines for the Battle of Chancellorsville, this historic crossroads is the location where several critical decisions were made. Here, Hooker decided to withdraw his army into a defensive posture on May 1, 1863. Here, Hooker decided the Confederates were retreating, and he did not further investigate reports of a dangerous movement approaching the right flank and the Eleventh Corps on May 2. Finally, it was here that Hooker's corps commanders and medical staff decided not to relieve him of command after a section of heavy column pillar fell on his head.

This clearing looked different in 1863. The road in front of you—the Orange Turnpike, now Route 3—would have been much narrower and "planked," in an effort to improve the road from mud patches.. The house, now in ruins and with just a foundation left after years of rebuilding and fires, stood welcomingly at the crossroads of the turnpike and Ely's Ford Road. The house itself was Chancellorsville, not a village or larger community.

Constructed in 1816, the multistory brick structure had been a celebrated tavern and favored stopping point for travelers in previous decades. At the time of the battle, widow Frances Chancellor and her daughters rented the house and resided here. Southern in sympathies, the white women seemed resentful about giving up their home as a military headquarters for the Union army.[5]

Across the road and to your right, the cannon at Fairview might be visible. (Sometimes they are obscured by tall crops in the fields.) A walled family cemetery is also there, and a house would have been at this location in 1863. Beyond Fairview to the southwest is the high ground of Hazel Grove, which offered a strong position for Confederate artillery to fire into the Chancellorsville clearing on May 3, 1863.

Troops from both sides had previously passed through Chancellorsville during the war. In the Chancellorsville Campaign, Union troops from Fifth and Twelfth Corps reached this crossroads clearing on April 30. That night Hooker paused the advance, intending to go forward in the morning.

Narrative of Capt. Francis Adams Donaldson, USA, 118th Pennsylvania, First Brigade, First Division, Fifth Corps, Army of the Potomac

The Chancellor House was a large two story brick building with porches and wooden pillows [pillars], and was in the centre of a cleared space surrounded with dense woods and thickets. It struck me at the time as being a large summer boarding house, although I did not go to it to ascertain, because, I presume, I felt that I was too soiled and dirty, although we were directly in front and but a few feet from the house. Upon the upper porch were many ladies dressed in light summer cloths, who, with characteristic Southern female bravado, reviled us audibly, and wanted to know why we did not go on as General Lee was anxious to extend the hospitalities of the country.[6]

At his comfortable headquarters, Maj. Gen. Joseph Hooker received and sent dispatches and did his best to stay informed about the battle. He also had communication lines with orderlies and telegraph wires connecting him to his chief of staff, Gen. Butterfield, who was on the other side of the Rappahannock and acting as a sort of go-between for Hooker and Sedgwick at Fredericksburg. In some ways, Hooker was in the right place: at his headquarters, monitoring information and reports and making decisions. However, Hooker began to make decisions blindly and without a clear understanding of the terrain.

In the afternoon of May 1, 1863, Hooker made a critical decision to stop advancing out of the Wilderness. Instead, he brought all his available troops into a defensive perimeter in the woods and fields around the Chancellorsville Crossroads. This decision ceded terrain advantage to the east and gave the advantage of movement and initiative to the Confederates.

On May 2, Hooker decided that the observed movement of Confederate troops was his enemy's retreat. He did not fully confirm that theory. Hooker allowed Maj. Gen. Sickles to organize an advance south toward the Catharine Furnace, but he did not give much attention to reports from the Eleventh Corps, which was positioned on the right flank, that enemy movements had been detected nearby. Without confirming the destination of the observable Confederate column, Hooker left his army in a vulnerable situation. Soldiers from the Eleventh Corps raced along the Orange Turnpike from the west (from the right where you are standing). The chaos headed toward Hooker's headquarters, and the general rode out and took quick rallying actions. However, the successful Confederate flank attack resulted in the sudden retreat of the Eleventh Corps, and the hasty shift of the Union lines, and night fighting that brought combat closing around the Union defenses near Chancellorsville.

By the morning of May 3, 1863, the divided Confederate army attacked, putting pressure on both the east- and west-facing portions of the Union lines circling Chancellorsville.

Narrative of Pvt. Martin W. Brett, CSA, Twelfth Georgia, Doles's Brigade, Rodes's Division, Jackson's Corps, Army of Northern Virginia

On Sunday morning, May 3rd, the engagement was terrific. On the previous night the Yankees had strengthened their breast-works, and reunited their lines in every possible way, and early Sunday morning we found their position bristling with all the artillery, small arms, and men they could bring up. We were in position to see the work before us, which we began at once and continued well up into the day, knowing that our only relief was to silence their batteries and

The Chancellorsville House burned several times in the nineteenth century, not just during the May 1863 battle. Today, this brick outlining shows the foundations of the original structure, which was used as Hooker's headquarters.

break the lines of solid fire from their small arms. We made one desperate charge after another, at times beating down their cannoneers with our clubbed muskets and killing many of them outright with the bayonet while they were making valiant efforts to man their guns. We succeeded in breaking their lines; but oh! the horrors of war. When that awful scene flits through my mind my eyes fill with irrepressible tears, and I pause before proceeding—The Chancellorsville Hotel, which was being used by the Yankees as a hospital, and where they had gathered many of their wounded, took fire and numbers who were helpless perished in the flames. There was also an extensive tract of woodland where a carpet of dry leaves, the accumulation of years, had become very thick on the ground, and adjoining that was a field covered with a dense growth of dry grass in condition to burn like tinder. We had done considerable fighting over the place that day, and there were many wounded, dying, and dead men and horses scattered about over the ground when it took fire. Lying, as it did, between our lines and those of the enemy, we could not extinguish the flames nor render the sufferers any assistance, so there were many burned to death who might otherwise have lived and recovered from their wounds.[7]

During the morning attacks, artillery fire into the crossroads intensified. While standing on or near the porch of the Chancellor House, Hooker was struck on the head with a piece of an artillery-damaged pillar. Knocked unconscious, he recovered and determined to carry on. However, his injuries were probably more severe than initially realized, and he exhibited signs of confusion, pain, and exhaustion as the day continued. These symptoms led to periods when he was not in command and decisions fell to subordinates. The decision to let Hooker continue as the commander left the Union army at Chancellorsville without overall leadership at a moment when the force was under heavy attack.

Union artillery ran out of ammunition, then Union infantry retreated to the north (behind you) to establish new defensive lines. The Chancellor House caught fire, and flames ripped through some of the surrounding woods. In this fiery scene, Union soldiers made last-ditch resistance efforts, rescued artillery, and retreated. Confederates charged into the clearing, cheering and recognizing their victory by capturing this position and reuniting their army at Chancellorsville.

Appendix I

The risks the Confederates took and the decisions they made led to their breakthrough here at the crossroads. To further explore places connected with those decisions on May 1, 2, and 3, please continue the tour.

To Tour Stop 4. Exit the Chancellorsville House Site parking lot, turning right (south) onto Ely's Ford Road. Proceed for 1.2 miles, crossing through the traffic light at the intersection with Plank Road (historic Orange Turnpike) and continuing straight on Old Plank Road. Make a sharp right turn onto Furnace Road, and pull into the designated roadside parking for the Lee-Jackson Bivouac Site. Walk to the interpretive area, then face the intersection.

Tour Stop 4: Lee-Jackson Bivouac Site

This site relates to:
  Critical Decision 6—Lee Allows Jackson to Initiate a Flank Attack

Somewhere in the woods surrounding this intersection of the historic Orange Plank Road (now Old Plank Road) and Catharine Furnace Road, Gen. Robert E. Lee and Lieut. Gen. Thomas J. "Stonewall" Jackson met during the night of May 1–2, 1863. It is unclear whether the Confederate officers' campfire and seating was on this corner where you stand or diagonally across the intersection. Just over a mile to your left is the Chancellorsville Crossroads where the Chancellor House stood, used as Union Maj. Gen. Hooker's headquarters during the battle. The road ahead of you will run northeast along McGee Ridge and toward the open fields of the First Day at Chancellorsville Battlefield. The road to the right was known as the Orange Plank Road during the war, and it turns to run parallel to the Orange Turnpike (modern Route 3). Catharine Furnace Road extends beside and behind you, leading about 1.5 miles west to an iron furnace that was there at the time of the battle.

During the afternoon of May 1, 1863, Union troops from the Fifth Corps and Twelfth Corps suddenly gave ground and retreated toward the Chancellorsville Crossroads. Confederates pursued until reaching their enemy's defensive position, and darkness and skirmishing settled over the Virginia Wilderness. Lee pondered what to do next. Clearly, Hooker had given up the military initiative, but how could Lee exploit the opportunity? Receiving information from Maj. Gen. James E. B. Stuart and his cavalry that the Union army's right flank was relatively unprotected, Jackson advocated finding a way to reach that position and launch a flank attack. Lee continued to gather information and weigh the options. If he allowed Jackson to proceed with the flank attack, he would be dividing his army again: a portion at Fredericks-

In the vicinity of this National Park Service tour stop site, Lee and Jackson met to plan the flank attack for May 2, 1863.

burg, a portion creating a diversion near Chancellorsville, and the majority marching with Jackson to the west for the flank attack.

Narrative of Maj. T. M. R. Talcott, CSA, Aide-de-Camp to Robert E. Lee, Army of Northern Virginia

About sunset General Jackson sent word to General Lee (by me) that his advance was checked and that the enemy was in force at Chancellorsville. This brought General Lee to the front and General Jackson met him in the southeast angle of the Chancellorsville and Catherine's Furnace Roads.

General Lee asked General Jackson whether he had ascertained the position and strength of the enemy on our left, to which General Jackson replied by stating the result of an attack made by Stuart's Cavalry near dusk. The position of the enemy directly in front was then discussed, and Capt Boswell and myself were sent to make a moonlight reconnaissance the result of which was reported about ten P.M. and was not favorable to an attack in front.

At this time Generals Lee and Jackson were together and General Lee who had a map before him asked General Jackson "How can we get at those people," to which General Jackson replied in effect "you know best. Show me what to do and we will try to do it." General Lee looked thoughtfully at the woods, then indicated [to] sit and explained the movement he desired General Jackson to make and closed by saying, "General Stuart will cover your movement with his Cavalry." General Jackson listened attentively and his face lighted up with a smile while General Lee was speaking then rising and touching his cap he left saying "My troops will move at four o'clock."[8]

Narrative of Pvt. Benjamin B. Carr, CSA, Twentieth North Carolina, Iverson's Brigade, Rodes's Division, Jackson's Corps, Army of Northern Virginia

We then started on that famous march to the rear of the Federal Army then commanded by Gen. Joe Hooker. But we thought it a retreat or a fall back for a better position until about 2 or 3 o'clock, while arching along a narrow road winding through a dense wilderness not seeing a house or clearing or other sign that the section was inhabited by human beings except the narrow road we were traveling when we saw a lone horseman coming with all the speed his horse was [capable] of, holding aloft a large yellow envelope. We stepped to the side of the road to let him pass. In a short time another courier came riding from the rear saying Gen. Jackson is coming, but no cheering. We stepped to the side of the road again and along came Gen. Jackson on his long, gaunt sorrel horse in a long gallop with his hat raised and each soldier with his hat raised but not a word spoken. We knew then something of importance was on hand. We marched on and on gradually bearing to the right.

About an hour before sunset we came to Gen. Stuart's cavalry pickets, but passing on farther to the right for a mile or more we stopped and formed a line of battle. Our Brigade, being in the lead was the first to form, the rest forming as they came up, the line was soon formed, and the order to advance was given. It was then near sunset. The attack was a complete surprise to the Federals. This line (which was their rear line) was formed across a field (which was the first field or clearing that we saw in all that long trip we made that day) and was about 400 yards from the woods from which we emerged charging with a yell over their cooking detail routing their rear line which retreated with firing only a few shots at us a great many of them not taken their guns which were stacked. It soon resulted in a running fight until night stopped it.⁹

Lee's decision to divide the Confederate force again put Jackson's flank march and attack in motion. It divided his army at a risk, but it also took advantage of the opportunity Hooker had created by holing up into a defensive position and leaving a weak place.

To further explore the results of Lee allowing Jackson's march, you have two options. The first set of driving directions will take you on the National Park Service roads, closely following Jackson's circuitous route. This approach is suggested because it will allow you to see and explore the distance and terrain of this flank march. However, if you would prefer a quicker option to reach the point of attack, follow the second set of directions.

To Tour Stop 5 via the Driving Route of Jackson's Flank March. This option will take you along Jackson's historic route on May 2, 1863. If you would prefer a faster trip to Stop 5, please travel via Route 3 as explained below.

Pull out of the parking area at the Lee-Jackson Bivouac Site, and continue straight on Furnace Road. Continue for 1.4 miles, then keep left toward Catharine Furnace and Jackson Trail East. As of the early 2020s, the route beyond Catharine Furnace is unpaved. Proceed for 2.8 miles on Jackson Trail East, which ends at a T intersection with Brock Road / Route 613. Turn left onto Brock Road / Route 613, and continue for 0.3 mile. Turn right onto Jackson Trail West, and continue for 2.3 miles. Jackson Trail West ends in a merging intersection with Brock Road. Make a slight left turn onto Brock Road / Route 613, and continue for 2.7 miles. At the traffic signal intersection, turn right onto Plank Road / Route 3. You are now heading east. Continue for 1.7 miles, then make a sharp left turn into the highway crossing to make a U-turn onto westbound Plank Road / Route 3. Turn into the gravel driveway to the right, and follow the lane to the parking area in the flank attack fields.

Please note that if you miss the U-turn on Plank Road / Route 3, you can make a U-turn at the traffic signal intersection ahead or at other highway crossings.

To Tour Stop 5 via Route 3. This option is the quickest and most direct way to Tour Stop 5, but you will not drive the Flank Attack Route. If you would prefer the historic route marched by the Confederates on May 2, 1863, please refer to the previous option.

Appendix I

Today, a National Park Service road traces portions of Jackson's flank march, allowing visitors to gain a better understanding of the distance and terrain that Confederate troops covered on May 2, 1863.

Carefully make a U-turn out of the parking area at the Lee-Jackson Bivouac Site. At the intersection, turn left (north) onto Old Plank Road, and continue for 1.1 miles to the Chancellorsville Crossroads. At the traffic light, turn left (west) onto Plank Road / Route 3, and proceed for 2.7 miles. Turn right into the gravel lane marked for the flank attack fields. Follow the lane to the parking area. Walk to the interpretive panels near the large tree and parking area, and face east (Route 3 will be in the distance to your right).

Tour Stop 5: Union Eleventh Corps' Camp

This site relates to:
  Critical Decision 6—Lee Allows Jackson to Initiate a Flank Attack
  Critical Decision 7—Hooker Decides the Confederates are Retreating
  Critical Decision 8—Jackson Cuts Off the Federals from US Ford

The open ground in the distance and generally along the road corridor today was fields surrounded by Wilderness woods at the time of the battle. These fields and the wooded terrain were the position and camp of the Union Eleventh Corps through the night of May 1 and day of May 2. To your right, modern-day Route 3 roughly follows the narrower span of the historic Orange Turnpike. Many of the Union regiments set up their positions facing south and paralleling this road, making them more vulnerable to the Confederates' flank attack coming from the west.

In the distance to the east, you might see a traffic signal. That intersection with historic Orange Plank Road saw some resistance as Union troops fought back, and it later became a Confederate horse artillery position. A little farther east, the most significant Union defensive line against the flank attack formed: the Buschbeck Line. Ultimately, whether they ran or retreated with resistance, most of the Union soldiers of the Eleventh Corps headed

Union soldiers from the Eleventh Corps encamped in the fields along the Orange Turnpike and had not reinforced their line toward the west.

east along the turnpike toward the Chancellorsville Crossroads, almost three miles distant.

> ### Narrative of Pvt. Darwin Cody, USA, Battery I, First Ohio Artillery, Third Division, Eleventh Corps, Army of the Potomac
>
> They massed their troops right on our extreme right where we did not expect them. They soon drove in our pickets. Then we poured the shell into them. The bullets came in like hailstones. Then they opened 2 Batteries on ours which made it pretty hot for us. Our Infantry soon commenced to run. Our support was all germans. They run without firing a gun. Such yelling I never heard before as the Rebs made. Our Battery was soon left alone. We stayed until they were within 15 rods of us. Then we were ordered to Limber up which we soon done. We fell back about a hundred rods where we unlimbered again. Our Infantry running in every direction. At this our Infantry were in the entrenchments in front of us. We gave them (the enemy) double canister which soon checked them in the center. We killed a good many of them in a short time. Our Infantry soon run and left us. Then the Rebbels soon commenced to charge on our Battery. Then they made out to get one of our guns. They shot the wheel horses, then we was down. We done all we could to save it. Our Infantry had all left us. We had one killed and nine wounded there, and six horses killed and 10 or 14 wounded. . . . We fell back for half mile. That was the nearest point where we could get our battery in position. I say dam the DUTCH. Gen. Hooker soon ordered the 12th corps to kill every man that run in the 11th. . . . If I ever run I am willing to have them shoot me.[10]

Turn and face west (Route 3 should be to your left now). Confederate lines of battle crested that ridgeline, which was wooded at the time, and charged toward the Union camps. The surprise attack began shortly after 5:00 p.m., and the springtime sun would have been shining behind the Confederates and into the eyes of the Union soldiers.

Report of Maj. Gen. Robert E. Rodes, CSA, Commanding D. H. Hill's Division, Jackson's Corps, Army of Northern Virginia

At 5:15 p.m. the word was given to move forward. . . . At once the line of battle rushed forward with a yell, and Doles at this moment debouched from the woods and encountered a force of the enemy and a battery of two guns intrenched. Detaching two regiments to flank the position, he charged without halting, sweeping everything before him, and pressing on to Talley's, gallantly carried the works there, and captured five guns by a similar flank movement of a portion of his command. So complete was the success of the whole maneuver, and such was the surprise of the enemy, that scarcely any organized resistance was met with after the first volley was fired. They fled in the wildest confusion, leaving the field strewn with arms, accouterments, clothing, caissons, and fieldpieces in every direction. The larger portion of his force, as well as intrenchments, were drawn up at right angles to our line, and, being thus taken in the flank and rear, they did not wait for the attack.[11]

This attack was the result of Lee's decision to divide his army again. The long march forming in the woods and charging forward culminated Lee's choice with a swift victory. But the Confederates were still divided, and the next critical decisions stemmed from the disorganization and confusion in the Union and Confederate ranks because of the flank attack.

To continue exploring the decisions on May 2, please continue to the next tour stop. You will be traveling east on Route 3, passing through more battlefield on your way.

To Tour Stop 6. Follow the gravel lane back to Plank Road / Route 3. You can only turn right (west), so turn right and take the left lane. In 0.3 mile, turn left into the highway crossing, and make a U-turn to head east on Plank Road / Route 3. Proceed for 2.1 miles, and use the left turn lane to turn onto Bullock Road and into the Chancellorsville Battlefield Visitor Center entrance. Keep right to enter the parking lot.

Park, and walk to the pathway leading into the woods at the left of the visitor center. This historic roadbed is Mountain Road, and you will find interpretive signs here. Face east, and the visitor center should be behind you.

If you have not already explored the Chancellorsville Battlefield Visitor Center, you may want to do so during this stop. In addition, an interpretive trail loops several miles through the Chancellorsville Battlefield and passes the remains of earthworks. If you are interested in walking the trail, check at the visitor center or trailhead (north side of the parking lot) for a free trail guide brochure.

Tour Stop 6: Jackson's Wounding Site

This site relates to:

Critical Decision 8—Jackson Cuts Off the Federals from US Ford

Critical Decision 9—Lee Puts J. E. B. Stuart in Command of the Second Corps

As darkness settled over the clearings and woods on May 2, 1863, the Union Eleventh Corps had been pushed into a frightened retreat that threw the Federal lines around Chancellorsville into temporary confusion too. Confederate Lieut. Gen. Thomas J. "Stonewall" Jackson carried out the march and surprise attack that Lee had approved. However, the dense woods and darkness began to work against the enthused Confederates, breaking up their battle lines and creating confusion that slowed their advance and effectiveness.

Jackson was anxious to press the attack. He also began taking an interest in moving farther north—farther away from Lee—but getting into a position that might block the Union's access to the river fords and lead to a decisive, army-crushing victory. To gather information, Jackson and a few staff officers and couriers rode through the Confederate infantry lines into no-man's-land. Using Mountain Road, which parallels Orange Turnpike (Route 3, to your right), he headed east on a scouting mission—the wrong role for a corps commander.

Capt. James Power Smith, CSA, Aide-de-Camp, Jackson's Corps, Army of Northern Virginia

When Jackson had reached the point where his line now crossed the turnpike, scarcely a mile west of Chancellorsville, and not half a mile from a line of Federal troops, he had found his front line unfit for the farther and vigorous advance he desired, by reason of the irregular character of the fighting, now right, now left, and because of the dense thickets, through which it was impossible to preserve align-

The Mountain Road was a narrow forest path that paralleled the Orange Turnpike; during the night of May 2, 1863, Jackson used this road as he scouted beyond his lines.

ment. Division commanders found it more and more difficult as the twilight deepened to hold their broken brigades in hand. Regretting the necessity of relieving the troops in front, General Jackson had ordered A. P. Hill's division, his third and reserve line, to be placed in front. While this change was being effected, impatient and anxious, the general rode forward . . . followed by two or three of his staff and a number of couriers and signal sergeants. He passed the swampy depression and began the ascent of the hill toward Chancellorsville, when he came upon a line of Federal infantry lying on their arms. . . . He turned and came back toward his line. . . . As he rode near to the Confederate troops, just placed in position and ignorant that he was in the front, the left company began firing to the front, and two of his party fell from their saddles dead—Captain Boswell, of the Engineers, and Sergeant Cunliffe, of the Signal Corps. Spurring his horse . . . he was met by a second volley. . . . Under this volley, when not two rods from the troops, the general received three balls at the same instant.[12]

Appendix I

Walk down (east) along Mountain Road. At the right turn, look behind you. The visitor center building will block your view, but on the other side of that building and in the woods along Bullock Road (a historic lane), the North Carolina line fired on Jackson and his group as they returned.

Jackson was wounded and forced to leave the battlefield. His decision to pursue a night attack and collect information for a movement toward the fords led to his wounding. It also created a command crisis for the Confederate Second Corps in the middle of a battle.

Continue to follow the trail, which will go past two monuments to Jackson and then lead to the visitor center porch. While many narratives of Chancellorsville keep the spotlight on wounded Jackson and gloss over the results and remainder of the battle, this book turns to the continuing influence of Jackson's decision on the Confederate army. This focus also leads to Lee's next critical decision.

Staff officers, Second Corps division commanders, and eventually Lee knew strong leadership was needed. Lee made the critical decision to allow his cavalry commander, Maj. Gen. James Ewell Brown Stuart, to take charge of the infantry and fight to reunite with the rest of Lee's army.

Report of Maj. Gen. James Ewell Brown Stuart, CSA, Commanding Jackson's Corps, Army of Northern Virginia

Captain [R. H. T.] Adams, of General A. P. Hill's staff, reached me post-haste, and informed me of the sad calamities which for the time deprived the troops of the leadership of both Jackson and Hill, and the urgent demand for me to come and take command as quickly as possible. I rode with rapidity back 5 miles, determined to press the pursuit already so gloriously begun. General Jackson had gone to the rear, but General A. P. Hill was still on the ground, and formally turned over the command to me. I sent a staff officer to General Jackson to inform him that I would cheerfully carry out any instructions he would give, and proceeded immediately to the front, which I reached at 10 p.m.[13]

Lee's critical decision to put Stuart in command set the focus for the next day of battle. The Confederate army would continue to fight on the offensive and had to find a way to reunite. Fortunately for the generals in gray, Hooker's next critical decision would assist their goals for May 3.

To Tour Stop 7. Exit the Chancellorsville Battlefield Visitor Center by taking the driveway heading east. Turn right (west) onto Route 3, and move over to the left lane. Use the left turn lane to turn left (south) onto Stuart Drive. Enter Stuart Drive, and continue for 0.5 mile. Park in the parking spaces for Hazel Grove.

(If you miss the left turn lane, continue west on Route 3. Then use the left turn lane to turn left into Wilderness Presidential Resorts. Turn around there, make a right onto eastbound Plank Road, and then turn right onto Stuart Drive.)

At Hazel Grove, walk along the road and then up the grass slope to your right. Stand near one of the cannon and face northeast, looking over the cleared space toward the Chancellorsville Crossroads.

Tour Stop 7: Hazel Grove

This site relates to:
    Critical Decision 9—Lee Puts J. E. B. Stuart in Command
       of the Second Corps
    Critical Decision 13—Hooker Orders Sickles to Abandon
       Hazel Grove

This plateau-like terrain you are standing on is Hazel Grove. In 1863, the cleared area immediately around you was larger, allowing Confederate artillery to mass here on May 3, 1863, and bombard Fairview and the Chancellorsville Crossroads ahead of you. You may be able to see the modern traffic light at the crossroads, and the Chancellor House would have been just to the left of that intersection. Fairview is closer, just over a half mile ahead of you where the terrain rises and flattens.

The offensive tactics for the morning of May 3 were dictated by Lee's critical decision to put Stuart in command of the Confederate Second Corps after Jackson's wounding, and by the need to reunite the Confederate forces near Chancellorsville before Hooker realized and exploited the division. This high ground at Hazel Grove sat between the divisions with Lee and the Second Corps divisions. Union troops from the Third Corps and some cavalry regiments had occupied this ground a on May 2, using it as an observation area and launching point for General Sickle's Union probe toward the Confederate marching column at Catharine Furnace (not visible and about a mile to the south).

Appendix I

Narrative of Maj. Gen. Alfred Pleasonton, USA, Commanding First Cavalry Division, Cavalry Corps, Army of the Potomac

On the afternoon of May 2nd, Sickles sent word that the Rebels were retreating towards Gordonsville. It was about three o'clock. Hooker sent for me, said he wanted an officer experienced in that part of the field, and wished me to take my command there....

I had a Battery and three Regiments. I went on to Hazel Grove, saw Mr. Sickles. We saw the Rebels about three miles off. They were going in a North Western direction. I gave him one regiment of cavalry, 6th New York, to protect his flanks, leaving me the 8th Pennsy., 17th Pennsy., and Martin's N.Y. Battery.

I posted my command near Hazel Grove. Shortly after, Mr. Sickles sent word the enemy were retreating and ordered me to follow. I rode out alone but saw it was no place for cavalry. Mr. Sickles went ahead, I returned. Half way back I saw the Eleventh Corps in full retreat. On they came, horses, caissons, ambulances. They would cut the trace and leave the guns. They dashed past into a swamp on the other side and the debris was piled in the swamp several feet high.[14]

In the night of May 2, Sickles consolidated and changed fronts for his brigades, using Hazel Grove as a point to hold. He launched a night counterattack against Confederates in the dense woods to the northwest without significant results. By the early morning of May 3, Union troops held Hazel Grove, but this position created an unsupported extension from the rest of Hooker's encircling line.

Hooker's order for Sickles to leave Hazel Grove opened that high-ground position for Confederate occupation. While his choice unified his lines and shifted the Third Corps back to Fairview, it also handed the rebels a key position to reunite their forces and a strong artillery position with a line of fire into the Chancellorsville Crossroads.

Though Hooker's decision put his army in a position more exposed to artillery fire, hours of fierce combat unfolded. Confederate regiments charged repeatedly against the Union earthworks of the Chancellorsville lines. It was the worst day of fighting at Chancellorsville, and casualty numbers increased horrifically—leading to the calculation of one soldier falling every second for what must have seemed like endless hours.

Cannon at Hazel Grove point toward Fairview and the Chancellorsville Crossroads beyond.

Narrative of Sgt. Albert M. White, CSA, Fourth North Carolina, Ramseur's Brigade, D. H. Hill's Division, Jackson's Corps, Army of Northern Virginia

Next morning at sun rise we started again to get in rear of the enimy aganst 2 oclock in the evening we had marched about 15 miles and come up in thear rear verry unexpectedly thoug they ware prepaired to run or if not they sure got ready any way they soon went we drove them about 3 mies that evening then stoped for the night but the fiteing did not stop they ware fireing back and foart till midnight net morning at sun rise we started again and soon got in warm quarters I have been in service now 2 years but this was the hardest fite ever 4 NC was in and this makes 8 fites I never saw men fall as fast in my life and I hope I never will again.[15]

To continue exploring the locations and results of critical decisions on May 3, 1863, return to your vehicle, and continue the tour to Fairview. If you prefer to walk to Fairview, the route is nearly two miles round trip, and you can simply follow the national park trail that crosses the rolling terrain between Hazel Grove and Fairview. You can return the same way after visiting Fairview.

To Tour Stop 8. Exit the parking at Hazel Grove, and continue southeast on Stuart Drive. In approximately 400 feet, keep left to veer onto Berry-Paxton Drive, following signs for Fairview. The road will end at a parking lot in 0.6 mile.

Walk along the trails cut in the field to the artillery line and marker cannon. You may want to explore the family cemetery or interpretive panels in the area. When you reach the artillery line, face southwest, looking back through the opening toward Hazel Grove.

Tour Stop 8: Fairview

This site relates to:
  Critical Decision 13—Hooker Orders Sickles to Abandon
    Hazel Grove
  Critical Decision 14—Union Officers Do Not Replace Hooker
    after His Injury

Although no dwelling stands here today, this site featured a wooden, possibly log, house and a nearby orchard in 1863. The home had been used by the Chancellor family prior to the construction of their large brick home, which stood about seven hundred yards away in the same clearing.[16]

Union troops had been positioning around Fairview and in the surrounding woods for days, but on the morning of May 3, 1863, the Union Third Corps came into this area as its troops retreated from Hazel Grove. Infantry and artillery packed closely along the corps' west- and south-facing lines, which formed part of the defensive perimeter around the Chancellorsville Crossroads.

Notice the remains of the artillery lunettes around the cannon. These earthworks were erected to protect cannon and artillerymen during the battle and would have been taller at the time of the battle. The lunettes here at Fairview are unique because some of them were initially built to face south, but then they were refashioned to face west on May 2. Artillerymen realized that the main Confederate attack was crashing toward them from that direction and so made the change. This area saw intense artillery dueling on the morning of May 3, especially after the Confederate guns came into position at Hazel Grove, which is just over a half mile away.

The tree line to the west would have been there in 1863, a border of the Wilderness and the location where Confederates charged toward the Union

Cannon near Fairview are still "protected" by lunettes (earthworks).

infantry and guns on May 3. Turn a little to your right. Modern-day Route 3 (historic Orange Turnpike) is visible. You may be able to see the traffic light at the intersection / Chancellorsville Crossroads. This position at Fairview would have been within sight of Hooker's headquarters at the Chancellor House. Continue turning to the right. The Union Twelfth Corps and Third Corps occupied this area around Fairview and the woods.

Hooker's decision to pull troops out of Hazel Grove and consolidate his defensive position brought more soldiers and artillery into the Fairview area and strengthened his western-facing lines. However, it also brought this whole position under heavy artillery fire from Confederate cannon that wheeled into position at Hazel Grove. As the rebel attacks raged through the morning hours, Union artillery struggled to maintain their supply of ammunition. In this crucial period of attack, Hooker suffered his head injury, adding to the command difficulties for the US Army.

Report of Brig. Gen. Stephen D. Ramseur, CSA, Commanding Ramseur's Brigade, D. H. Hill's Division, Jackson's Corps, Army of Northern Virginia

At the command "Forward," my brigade, with a shout, cleared the breastworks, and charged the enemy. . . . The charge of the brigade, made at a critical moment, when the enemy had broken and was hotly pressing the center of the line in our front with apparently overwhelming numbers, not only checked his advance, but threw him back in disorder, and pushed him with heavy loss from the last line of works.[17]

Narrative of Sgt. Henry Morhous, USA, 123rd New York, Second Brigade, First Division, Twelfth Corps, Army of the Potomac

The 123d was in the front line, in the edge of a wood, while behind them was an open field, the ground ascending back to the Chancellorsville House. . . . At length Sunday morning dawned, a day destined to be invested through all coming time with a melancholy and imperishable interest. . . . Fired to an almost divine potency, with a majestic madness, this band of soldiers shook the air with their battle cries, and for over four long hours fought like Spartans. The Rebels charged up in solid columns and were repulsed; rushed up again and again, receiving terrific fire square in their faces, but still pushed forward unto death as if they coveted it. The lines in the rear of the Regiment began to fade out, and there is nothing between its right and the plank road. Soon there is nothing on their left, and soon, too, nothing can be seen behind them but the artillery. Our batteries, at short range, hurled upon them grape and canister. The advancing column was cut and gashed as if pierced . . . plowed by lightning strokes. Companies and Regiments melted away yet still they came. . . . With the immense odds the preponderance of numbers must eventually tell, and the weaker party be forced back by the sheer weight of the foe. . . . The enemy finally sweep down and try to turn the right flank. The right wing of the Regiment swings back, but they come to the front again. The boys were ordered to unsling knapsacks and charge over the works. They did so, but having no support on either right or left, were ordered back behind the rude works where many of their brave comrades lay dead and many more wounded. . . . Up the hill towards the Chancellorsville House they went [retreated], through a perfect show of shot and shell. . . . The Regiment became divided, some going to the right and some to the left of the Chancellorsville House. And here, also the colors of the Regiment were lost.[18]

Repeated Confederate attacks eventually broke through points of the Union lines. The assaults were compounded by artillery supply difficulties, and the Federal line began to cave in. Some units withdrew in an orderly fashion, others retreated hastily, and still others fought rearguard actions as the Union corps pulled back out of the Chancellorsville Crossroads position and set up a new defensive position. The new location covered the corps' access to fords on the Rappahannock River.

The harsh combat on May 3 and the Union retreat from the crossroads were the results of Lee's decision to put Stuart in command, Hooker's decision to give up Hazel Grove, and the decision to leave Hooker in command though he struggled to lead due to his injury.

To explore the new defensive lines created and held by the Federals, return to your vehicle, and continue the tour.

To Tour Stop 9. Exit the parking lot at Fairview, and drive south on Berry-Paxton Drive for 0.6 mile. Keep left at the intersection, and merge onto Stuart Drive. In 0.2 mile, keep left at the intersection, and continue onto Slocum Drive. Follow Slocum Drive for 0.7 mile to the T intersection with Old Plank Road. Turn left (north) on Old Plank Road, and continue for 0.1 mile to the traffic light intersection. At the light, turn left (west) on Plank Road / Route 3, and continue for 0.9 mile. Make a right turn (north) into Bullock Road, and continue for 0.8 mile. Pull into the designated roadside parking for the Bullock House Site.

Walk toward the intersection ahead of you (Bullock Road / Ely's Ford Road). Stand well away from the road, since Ely's Ford Road can be a busy thoroughfare. Face the intersection, and note the trailhead visible across the road.

Tour Stop 9: Bullock House Site and Hooker's Last Line

This site relates to:
  Critical Decision 14—Union Officers Decide Not to Replace
    Hooker after His Injury
  Critical Decision 15—Hooker Brings Hunt from the Rear
  Critical Decision 16—Hooker Retreats

In 1863, a two-and-a-half-story wooden frame house, painted white, stood near this site. Oscar Bullock's family lived here, surrounded by his three hundred acres of farm- and woodland, but he was absent in 1863, serving in the Thirtieth Virginia Infantry. During the early part of the battle, surgeons used the house as a field hospital until the fighting drew too close.

The home was uninhabitable after the battle, forcing the civilians to seek residence elsewhere.[19]

When the Union corps retreated from their positions around Chancellorsville, they moved north and established a new defensive position, often called Hooker's Last Line. This area around the site of the Bullock House is the apex of that curving defensive line. Union soldiers dug new earthworks that circled north toward the Rappahannock approximately two miles away.

You might want to carefully cross the road and enter the wooded trail to see some of the remains of the earthworks.

Report of Maj. Gen. Winfield S. Hancock, USA, Commanding First Division, Second Corps, Army of the Potomac

At 10 a.m., I received the order to withdraw my forces. I first sent orders to the batteries to retire. After that had been accomplished, I marched my command in good order and without molestation, save by artillery to a point about half a mile to the rear, toward the United States Ford, where a new line was established. . . .

Rifle-pits were immediately thrown up on our new front, abatis felled, and the position made as strong as practicable. I have no doubt that we could have successfully resisted any assault. . . .

We awaited the attack of the enemy in or new position until 3:30 a.m. on the morning of the 6th.[20]

Within this new line, Brig. Gen. Henry Hunt readied the Union artillery. Infantry units were layered, creating deep positions that would be difficult for attacking Confederates to breach. Here, Hooker had to decide what do next. His campaign plans were falling apart, but his army was still intact and—aside from the Eleventh Corps—in strong spirits and seeming ready to continue fighting.

Narrative of Capt. Charles Bowers, USA, Thirty-Second Massachusetts, Second Brigade, First Division, Fifth Corps, Army of the Potomac

Our regiment has the advance at this point occupying the trenches. Behind us are some five lines ready to occupy . . . if necessary. The advance must come from the woods in our front across a plain some 300 yards deep. Our skirmishers are in the edge of the woods and at the approach of the foe will fire upon them and gradually return to our lines. As soon as they are safe and the rebels approach in sufficient numbers, our batteries will open upon them with a terrific show of round and grape shot. We are ordered to wait until they are within . . . rifle distance and then fire into them as rapidly as possible. . . . General Hooker is here. . . . The men are encouraged . . . confident that he is the man to direct.[21]

Three critical decisions are connected to this area. When Union generals and surgeons let Hooker continue in command despite his need to rest on the afternoon of May 3 after his injury, they created command issues that influenced the remainder of the morning fight. These issues continued to affect the army through the rest of May 3, even as the new lines were established. The new defensive lines were well built, but there were times when corps commanders continued making decisions that should have been made by an army commander.

The next critical decision directly affected Hooker's Last Line. Hooker's choice to bring Hunt from the rear and put him at his proper post as chief

Trenches from Hooker's Last Line are hidden in the trees near Ely's Ford Road and extend toward the Rappahannock River.

of artillery meant that the Union cannon would be well positioned and—more importantly—supplied with ammunition for any coming battle. Hunt's return helped to restore confidence among the battery commanders. Also, well-positioned artillery helped to instill and maintain confidence among the infantrymen that they were in a strong and relatively safe position to continue a defensive fight.

The final critical decision that ended the Chancellorsville Campaign is also connected to this position. After waiting out May 4 and corresponding rather frantically with Major General Sedgwick at Salem Church and Banks' Ford, Hooker gathered opinions from his corps commanders about what to do next. He ultimately retreated, withdrawing the army across the Rappahannock River. This decision went against the preference to fight held by a majority of his generals and created ongoing conflict between Hooker and his corps commanders. However, Hooker's retreat led to the end of the campaign, leaving victory to the Confederates.

To explore the fighting at Fredericksburg and Salem Church, which involved additional critical decisions and contributed to Hooker's last critical decision, this tour will head east.

Second Fredericksburg Battlefield

To Tour Stop 10. Exit the parking area at the Bullock House Site, and continue straight to the stop sign. Turn right (southeast) onto Ely's Ford Road, and continue for 0.7 mile. At the traffic light, turn left (east) onto Plank Road / Route 3 / Blue and Gray Parkway, and continue east for 9.2 miles. At the traffic signal, turn left (northeast) onto Lafayette Boulevard, and continue for 0.4 mile. Turn left into the parking lot of Fredericksburg Battlefield Visitor Center.

You might want to explore the visitor center. Most of the displays and interpretation will focus on the First Battle of Fredericksburg (December 11–13, 1862), and they are good ways to explore the layers of battle history at this site. Memories of the December battle certainly haunted the minds of many soldiers who fought here at the Second Battle of Fredericksburg on May 3, 1863.

Walk up into the Sunken Road, which is just beyond the stone wall visible from the main parking lot. If facing Marye's Heights (high ground), turn to the right, and walk toward the small historic frame house. Stop anywhere you like in the Sunken Road, and face toward town (high ground behind you).

Tour Stop 10: The Sunken Road and Marye's Heights

This site relates to:
    Critical Decision 10—Griffin Grants a Temporary Truce
    Critical Decision 11—Sedgwick's Troops Move Forward

When Hooker began his march that stalled at the Chancellorsville Crossroads, the other part of his plan had Maj. Gen. John Sedgwick, the Sixth Corps, and elements of other corps acting as a diversion to distract the Confederates. Once Lee decided to turn and fight Hooker and the combat centered around Chancellorsville, Sedgwick's role and importance began to shift. Sedgwick moved slowly—due partly to personality, partly to logistics, and partly to unclear communications. However, by the early morning of May 3, four Union divisions readied to attack the Confederate position along Marye's Heights and Lee's Hill farther to the south.

You are standing in the Sunken Road at the base of Marye's Heights. The white frame house is the Innis House, and nearby is the foundation footprint of the Stephens House. Both structures were standing at the time of the battles in 1862 and 1863. The large house on the heights is Brompton, and it was also here at the time of the battles. Now a private residence for the president of the University of Mary Washington, it is not open to the public.

The ground in front of you as you face the Sunken Road's wall would have been open and stretching for a little over a half mile toward the edge of the town of Fredericksburg. Confederate artillery sat on Marye's Heights. Here, in the Sunken Road, Mississippi infantry waited. However, unlike the near-perfect artillery cross fire and densely packed infantry holding this position in December 1862, the cannon and troops here in May 1863 had a lot of ground to cover.

The wall bordering the Sunken Road has been mostly rebuilt by the National Park Service. One section of the original Sunken Road still exists; if you look beyond the Innis House, the section of wall lining the dirt bank near the Sergeant Kirkland statue dates to the Civil War.

To your right and not visible from this location is Lee's Hill, another Confederate defensive position, covering Telegraph Road and other access points toward the west and Chancellorsville. Stretched-thin Confederate lines also held Lee's Hill.

The first critical decision connected to this location was the Confederate choice to allow a flag of truce. After several repulsed attacks, Union officers requested a flag of truce to retrieve their wounded. Primary sources do not make it clear whether the request began as a deception or turned into one once the rebel line in the Sunken Road had been observed. Either way, the decision to permit a flag of truce revealed the vulnerabilities of the Confederate

Appendix I

position and convinced Union troops that they could actually take the position.

Narrative of Pvt. William H. Moore, CSA, Twenty-First Mississippi, Barksdale's Brigade, McLaws's Division, Longstreet's Corps, Army of Northern Virginia

On Sunday morning about day light they made their first attack here on us and we repulsed them three times. They then sent a flag of truce requesting permission to get off their wounded and buy their dead. Unfortunately for us, Gen. Griffin of the 19th Miss Regt., granted it and under cover of this, they come up close to our works and discover what a small force we had here and all the time the flag of truce was flying, they were arranging their plans to flank us both right and left and attack us with an over whelming force in front. And in five minutes after the flag of truce was taken down They made the attack.[22]

Marye's Heights rises behind the Sunken Road, and the high ground is visible in the left of this photo.

If you would like, walk to the top of Marye's Heights. There is a paved service road (not accessible for public vehicles) near the Innis House. Notice the steepness of the face of the hill; Union soldiers charged up this slope on May 3, 1863. A trail will take you across Willis Hill (part of Marye's Heights) and toward Fredericksburg National Cemetery. Choose a place to overlook the Sunken Road—there are many excellent options—and explore the next critical decision.

After several repulsed attacks, Union soldiers began to realize several things about the Confederate defense at Marye's Heights. First, the rebels did not have a lot of infantry or artillery as compared with the December battle nightmare. Second, it might be possible to take the high ground with a concerted, nonstop, determined rush. The critical decision fell to soldiers and officers in the ranks who decided to go forward and take the position.

The result of their choice was a fierce charge that broke through the Confederate lines at several points, including here on Willis Hill / Marye's Heights. Confederate infantry, artillerymen, and cannon were captured, and for the first time in battle, a triumphant Union flag waved on the deadly high ground. The capture of Marye's Heights forced the Confederate defenders into a confused retreat and opened the road for Sedgwick and his soldiers to advance toward Chancellorsville, where Hooker desperately needed something to distract Lee.

Diary of Pvt. Bailey Smith, USA, Sixth Vermont, Second Brigade, Second Division, Sixth Corps, Army of the Potomac

12M. Hurra! Hurra! We have taken the heights. Our forces between us and the city have advanced straight up the heights and the stars and stripes wave in triumph on rebel fortifications. Our artillery has advanced and taken up a positions there, and are pouring into the flying enemy. . . .

French is dead. How I pity his poor wife and little boy.

We are all jubilant, but there is no cheering. We have learned better than to indulge in cheering.[23]

If you have walked to the top of the high ground, continue along the crest and into Fredericksburg National Cemetery. Authorized in 1865, this burial ground became the final resting place for many Union soldiers who perished in this region at various skirmishes and the Battles of Fredericksburg,

Appendix I

Union troops charged up Marye's Heights on May 3, 1863, after capturing the Sunken Road during the Second Battle of Fredericksburg.

Chancellorsville, the Wilderness, and Spotsylvania Court House. You can follow the brick pathway down to the visitor center and parking lot. Or you can extend your walk farther into the cemetery. At the far end of the ridgeline you have been walking, there is a small marker for Parker's Battery (Confederate) during the Battle of Second Fredericksburg.

When you have finished walking in the cemetery, follow the brick path down to the visitor center and parking lot. As you follow the directions toward Salem Church, you will be roughly following the route of Sedgwick's advance to the west. The terrain would have been open, rolling ground—not the cityscape of the modern era.

To Tour Stop 11. Exit the parking lot of Fredericksburg Battlefield Visitor Center, and turn right (southwest) onto Lafayette Boulevard. Continue for 0.4 mile. At the traffic light, turn/merge right onto Blue and Gray Parkway / Route 3, and continue for 3.4 miles. Use the inside left turn lane to turn left (south) on Salem Church Road / Route 639, and continue for 0.2 mile. At the traffic light, turn left (east) onto General Semmes Road. In approximately 275 feet, turn left (north) at the stop sign onto Old Salem Church Road, and continue for 0.2 mile. Turn left into the parking lot. (If you make the forced right turn in the road, you've just missed the parking lot; turn around in the modern church parking lot ,and return to the National Park Service lot.)

Walk to the church structure, which is a National Park Service site. The building is occasionally open to explore inside. If it is not, peek through the windows, or read the interpretive signs. Then stand on the side of the church so that the church is between you and the parking lot. Look east toward the modern cemetery, modern church, and busy roadway (Route 3).

Tour Stop 11: Salem Church

This site relates to:
  Critical Decision 12—Lee Divides His Army Again

A house of worship since its construction in 1844, Salem Church served as a meeting place for a Baptist congregation. Located approximately four miles from historic Fredericksburg, the church had been a shelter for refugees during the Battle of Fredericksburg in December 1862.[24]

By the afternoon of May 3, 1863, Maj. Gen. John Sedgwick and his brigades marched west, intending to head to Chancellorsville and threaten the rear of Lee's army. However, Brig. Gen. Cadmus Wilcox and his Alabama brigade made their most significant delaying action on this ridge. Messengers had already galloped into the Wilderness, carrying the news to Lee that Sedgwick had taken Marye's Heights.

Lee's critical decision raced three brigades from McLaws's Division and one brigade from Anderson's Division to supply much-needed reinforcements to Wilcox at Salem Church. Lee had to divide his newly reunited army at Chancellorsville to counter this new threat. When the reinforcements arrived, about ten thousand Confederates on good terrain opposed Sedgwick.

Report of Gen. Robert E. Lee, CSA, Commanding Army of Northern Virginia

Information of the state of affairs in our rear having reached Chancellorsville . . . General McLaws, with his three brigades and one of General Anderson's, was ordered to re-enforce General Wilcox. He arrived at Salem Church early in the afternoon, where he found General Wilcox in line of battle, with a large force of the enemy— consisting, as was reported, of one army corps and part of another, under Major-General Sedgwick—in his front. . . . The enemy's artillery played vigorously upon our position for some time, when his infantry advanced in three strong lines, the attack being directed

Appendix I

Salem Church still stands, a sanctuary on the limited acreage preserved at Salem Church battlefield.

mainly against General Wilcox, but partially involving the brigades on his left. The assault was met with the utmost firmness, and after a fierce struggle the first line was repulsed with great slaughter. The second then came forward, but immediately broke under the close and deadly fire which it encountered, and the whole mass fled in confusion to the rear. They were pursued by the brigades of Wilcox and Semmes, which advanced nearly a mile, when they were halted to reform in the presence of the enemy's reserve, which now appeared in large force. It being quite dark, General Wilcox deemed it imprudent to push the attack with his small numbers....[25]

Narrative of Pvt. Fred H. West, CSA, Fifty-First Georgia, Semmes's Brigade, McLaws's Division, Longstreet's Corps, Army of Northern Virginia

When the fight was ended, we heard the enemy had crossed in force at Fredericksburg and occupied our height, having taken some prisoners and a portion of the Washington Artillery. We were again ordered to confront this new force, and immediately commenced the march. Having gone to within 3 miles of the city, we went into line of battle very near the lines of the enemy. They advanced against us, but we drove them back with considerable loss, and were ordered to charge, and raising a shout we rushed to the front. The terrified Yanks thew off knapsacks and incumberances and ran for life. We rushed ahead after them to the top of a ridge in an open field and discovered that but two regiments, the 10th and 51st Georgia, had joined in a charge intended for several brigades. The battery we were charging was in our front and we exposed to its fire. . . . It was a terrible, an awful place, and when we returned we found that more than half our regiment was missing.[26]

The terrain has significantly changed, and this small tract is all that remains preserved of Salem Church battlefield. However, if you turn and look around the area, you may catch a glimpse of the ridgeline that runs north to south, dominated by the historic church and the traffic light and shopping center.

The battle delay that Wilcox and the arriving reinforcements created forced Sedgwick to pause. His pause through the night allowed more Confederates to gather, and by the morning of May 4, Sedgwick started pulling back toward the Rappahannock River while the Confederates closed in.

Lee's decision to divide his army again had been forced by Sedgwick's initially bold advance. Shifting troops to the east was necessary and successfully pinned Sedgwick into ineffectiveness. But the move added to the soldiers' exhaustion and gave Hooker's troops time to significantly strengthen their Last Line.

Report of Maj. Gen. John Sedgwick, USA, Commanding Sixth Corps, Army of the Potomac

At Salem Chapel the enemy were re-enforced by a brigade from Banks' Ford and by troops from the direction of Chancellorsville, and made determined resistance. . . . After a sharp and prolonged contest, we gained the heights, but were met by fresh troops pouring in upon the flank of the advanced portion of the line. . . .

During the night the enemy were re-enforcing heavily. . . . The following morning, at an early hour, I was informed that a column of the enemy, 15,000 strong, coming from the direction of Richmond, had occupied the heights of Fredericksburg, cutting off my communications with the town. . . .

While these things were occurring on my left, I received a dispatch from the major-general commanding, informing me that he had contracted his lines; that I must look well to the safety of my corps, preserve my communications with Fredericksburg and Banks' Ford, and suggesting that I fall back upon the former place, or recross, in preference, at Banks' Ford, where I could more readily communicate with the main body.[27]

Lee's prompt critical decision to reinforce a delaying battle at Salem Church bought him time and eventually trapped both Hooker and Sedgwick, keeping them separate. Ultimately, Lee was not able to destroy either of the Union forces decisively, but he would force both of them to recross the Rappa-

The Twenty-Third New Jersey Monument keeps watch over the lanes of traffic cutting across Salem Church battlefield.

hannock River. To explore Sedgwick's crossing and the Rappahannock River, head to the final tour stop.

If you want, linger and explore the Salem Church site further before heading to the river. On this side of the highway stands the Twenty-Third New Jersey Monument, placed in 1906. On the north side of Route 3 and a little farther east, the Fifteenth New Jersey Monument was erected in 1908. If you want to see the Fifteenth New Jersey Monument, please drive to the location and park in the strip-mall lot. Do not attempt to walk there, since (at the time of this writing) there is no good sidewalk system to make the trip safe.

To Tour Stop 12. Exit the Salem Church parking lot, and turn right on Old Salem Church Road. In 0.2 mile, turn right (west) onto General Semmes Road. In approximately 275 feet, turn right (north) at the traffic light onto Salem Church Road. In 0.2 mile, use the second lane from the right to turn right (east) onto Plank Road / Route 3, and continue for 0.7 mile. Use the inside left turn lane to turn left (north) onto Bragg Road, and continue for 0.9 mile. At the traffic light, turn left (west) onto River Road / Route 618, and continue for 1.5 miles. Turn right at the Mott's Run Boat Launch, and park in the parking area.

Walk to a point where you can safely overlook the Rappahannock River, and face the river.

Tour Stop 12: Rappahannock River near Banks' Ford

This site relates to:
   Critical Decision 12—Lee Divides His Army Again
   Critical Decision 16—Hooker Retreats

There were several fords along the Rappahannock River that were particularly convenient for the construction of pontoon bridges and army crossings during the Civil War. Banks' Ford, located upstream from Fredericksburg, was one of these options.

Today, Banks' Ford is not easily accessible to the public on land, and taking a paddling trip is beyond the scope of this battlefield tour. It is located a little farther downriver from your location at this river access point. However, turn and look behind you and also recall the steep slope you drove down as you accessed river-level. Bluffs and ravines like these on both sides of the river created shelter and difficulties for Union soldiers.

By May 4, Sedgwick and his brigades had their backs to the river, and Confederates were holding them in place. Banks' Ford could be the Federals' retreat route to the opposite shore. Messages traveled between Hooker and

Sedgwick, with a confusing array of ideas calling for Sedgwick to either reinforce Hooker, fight the Confederates, retreat, or hold his position. Though his choice is not ranked as a critical decision, Sedgwick withdrew his troops across pontoon bridges during the night of May 4–5.

Narrative of Surgeon Edwin Buckman, USA, Ninety-Eighth Pennsylvania, Third Brigade, Third Division, Sixth Corps, Army of the Potomac

At about 5 o'clock firing commenced all along the lines on the left—the Batteries opened with all their forces and in crossfire with about 30 cannon upon the advancing enemy. Their loss must have been great at this time and place.

While this was going on the infantry commenced retreat the 23rd [Pennsylvania] being apparently the rear guard—and occasionally required to form to protect the battery from capture—The retreat was conducted with moderate degree of regularity—The columns being with few exceptions kept in form—we continued the retreat . . . to Banks Ford which we found under cover of Rebel batteries—but crossed in the night—and rested in the ravines and woods beyond until morning when we moved a couple of miles and encamped in the woods two night and days during which time it rained a good deal making the camp abominably muddy.[28]

Sedgwick's decision to cross the river factored into Hooker's final critical decision: to override his generals' preferences and also take his force across the Rappahannock. Many generals and soldiers in the ranks were surprised by Hooker's choice, believing that the fight at Chancellorsville had not been fair, and that the Union army had not fully unleashed its strength against the Confederates. But Hooker had made his final decision, and once his force was safely across the river, the campaign came to an end.

Report of Maj. Gen. George G. Meade, USA, Commanding Fifth Corps, Army of the Potomac

This day (5th) was occupied in awaiting and expecting an attack from the enemy, and in opening roads from the advanced lines to the United States Ford, for more complete and speedy communications. The commanding general having directed the withdrawal of the army to the left bank of the Rappahannock, and having designated the Fifth Corps as rear guard, Humphreys' and Sykes' divisions were put in motion just before daylight, followed by Griffin, who kept constantly a brigade deployed in line of battle, to cover the rear. The troops were all crossed by 9 a.m., without any molestation from the enemy . . . even the withdrawal of the pickets. . . . The whole command, with the exception of [a brigade left to help with pontoon bridges], reached the old camp near Stoneman's Switch by 6 p.m. of this date, the 6th instant."[29]

On this side of the Rappahannock River, Confederates grasped the idea that they had won a victory and Hooker and Sedgwick had retreated. It had taken days of intense marching, combat, and casualties, but victory was theirs. Not an army-crushing victory, but a success that would be celebrated in newspapers and eventually crowned as Lee's greatest battlefield victory in the war's memory.

Though Banks Ford is not accessible by public land today, this view of the Rappahannock River is in the vicinity of where Sedgwick's troops waited to make their crossing.

On the opposite side of the river, Union soldiers grumbled. They knew they had retreated, but many did not feel defeated. Generals, officers, and men in the ranks tried to make sense of what happened or looked for scapegoats for their loss, but they generally continued to have high morale and an intensifying desire to fight again.

Narrative of Capt. Henry L. Abbott, USA, Twentieth Massachusetts, Third Brigade, Second Division, Second Corps, Army of the Potomac

I have just heard from the best sources that the whole army is on the retreat. Many a man here would give up his life to hear that the news is false but there can be no doubt about it. It is horrible awful. Every man in Sigel's Corps [Eleventh Corps] ought to be hauled off the face of the Earth. I am afraid we shall never lift our heads out of this terrible infamy. Hooker has done gallantly, according to his ideas, & I feel less inclined to hit him now than ever, but I must say that it seemed from the first very strange, dividing our forces into ... two equal parts.[30]

The fighting at Chancellorsville, Second Fredericksburg, and Salem Church ended, but the war continued. The Army of Northern Virginia and the Army of the Potomac would fight again, and they would cross and recross the Rappahannock River several more times in the coming two years of war.

This concludes the battlefield guide to the critical decisions at Chancellorsville.

APPENDIX II

CHANCELLORSVILLE AND THE LOST CAUSE

Historical memory and historical interpretation are influencers of fact. Discerning fact from fiction—or fact from simple misremembering—becomes challenging with the passing of time, the telling and retelling of stories, and the armchair historians' wished-for outcomes. The Battle of Chancellorsville has its own continuing story in memory and interpretation, extending from the soldiers' memories through veterans' stories and into twenty-first-century perspectives.

The Battle of Chancellorsville gained particular significance in the Southern Lost Cause memory. This perspective has surrounded decades of monumentation, writings, and battlefield interpretation. It also continues to influence some of the ways the military decisions and outcomes of the battle have been traditionally viewed. This book attempts to break away from some of the customary emphases and refocus on choices and outcomes through the study of primary sources written mostly during or close to the time of battle. However, a brief outline of Civil War memory around the Battle of Chancellorsville may be helpful when considering how decisions might have been viewed in the past. Historical memory touches everything, and understanding its influence can be useful when considering a particular battle.

Civil War veterans and contemporary writers made the first contributions to how their battles and other war-era events would be remembered. Primary sources including opinion and interpretation of facts were the earliest efforts to portray events from certain perspectives. Both sides created such sources, and this phenomenon is not unique to the American Civil War experience. Explaining facts in ways that pass blame or elevate certain people or incidents is a hallmark of how humans explain, justify, and make sense of the world around them in positive and negative situations. The experience of war seems to increase the need for rationalization, while particular groups also interpret the outcomes of battles or wars in ways that fit their reasons for fighting.

In the aftermath of the Confederate surrenders in 1865, many Southern civilians and Confederate veterans privately grappled with the losses they had endured, the reasons for the war, and the outcomes of their defeat. A thought pattern referred to as the Lost Cause took root and evolved in the following decades. This became a way of explaining the war from a Southern perspective. Some of its hallmarks included deemphasizing or denying slavery as a cause of the war, bestowal of high hero status on many Confederate generals, and the idea that Southern civilization had been destroyed. There were other components of the Lost Cause, and layers of this thinking reached into many aspects of Southern society, historical memory, and—for many years of the twentieth century—the teaching, remembrance, and celebration of the Civil War in American culture.

Union veterans developed memory patterns too. Some of them focused on the war's meaning, aligning it with Lincoln and Republican visions for emancipation and early civil rights.[1] Many former servicemen leaned into historical memory that countered the points of the Lost Cause, emphasizing the rebelliousness of the Confederacy, highlighting the evils of slavery, and portraying the Union as the right cause. It troubled many Union veterans that though they had won the war, their former enemies were literally writing history books painting Confederates as the heroes of a lost war. For decades, though, Union memory narrative was in most circumstances drowned out by Lost Cause ideas in national remembrance and academic instruction.

The Battle of Chancellorsville ended with a Confederate victory, important but not as decisive as Gen. Robert E. Lee had desired. However, with the passage of a few more weeks and the events of the Pennsylvania Campaign, Chancellorsville gained significance in the rebels' minds. Growing Confederate losses and the eventual surrender of the Army of Northern Virginia at Appomattox Court House in April 1865 raised the importance of Chancellorsville in historical memory, particularly Southern memory. Chancellorsville was the location of—arguably—Lee's greatest victory. But Chancellorsville was also the battle where Stonewall Jackson was wounded, and where Confederate units took massive casualties that would be difficult to replace. With hindsight after losses at Gettysburg and the Overland Campaign, Chancellorsville and the demise of Jackson became touchstones of Confederate memory and Lost Cause myth.

In many books and perspectives on Chancellorsville written after the war's end, Confederate general Thomas J. "Stonewall" Jackson is the figurehead of the battle. Great emphasis has been placed on his flank march and attack on May 2, 1863.[2] Following Jackson's wounding by friendly fire that evening, many accounts continue the Stonewall narrative through to the field hospital and his death on May 10, 1863. The rest of the Battle of Chancellorsville often becomes an afterthought and a victory that Lee regretted solely because of Jackson's death. In the books that further examine the battle, Jackson's death is usually listed as one of the highly significant outcomes. The what-if question about Jackson's absence from Gettysburg lingers in books, internet forums, and battlefield visitors' minds. Making Jackson the face of Chancellorsville aligns with Lost Cause vision. Jackson's death typically receives high emphasis as a reason why Lee's string of victories was broken after Chancellorsville, so his death has also been seen as contributing deeply to the Confederacy's loss of the war. Jackson's surviving staff officers contributed to their general's high stature, helping to craft his image as a martyr of the Lost Cause.[3]

Today, the Chancellorsville Battlefield Visitor Center is located where Jackson rode along the wooded road trace, and within a few yards of where the North Carolinians accidentally fired at him. Two monuments and several interpretive markers unfold this moment and impress visitors with its perceived high importance. While the wounding and later death of General Jackson certainly influenced the Battle of Chancellorsville and other aspects of the Civil War, there is much more to the battle. Fortunately, the suggested driving tour and stops created by the National Park Service expand visitors' understanding of the engagement, though May 2 receives a high portion of the focus.

The Confederate victory at Chancellorsville and the so-called martyrdom of Jackson fit the Lost Cause narrative. However, the successful Union attacks during the Second Battle of Fredericksburg on May 3, 1863, and the threatening of Lee's divided army have been traditionally brushed aside in the Chancellorsville story. Particularly concerning the attack on Marye's Heights, Confederates writing afterward preferred to capitalize on the trickery of the Union flag of truce. There are complications around understanding the flag of truce moment, particularly the timing and outcome. However, the accounts of the event become suspicious when the loudest denouncers were the Confederate officers who bungled their response to the request and did not notify superior officers. The rush of attack against Marye's Heights and the Union victory there were easiest to ignore in the Lost Cause telling of the battle. Alternatively, if the truce had to be addressed, an emphasis on Yankee trickery instead of Confederate numerical weakness or poor judgment seemed to conveniently explain the moment.[4]

Battlefield preservation losses reflect the de-emphasizing of Second Fredericksburg and Salem Church in historical memory. Though parts of the Second Fredericksburg Battlefield are preserved because the locations relate to the First Battle of Fredericksburg (December 1862), interpretation of the successful Union attacks in May 1863 is currently limited. Salem Church battlefield is almost entirely lost to pavement and modern shopping centers. Only the historic brick structure, limited acreage around the church, and two New Jersey monuments remain as reminders of the fight at Chancellorsville. Unfortunately, due to the traditional interpretation of Chancellorsville and focus on that fighting, an opportunity to purchase and preserve land around the historic church was declined in the late 1970s. Preservation emphasis at that time followed and mirrored the Antietam Plan, which focused on preserving essential strips of land, rather than larger parcels of battlefield; due in part to this type of planning and the heavy Lee-Jackson emphasis on Chancellorsville, Salem Church battlefield was lost for preservation.[5]

Like past preservation efforts, the placement of monuments at Chancellorsville reflects a Confederate and Lost Cause interpretation. Some of this stems from Chancellorsville's location as a battlefield in Virginia, and from the fact that most Union regiments fighting in the Eastern Theater preferred to put their monuments at Gettysburg or Antietam Battlefields. Around 1876, James Power Smith and Rev. Beverly Tucker Lacy, former staff officers for Stonewall Jackson, placed a boulder near the location of the general's wounding. Later, Smith also placed ten engraved stone markers at battlefield sites near Fredericksburg, Chancellorsville, and the Wilderness, noting the locations of Confederate officers during combat. A second monument near Jackson's wounding was later placed, and other Confederate memorials at Chancellorsville include a monument to Gen. Elisha F. Paxton and cedar trees planted in honor of Lee and Jackson's bivouac and flank attack planning. Union monuments at Chancellorsville are generally tucked out of the way and are more challenging to find and visit; they include the regimental memorials for the 27th Indiana Infantry, 114th Pennsylvania Infantry, and 154th New York Infantry.

Chancellorsville occupies a comparatively small place in Civil War popular culture. Novelist Stephen Crane's classic book *The Red Badge of Courage* was published in 1895, and it probably drew inspiration from Union veterans' stories about the Battle of Chancellorsville. Clues sprinkled throughout the text indicate that the unnamed battle is Chancellorsville, and Crane confirmed these hints in a follow-up short story about the same main character.

The Red Badge of Courage has been adapted for film twice. The 1951 movie version features World War II veteran and most decorated American hero Audie Murphy as the main character, while the 1974 version was a made-for-television production. The story focuses on the individual experience in warfare and does not highlight the Chancellorsville battle or military outcomes on the large scale. Still, for some novel and film enthusiasts, *The Red Badge of Courage* is a link to building more curiosity about Chancellorsville.

Michael Shaara's Pulitzer Prize–winning novel *The Killer Angels* (1974) focuses on the Battle of Gettysburg; his son, Jeff Shaara, penned a prequel novel, *Gods and Generals*, published in 1996. Director Ron Maxwell adapted *Gods and Generals* (2003) into a lengthy movie following parts of Stonewall Jackson's life and Civil War battles. A version of Chancellorsville and Jackson's death finishes the film, offering a cinematic telling of historical events heavily influenced by Lost Cause points.[6] Over the years, other fiction books include or focus on the Battle of Chancellorsville, but *The Red Badge of Courage* and *Gods and Generals* have received the most attention.

The Battle of Chancellorsville continues to rank high in historical interpretation and memory, with an emphasis on Confederate stories. Lee and Jackson continue to hold much of the spotlight. They did achieve a victory, but it was not as significant as Lee desired, nor was it as flawless as memory makers sometimes wanted it to be.

However, the fields of history and historical interpretation are beginning to look more closely at aspects of Chancellorsville beyond the traditional stories. Interest in the experience of German American immigrants lends new attention to the Eleventh Corps' position, retreat, and brief resistance on May 2, 1863. Some historians are reassessing the importance of Second Fredericksburg and Salem Church.

Chancellorsville—like most Civil War battles—holds the opportunity to investigate the traditional stories, question some of the historical memory, and explore additional ways to understand the decisions and outcomes of this fight in the Virginia Wilderness in 1863.

APPENDIX III

UNION ORDER OF BATTLE

ARMY OF THE POTOMAC
  Maj. Gen. Joseph Hooker

FIRST ARMY CORPS
  Maj. Gen. John F. Reynolds

FIRST DIVISION
  Brig. Gen. James S. Wadsworth

First Brigade
  Col. Walter Phelps Jr.
    22d New York
    24th New York
    30th New York
    84th New York
Second Brigade
  Brig. Gen. Lysander Cutler
    7th Indiana
    76th New York
    95th New York
    147th New York
    56th Pennsylvania

THIRD BRIGADE
  Brig. Gen. Gabriel R. Paul
    22d New Jersey
    29th New Jersey
    30th New Jersey
    31st New Jersey
    137th Pennsylvania
FOURTH BRIGADE
  Brig. Gen. Solomon Meredith
    19th Indiana
    24th Michigan
    2d Wisconsin
    6th Wisconsin
    7th Wisconsin
DIVISION ARTILLERY
  Capt. John A. Reynolds
    New Hampshire Light, 1st Battery
    1st New York Light, Battery L
    4th United States, Battery B

SECOND DIVISION
Brig. Gen. John C. Robinson

FIRST BRIGADE
  Col. Adrian R. Root
    16th Maine
    94th New York
    104th New York
    107th Pennsylvania
SECOND BRIGADE
  Brig. Gen. Henry Baxter
    12th Massachusetts
    26th New York
    90th Pennsylvania
    136th Pennsylvania
THIRD BRIGADE
  Col. Samuel H. Leonard
    13th Massachusetts
    83d New York

    97th New York
    11th Pennsylvania
    88th Pennsylvania
 Division Artillery
   Capt. Dunbar R. Ransom
    Maine Light, 2d Battery (B)
    Maine Light, 5th Battery (E)
    Pennsylvania Light, Battery C
    5th United States, Battery C

THIRD DIVISION
 Maj. Gen. Abner Doubleday

 First Brigade
   Brig. Gen. Thomas A. Rowley
    121st Pennsylvania
    135th Pennsylvania
    142d Pennsylvania
    151st Pennsylvania
 Second Brigade
   Col. Roy Stone
    143d Pennsylvania
    149th Pennsylvania
    150th Pennsylvania
 Division Artillery
   Maj. Ezra W. Matthews
    1st Pennsylvania Light, Battery B
    1st Pennsylvania Light, Battery F
    1st Pennsylvania Light, Battery G

SECOND ARMY CORPS
 Maj. Gen. Darius N. Couch

FIRST DIVISION
 Maj. Gen. Winfield S. Hancock

 First Brigade
   Brig. Gen. John C. Caldwell
    5th New Hampshire

  61st New York
  81st Pennsylvania
  148th Pennsylvania

SECOND BRIGADE
 Brig. Gen. Thomas F. Meagher
  28th Massachusetts
  63d New York
  69th New York
  88th New York
  116th Pennsylvania

THIRD BRIGADE
 Brig. Gen. Samuel K. Zook
  52d New York
  57th New York
  66th New York
  140th Pennsylvania

FOURTH BRIGADE
 Col. John R. Brooke
  27th Connecticut
  2d Delaware
  64th New York
  53d Pennsylvania
  145th Pennsylvania

DIVISION ARTILLERY
 Capt. Rufus D. Pettit
  1st New York Light, Battery B
  4th United States, Battery C

SECOND DIVISION
 Brig. Gen. John Gibbon

FIRST BRIGADE
 Brig. Gen. Alfred Sully
 Col. Henry W. Hudson
 Col. Byron Laflin
  19th Maine
  15th Massachusetts
  1st Minnesota
  34th New York
  82d New York

SECOND BRIGADE
    Brig. Gen. Joshua T. Owen
        69th Pennsylvania
        71st Pennsylvania
        72d Pennsylvania
        106th Pennsylvania

THIRD BRIGADE
    Col. Norman J. Hall
        19th Massachusetts
        20th Massachusetts
        7th Michigan
        42d New York
        59th New York
        127th Pennsylvania

DIVISION ARTILLERY
        1st Rhode Island Light, Battery A
        1st Rhode Island Light, Battery B

THIRD DIVISION
    Maj. Gen. William H. French

FIRST BRIGADE
    Col. Samuel S. Carroll
        14th Indiana
        24th New Jersey
        28th New Jersey
        4th Ohio
        8th Ohio
        7th West Virginia

SECOND BRIGADE
    Brig. Gen. William Hays
    Col. Charles J. Powers
        14th Connecticut
        12th New Jersey
        108th New York
        130th Pennsylvania

THIRD BRIGADE
    Col. John D. MacGregor
    Col. Charles Alright
        1st Delaware

    4th New York
    132d Pennsylvania

Division Artillery
    1st New York Light, Battery G
    1st Rhode Island Light, Battery G

Reserve Artillery
    1st United States, Battery I
    4th United States, Battery A

THIRD ARMY CORPS
Maj. Gen. Daniel E. Sickles

FIRST DIVISION
Brig. Gen. David B. Birney

First Brigade
 Brig. Gen. Charles K. Graham
 Col. Thomas W. Egan
    57th Pennsylvania
    63d Pennsylvania
    68th Pennsylvania
    105th Pennsylvania
    114th Pennsylvania
    141st Pennsylvania

Second Brigade
 Brig. Gen. J. H. Hobart Ward
    20th Indiana
    3d Maine
    4th Maine
    38th New York
    40th New York
    99th Pennsylvania

Third Brigade
 Col. Samuel B. Hayman
    17th Maine
    3d Michigan
    5th Michigan
    1st New York
    37th New York

Division Artillery
  Capt. A. Judson Clark
    New Jersey Light, Battery B
    1st Rhode Island Light, Battery E
    3d United States, Battery F
    3d United States, Battery K

SECOND DIVISION
  Maj. Gen. Hiram G. Berry
  Brig. Gen. Joseph B. Carr

First Brigade
  Brig. Gen. Joseph B. Carr
  Col. William Blaisdell
    1st Massachusetts
    11th Massachusetts
    16th Massachusetts
    11th New Jersey
    26th Pennsylvania

Second Brigade
  Brig. Gen. Joseph W. Revere
  Col. J. Egbert Farnum
    70th New York
    71st New York
    72d New York
    73d New York
    74th New York
    120th New York

Third Brigade
  Brig. Gen. Gershom Mott
  Col. William J. Sewell
    5th New Jersey
    6th New Jersey
    7th New Jersey
    8th New Jersey
    2d New York
    115th Pennsylvania

Division Artillery
  Capt. Thomas W. Osborn

1st New York Light, Battery D
New York Light, 4th Battery
1st United States, Battery H
4th United States, Battery K

THIRD DIVISION
Maj. Gen. Amiel W. Whipple
Brig. Gen. Charles K. Graham

First Brigade
Col. Emlen Franklin
86th New York
124th New York
122d Pennsylvania

Second Brigade
Col. Samuel M. Bowman
12th New Hampshire
84th Pennsylvania
110th Pennsylvania

Third Brigade
Col. Hiram Berdan
1st United States Sharpshooters
2d United States Sharpshooters

Division Artillery
Capt. Albert A. Von Puttkammer
Capt. James F. Huntington
New York Light, 10th Battery
New York Light, 11th Battery
1st Ohio Light, Battery H

FIFTH ARMY CORPS
Maj. Gen. George G. Meade

FIRST DIVISION
Brig. Gen. Charles Griffin

First Brigade
Brig. Gen. James Barnes
2d Maine

18th Massachusetts
22d Massachusetts
2d Co. Massachusetts Sharpshooters
1st Michigan
13th New York
25th New York
118th Pennsylvania

Second Brigade
  Col. James McQuade
  Col. Jacob B. Sweitzer
    9th Massachusetts
    32d Massachusetts
    4th Michigan
    14th New York
    62d Pennsylvania

Third Brigade
  Col. Thomas B. W. Stockton
    20th Maine
    Michigan Sharpshooters, Brady's Company
    16th Michigan
    12th New York
    17th New York
    44th New York
    83d Pennsylvania

Division Artillery
  Capt. Augustus P. Martin
    Massachusetts Light, 3d Battery (C)
    Massachusetts Light, 5th Battery (E)
    1st Rhode Island Light, Battery C
    5th United States, Battery D

SECOND DIVISION
Maj. Gen. George Sykes

First Brigade
  Brig. Gen. Romeyn B. Ayres
    3d United States, Companies B, C, F, G, I, and K
    4th United States, Companies C, F, H, and K
    12th United States, Companies A, B, C, D, and G
      (1st Battalion), and A, C, and D (2d Battalion)

14th United States, Companies A, B, D, E, F, and G (1st Battalion), and F and G (2d Battalion)

SECOND BRIGADE
Col. Sidney Burbank
2d United States, Companies B, C, F, I, and K
6th United States, Companies D, F, G, H, and I
7th United States, Companies A, B, E, and I
10th United States, Companies D, G, and H
11th United States, Companies B, C, D, E, F, and G (1st Battalion), and C and D (2d Battalion)
17th United States, Companies A, C, D, G, and H (1st Battalion), and A and B (2d Battalion)

THIRD BRIGADE
Col. Patrick H. O'Rorke
5th New York
140th New York
146th New York

DIVISION ARTILLERY
Capt. Stephen H. Weed
1st Ohio Light, Battery I
5th United States, Battery I

THIRD DIVISION
Brig. Gen. Andrew A. Humphreys

FIRST BRIGADE
Brig. Gen. Erastus B. Tyler
91st Pennsylvania
126th Pennsylvania
129th Pennsylvania
134th Pennsylvania

SECOND BRIGADE
Col. Peter H. Allabach
123d Pennsylvania
131st Pennsylvania
133d Pennsylvania
155th Pennsylvania

DIVISION ARTILLERY
Capt. Alanson M. Randol

1st New York Light, Battery C
1st United States, Battery E
1st United States, Battery G

SIXTH ARMY CORPS
Maj. Gen. John Sedgwick

FIRST DIVISION
Brig. Gen. William T. H. Brooks

First Brigade
Col. Henry W. Brown
Col. William H. Penrose
Col. Samuel L. Buck
Col. William H. Penrose
- 1st New Jersey
- 2d New Jersey
- 3d New Jersey
- 15th New Jersey
- 23d New Jersey

Second Brigade
Brig. Gen. Joseph J. Bartlett
- 5th Maine
- 16th New York
- 27th New York
- 121st New York
- 96th Pennsylvania

Third Brigade
Brig. Gen. David A. Russell
- 18th New York
- 32d New York
- 49th Pennsylvania
- 95th Pennsylvania
- 119th Pennsylvania

Division Artillery
Maj. John A. Tompkins
- Massachusetts Light, 1st Battery (A)
- New Jersey Light, Battery A
- Maryland Light, Battery A
- 2d United States, Battery D

SECOND DIVISION
Brig. Gen. Albion P. Howe

Second Brigade
Col. Lewis A. Grant
- 26th New Jersey
- 2d Vermont
- 3d Vermont
- 4th Vermont
- 5th Vermont
- 6th Vermont

Third Brigade
Brig. Gen. Thomas H. Neil
- 7th Maine
- 21st New Jersey
- 20th New York
- 33d New York
- 49th New York
- 77th New York

Division Artillery
Maj. J. Watts De Peyster
- New York Light, 1st Battery
- 5th United States, Battery F

THIRD DIVISION
Maj. Gen. John Newton

First Brigade
Col. Alexander Shaler
- 65th New York
- 67th New York
- 122d New York
- 23d Pennsylvania
- 82d Pennsylvania

Second Brigade
Col. William H. Browne
Col. Henry L. Eustis
- 7th Massachusetts

    10th Massachusetts
    37th Massachusetts
    36th New York
    2d Rhode Island
 THIRD BRIGADE
  Brig. Gen. Frank Wheaton
    62d New York
    93d Pennsylvania
    98th Pennsylvania
    102d Pennsylvania
    139th Pennsylvania
 DIVISION ARTILLERY
  Capt. Jeremiah McCarthy
    1st Pennsylvania Light, Battery C
    1st Pennsylvania Light, Battery D
    2d United States, Battery G

LIGHT DIVISION
 Col. Hiram Burnham
  6th Maine
  31st New York
  43d New York
  61st Pennsylvania
  5th Wisconsin
  New York Light Artillery, 3d Battery

ELEVENTH ARMY CORPS
 Maj. Gen. Oliver O. Howard

FIRST DIVISION
 Brig. Gen. Charles Devens Jr.
 Brig. Gen. Nathaniel C. McLean

FIRST BRIGADE
 Col. Leopold von Gilsa
  41st New York
  45th New York
  54th New York
  153d Pennsylvania

SECOND BRIGADE
    Brig. Gen. Nathaniel C. McLean
    Col. John C. Lee
        17th Connecticut
        25th Ohio
        55th Ohio
        75th Ohio
        107th Ohio
UNATTACHED
        8th New York (one company)
DIVISION ARTILLERY
        New York Light, 13th Battery

SECOND DIVISION
    Brig. Gen. Adolph von Steinwehr

FIRST BRIGADE
    Col. Adolphus Buschbeck
        29th New York
        154th New York
        27th Pennsylvania
        73d Pennsylvania
SECOND BRIGADE
    Brig. Gen. Francis C. Barlow
        33d Massachusetts
        134th New York
        136th New York
        73d Ohio
DIVISION ARTILLERY
        1st New York Light, Battery I

THIRD DIVISION
    Maj. Gen. Carl Schurz

FIRST BRIGADE
    Brig. Gen. Alexander Schimmelfennig
        82d Illinois
        68th New York
        157th New York

61st Ohio
74th Pennsylvania

SECOND BRIGADE
Col. Włodzimierz Krzyzanowski
58th New York
119th New York
75th Pennsylvania
26th Wisconsin

UNATTACHED
82d Ohio

DIVISION ARTILLERY
1st Ohio Light, Battery I

RESERVE ARTILLERY
Lieut. Col. Louis Schirmer
New York Light, 2d Battery
1st Ohio Light, Battery K
1st West Virginia Light, Battery C

TWELFTH ARMY CORPS
Maj. Gen. Henry W. Slocum

FIRST DIVISION
Brig. Gen. Alpheus W. Williams

FIRST BRIGADE
Brig. Gen. Joseph F. Knipe
5th Connecticut
28th New York
46th Pennsylvania
128th Pennsylvania

SECOND BRIGADE
Col. Samuel Ross
20th Connecticut
3d Maryland
123d New York
145th New York

THIRD BRIGADE
Brig. Gen. Thomas H. Ruger

27th Indiana
2d Massachusetts
13th New Jersey
107th New York
3d Wisconsin

DIVISION ARTILLERY
　Capt. Robert H. Fitzhugh
　　1st New York Light, Battery K
　　1st New York Light, Battery M
　　4th United States, Battery F

SECOND DIVISION
　Brig. Gen. John W. Geary

FIRST BRIGADE
　Col. Charles Candy
　　5th Ohio
　　7th Ohio
　　29th Ohio
　　66th Ohio
　　28th Pennsylvania
　　147th Pennsylvania

SECOND BRIGADE
　Brig. Gen. Thomas L. Kane
　　29th Pennsylvania
　　109th Pennsylvania
　　111th Pennsylvania
　　124th Pennsylvania
　　125th Pennsylvania

THIRD BRIGADE
　Brig. Gen. George S. Greene
　　60th New York
　　78th New York
　　102d New York
　　137th New York
　　149th New York

DIVISION ARTILLERY
  Capt. Joseph M. Knap
    Pennsylvania Light, Battery E
    Pennsylvania Light, Battery F

CAVALRY CORPS
  Brig. Gen. George Stoneman

FIRST DIVISION
  Brig. Gen. Alfred Pleasonton

FIRST BRIGADE
  Col. Benjamin F. Davis
    8th Illinois
    3d Indiana
    8th New York
    9th New York

SECOND BRIGADE
  Col. Thomas C. Devin
    1st Michigan
    6th New York
    8th Pennsylvania
    17th Pennsylvania

DIVISION ARTILLERY
  New York Light, 6th Battery

SECOND DIVISION
  Brig. Gen. William W. Averell

FIRST BRIGADE
  Col. Horace B. Sargent
    1st Massachusetts
    4th New York
    6th Ohio
    1st Rhode Island

SECOND BRIGADE
  Col. John B. McIntosh
    3d Pennsylvania

4th Pennsylvania
16th Pennsylvania

DIVISION ARTILLERY
2d United States, Battery A

THIRD DIVISION
Brig. Gen. David McMurtrie. Gregg

FIRST BRIGADE
Col. Judson Kilpatrick
1st Maine
2d New York
10th New York

SECOND BRIGADE
Col. Percy Wyndham
12th Illinois
1st Maryland
1st New Jersey
1st Pennsylvania

REGULAR RESERVE CAVALRY BRIGADE
Brig. Gen. John Buford
6th Pennsylvania
1st United States
2d United States
5th United States
6th United States

DIVISION ARTILLERY
2d United States, Battery B
2d United States, Battery L
2d United States, Battery M
4th United States, Battery E

ARMY ARTILLERY
Brig. Gen. Henry J. Hunt

ARTILLERY RESERVE
Capt. William M. Graham
Brig. Gen. Robert O. Tyler
1st Connecticut Heavy, Battery B

1st Connecticut Heavy, Battery M
New York Light, 5th Battery
New York Light, 15th Battery
New York Light, 29th Battery
New York Light, 30th Battery
New York Light, 32d Battery
1st United States, Battery K
3d United States, Battery C
4th United States, Battery G
5th United States, Battery K

[*Official Records*, vol. 25, pt. 1, pp.156–70.]

APPENDIX IV

CONFEDERATE ORDER OF BATTLE

ARMY OF NORTHERN VIRGINIA
    Gen. Robert E. Lee

LONGSTREET'S FIRST CORPS (present for duty at Chancellorsville)

MCLAWS'S DIVISION
    Maj. Gen. Lafayette McLaws

WOFFORD'S BRIGADE
    Brig. Gen. William T. Wofford
        16th Georgia
        18th Georgia
        24th Georgia
        Cobb's Georgia Legion
        Phillips's Georgia Legion

SEMMES'S BRIGADE
    Brig. Gen. Paul J. Semmes
        10th Georgia
        50th Georgia
        51st Georgia
        53d Georgia

KERSHAW'S BRIGADE
    Brig. Gen. Joseph B. Kershaw
        2d South Carolina
        3d South Carolina
        7th South Carolina
        8th South Carolina
        15th South Carolina
        3d South Carolina Battalion
BARKSDALE'S BRIGADE
    Brig. Gen. William Barksdale
        13th Mississippi
        17th Mississippi
        18th Mississippi
        21st Mississippi
DIVISION ARTILLERY
    Col. H. C. Cabell
        Carlton's (Georgia) Battery
        Frazer's (Georgia) Battery
        McCarthy's (Virginia) Battery
        Manly's (North Carolina) Battery

ANDERSON'S DIVISION
    Maj. Gen. Richard H. Anderson

WILCOX'S BRIGADE
    Brig. Gen. Cadmus M. Wilcox
        8th Alabama
        9th Alabama
        10th Alabama
        11th Alabama
        14th Alabama
WRIGHT'S BRIGADE
    Brig. Gen. Ambrose R. Wright
        3d Georgia
        22d Georgia
        48th Georgia
        2d Georgia Battalion
MAHONE'S BRIGADE
    Brig. Gen. William Mahone
        6th Virginia

    12th Virginia
    16th Virginia
    41st Virginia
    61st Virginia
POSEY'S BRIGADE
  Brig. Gen. Carnot Posey
    12th Mississippi
    16th Mississippi
    19th Mississippi
    48th Mississippi
PERRY'S BRIGADE
  Brig. Gen. Edward A. Perry
    2d Florida
    5th Florida
    8th Florida
DIVISION ARTILLERY
  Lieut. Col. J. J. Garnett
    Grandy's (Virginia) Battery
    Lewis's (Virginia) Battery
    Maurin's (Louisiana) Battery
    Moore's (Virginia) Battery

ARTILLERY RESERVE

ALEXANDER'S BATTALION
  Col. Edward Porter Alexander
    Eubank's (Virginia) Battery
    Jordan's (Virginia) Battery
    Moody's (Louisiana) Battery
    Parker's (Virginia) Battery
    Rhett's (South Carolina) Battery
    Woolfolk's (Virginia) Battery

WASHINGTON (LOUISIANA) ARTILLERY
  Col. J. B. Walton
    Eshleman's 4th Company
    Miller's 3d Company
    Richardson's 2d Company
    Squires's 1st Company

SECOND CORPS
    Lieut. Gen. Thomas J. Jackson
    Maj. Gen. Ambrose P. Hill
    Brig. Gen. Robert E. Rodes
    Maj. Gen. J. E. B. Stuart

HILL'S DIVISION
    Maj. Gen. Ambrose P. Hill
    Brig. Gen. Henry Heth
    Brig. Gen. William Dorsey Pender
    Brig. Gen. James J. Archer

Heth's Brigade
    Brig. Gen. Henry Heth
    Col. J. M. Brockenbrough
- 40th Virginia
- 47th Virginia
- 55th Virginia
- 22nd Virginia

Thomas's Brigade
    Brig. Gen. E. L. Thomas
- 14th Georgia
- 35th Georgia
- 45th Georgia
- 49th Georgia

McGowan's Brigade
    Brig. Gen. Samuel McGowan
    Col. O. E. Edwards
    Col. A. Perrin
    Col. D. H. Hamilton
- 1st South Carolina
- 1st South Carolina Rifles
- 12th South Carolina
- 13th South Carolina
- 14th South Carolina

Lane's Brigade
    Brig. Gen. James H. Lane
- 7th North Carolina
- 18th North Carolina

28th North Carolina
33rd North Carolina
37th North Carolina

ARCHER'S BRIGADE
Brig. Gen. James J. Archer
Col. B. D. Fry
13th Alabama
5th Alabama Battalion
1st Tennessee
7th Tennessee
14th Tennessee

PENDER'S BRIGADE
Brig. Gen. William Dorsey Pender
13th North Carolina
16th North Carolina
22d North Carolina
34th North Carolina
38th North Carolina

DIVISION ARTILLERY
Col. R. L. Walker
Brunson's (South Carolina) Battery
Crenshaw's (Virginia) Battery
Davidson's (Virginia) Battery
McGraw's (Virginia) Battery
Marye's (Virginia) Battery

D. H. HILL'S DIVISION
Brig. Gen. Robert E. Rodes
Brig. Gen. S. D. Ramseur

RODES'S BRIGADE
Brig. Gen. Robert E. Rodes
Col. E. A. O'Neal
Col. J. M. Hall
3d Alabama
5th Alabama
6th Alabama
12th Alabama
26th Alabama

Colquitt's Brigade
   Brig. Gen. Alfred H. Colquitt
- 6th Georgia
- 19th Georgia
- 23d Georgia
- 27th Georgia
- 28th Georgia

Ramseur's Brigade
   Brig. Gen. Stephen D. Ramseur
   Col. F. M. Parker
- 2d North Carolina
- 4th North Carolina
- 14th North Carolina
- 30th North Carolina

Doles's Brigade
   Brig. Gen. George Doles
- 4th Georgia
- 12th Georgia
- 21st Georgia
- 44th Georgia

Iverson's Brigade
   Brig. Gen. Alfred Iverson
- 5th North Carolina
- 12th North Carolina
- 20th North Carolina
- 23d North Carolina

Division Artillery
   Lieut. Col. T. H. Carter
- Reese's (Alabama) Battery
- Carter's (Virginia) Battery
- Fry's (Virginia) Battery
- Page's (Virginia) Battery

EARLY'S DIVISION
Gen. Jubal A. Early

Gordon's Brigade
   Brig. Gen. John B. Gordon
- 13th Georgia

        26th Georgia
        31st Georgia
        38th Georgia
        60th Georgia
        61st Georgia

HOKE'S BRIGADE
    Brig. Gen. Robert Hoke
    Col. Isaac E. Avery
        6th North Carolina
        21st North Carolina
        54th North Carolina
        57th North Carolina
        1st North Carolina Battalion

SMITH'S BRIGADE
    Brig. Gen. William Smith
        13th Virginia
        49th Virginia
        52d Virginia
        58th Virginia

HAYS'S BRIGADE
    Brig. Gen. Harry T. Hays
        5th Louisiana
        6th Louisiana
        7th Louisiana
        8th Louisiana
        9th Louisiana

DIVISION ARTILLERY
    Lieut. Col. R. S. Anderson
        Brown's (Maryland) Battery
        Carpenter's (Virginia) Battery
        Dement's (Maryland) Battery
        Raine's (Virginia) Battery

TRIMBLE'S DIVISION
    Brig. Gen. R. E. Colston

PAXTON'S BRIGADE
    Brig. Gen. E. F. Paxton
    Col. J. H. S. Funk

   2d Virginia
   4th Virginia
   5th Virginia
   27th Virginia
   33d Virginia

JONES'S BRIGADE
 Brig. Gen. J. R. Jones
 Col. T. S. Garnett
 Col. A. S. Vandeventer
   21st Virginia
   42d Virginia
   44th Virginia
   48th Virginia
   50th Virginia

COLSTON'S BRIGADE
 Col. E. T. H. Warren
 Col. T. V. Williams
 Lieut. Col. S. T. Walker
 Lieut. Col. S. D. Thruston
 Lieut. Col. H. A. Brown
   1st North Carolina
   3d North Carolina
   10th Virginia
   23d Virginia
   37th Virginia

NICHOLL'S BRIGADE
 Brig. Gen. Francis T. Nicholls
 Col. J. M. Williams
   1st Louisiana
   2d Louisiana
   10th Louisiana
   14th Louisiana
   15th Louisiana

DIVISION ARTILLERY
 Lieut. Col. H. P. Jones
   Carrington's (Virginia) Battery
   Garber's (Virginia) Battery
   Latimer's (Virginia) Battery
   Thompson's Battery (Louisiana Guard Artillery)

ARTILLERY RESERVE
  Col. Stapleton Crutchfield

BROWN'S BATTALION
  Col. J. Thompson Brown
    Brooke's (Virginia) Battery
    Dance's (Virginia) Battery
    Graham's (Virginia) Battery
    Hupp's (Virginia) Battery
    Smith's Battery (3d Richmond Howitzers)
    Watson's Battery (2d Richmond Howitzers)

MCINTOSH'S BATTERY
  Maj. D. G. McIntosh
    Hurt's (Alabama) Battery
    Johnson's (Virginia) Battery
    Lusk's (Virginia) Battery
    Wooding's (Virginia) Battery

RESERVE ARTILLERY
  Brig. Gen. William N. Pendleton

SUMTER'S BATTALION
  Lieut. Col. A. S. Cutts
    Patterson's Battery
    Ross's Battery
    Wingfield's Battery

NELSON'S BATTALION
  Lieut. Col. W. Nelson
    Kirkpatrick's (Virginia) Battery
    Massie's (Virginia) Battery
    Milledge's (Georgia) Battery

CAVALRY
  Maj. Gen. James E. B. Stuart

FIRST BRIGADE (South of the James River, recruiting)
  Brig. Gen. Wade Hampton
    1st North Carolina

   1st South Carolina
   2d South Carolina
   Cobb's Georgia Legion
   Phillips's Georgia Legion

SECOND BRIGADE
 Brig. Gen. Fitzhugh Lee
   1st Virginia
   2d Virginia
   3d Virginia
   4th Virginia

THIRD BRIGADE (opposing Stoneman's Raid)
 Brig. Gen. W. H. F. Lee
   2d North Carolina
   5th Virginia
   9th Virginia
   10th Virginia
   13th Virginia
   15th Virginia

FOURTH BRIGADE (on detached service)
 Brig. Gen. William E. Jones
   1st Maryland Battalion
   6th Virginia
   7th Virginia
   11th Virginia
   12th Virginia
   34th Virginia Battalion
   35th Virginia Battalion

HORSE ARTILLERY
 Maj. Robert F. Beckham
   Lynchburg Beauregards
   Stuart Horse Artillery
   Virginia Battery
   Washington (South Carolina) Artillery

[*Official Records*, vol. 25, pt. 1, pp. 789–94.

NOTES

Preface

1. The Army of Northern Virginia's casualties totaled nearly 13,500 dead, wounded, and missing. This figure included a significant number of regimental and command officers. Lee lost leaders at all levels of command whom he could not easily replace, and the thousands of fallen soldiers could not be replaced either, even with Confederate conscription. Chancellorsville broke the backbone of Lee's army. It was still a powerful fighting force, but Chancellorsville is often seen as the beginning of the end of Confederate military strength in Virginia.

Introduction

1. John W. Haley, April 9, 1863, in *The Rebel Yell and the Yankee Hurrah: The Civil War Journal of a Maine Volunteer*, ed. by Ruth L. Silliker (Camden, ME: Down East Books, 1985), 75.
2. John J. Hennessy, *The First Battle of Manassas: An End to Innocence, July 21, 1861*, rev. ed. (Mechanicsburg, PA: Stackpole Books, 2015), 153–65.
3. James McPherson, *The Battle Cry of Freedom: The Civil War Era* (Oxford: Oxford University Press, 1988), 392–416.
4. McPherson, *Battle Cry of Freedom*, 418–22.
5. McPherson, *Battle Cry of Freedom*, 515–20.

6. McPherson, *Battle Cry of Freedom*, 578–79.
7. McPherson, *Battle Cry of Freedom*, 579–83.
8. Stephen W. Sears, *Lincoln's Lieutenants: The High Command of the Army of the Potomac* (New York: Houghton Mifflin Harcourt, 2017), 132–77.
9. Peter Cozzens, *Shenandoah, 1862: Stonewall Jackson's Valley Campaign* (Chapel Hill: University of North Carolina Press, 2008), 1–6.
10. Douglas Southall Freeman, *Lee's Lieutenants: A Study in Command*, abridged to one volume by Stephen W. Sears (New York: Scribner, 1998), 144–45.
11. Cozzens, *Shenandoah, 1862*, 511–13.
12. Sears, *Lincoln's Lieutenants*, 229–328; Freeman, *Lee's Lieutenants*, 230–84.
13. John J. Hennessy, *Return to Bull Run: The Campaign of Second Manassas* (Norman: University of Oklahoma Press, 1993), 28–30.
14. Hennessy, *Return to Bull Run*, 456–72.
15. Stephen W. Sears, *The Landscape Turned Red: The Battle of Antietam* (Boston: First Mariner Books, 1983), 308–9.
16. Sears, *Landscape Turned Red*, 333–35.
17. Francis Augustin O'Reilly, *The Fredericksburg Campaign: Winter War on the Rappahannock* (Baton Rouge: Louisiana State University Press, 2006).
18. Freeman, *Lee's Lieutenants*, 418; O'Reilly, *Fredericksburg Campaign*, 452–53.
19. Haley, April 9, 1863, 75.

Chapter 1

1. Charles Engel to Charlotte Engel, January 26, 1863, Fredericksburg-Spotsylvania National Military Park Bound Volume 419-15. Fredericksburg-Spotsylvania National Military Park Bound Volume Collection. Fredericksburg & Spotsylvania National Military Park, Fredericksburg, Virginia.
2. Sears, *Lincoln's Lieutenants*, 468.
3. Sears, *Lincoln's Lieutenants*, 469.
4. Sears, *Lincoln's Lieutenants*, 472.
5. Sears, *Lincoln's Lieutenants*, 473–74.
6. Albert Z. Conner Jr. and Chris Mackowski, *Seizing Destiny: The Army of the Potomac's "Valley Forge" and the Civil War Winter That Saved the Union* (El Dorado Hills, CA: Savas Beatie, 2016), 34.

7. John F. Reynolds to sisters, January 23, 1863, Fredericksburg-Spotsylvania National Military Park Bound Volume 466-05. Fredericksburg-Spotsylvania National Military Park Bound Volume Collection. Fredericksburg & Spotsylvania National Military Park, Fredericksburg, Virginia.

8. United States War Department, *The War of the Rebellion: Official Records of the Union and Confederate Armies* (Washington, DC: United States Government Printing Office, 1874–180), volume 21, pages 989–99. Hereafter, this source will be cited in the following format: *OR*, vol. 21, pp. 989–99.

9. Abraham Lincoln, *Lincoln: Speeches and Writings, 1859–1865*, ed. Roy P. Balser. (New York: Library of America, 1989), 433-34.

10. Conner and Mackowski, *Seizing Destiny*, 45.

11. Conner and Mackowski, *Seizing Destiny*, 52–58.

12. Lincoln, *Speeches and Writings*, 433-34.

13. Charles Engel to Charlotte Engel, April 13, 1863, Fredericksburg-Spotsylvania National Military Park Bound Volume 419-15.

14. Walter H. Taylor, *Four Years with General Lee*, ed. James I. Robertston Jr. (Bloomington: Indiana University Press, 1996), 76–77.

15. Sears, *Lincoln's Lieutenants*, 32.

16. Freeman, *Lee's Lieutenants*, 422.

17. Sears, *Lincoln's Lieutenants*, 36.

18. O'Reilly, *Fredericksburg Campaign*, 33–34.

19. Freeman, *Lee's Lieutenants*, 448.

20. Walter H. Taylor, *Lee's Adjutant: The Wartime Letters of Colonel Walter Herron Taylor, 1862–1865*, ed. R. Lockwood Tower (Columbia: University of South Carolina Press, 1995), 52.

21. Henry Livermore Abbott, April 20, 1863, in *Fallen Leaves: The Civil War Letters of Major Henry Livermore Abbott*, ed. Robert Garth Scott (Kent, OH: Kent State University Press, 1991), 173.

22. Sears, *Lincoln's Lieutenants*, 64.

23. Sears, *Lincoln's Lieutenants*, 117.

24. Abbott, May (7?), 1863, in *Fallen Leaves*, 178.

Chapter 2

1. James I. Robertson Jr., *Stonewall Jackson: The Man, the Soldier, the Legend* (New York: Simon and Schuster, 1997), 697.

2. "Lee's Report," *Official Records*, vol. 25, pt. 1, p. 796.
3. "Lee's Report," *Official Records*, vol. 25, pt. 1, 796.
4. "Anderson's Report," *Official Records*, vol. 25, pt. 1, 849.
5. William J. Miller, *Mapping for Stonewall: The Civil War Service of Jed Hotchkiss* (Washington, DC: Elliott and Clark, 1993), 109.
6. "Lee's Report," *Official Records*, vol. 25, pt. 1, 796.
7. Confederate Captain in James H. Lane's Brigade.
8. Freeman, *Lee's Lieutenants*, 466–67.
9. "Barksdale's Report," *Official Records*, vol. 25, pt. 1, 839.
10. "McLaws's Report," *Official Records*, vol. 25, pt. 1, 824.
11. Ernest B. Furgurson, *Chancellorsville, 1863: The Souls of the Brave* (New York: Vintage House, 1992), 120.
12. Furgurson, *Chancellorsville*, 120.
13. "Anderson's Report," *Official Records*, vol. 25, pt.1, 850.
14. Freeman, *Lee's Lieutenants*, 469.
15. Edward Stanley Abbot, edited by Quincy S. Abbot, *From Schoolboy to Soldier: The Correspondence and Journals of Edward Stanley Abbot, 1853–1863* (West Hartford: Quincy Abbot, 2013), 194.
16. Stephen W. Sears, *Chancellorsville* (Boston: Houghton Mifflin Company, 1996), 192.
17. *Official Records*, vol. 25, pt. 2, Correspondence, 324.
18. Abbot, *From Schoolboy to Soldier*, 207.
19. *Official Records*, vol. 25, pt. 2, Correspondence, 326–27.
20. *Official Records*, vol. 25, pt. 2, Correspondence, 327.
21. Sears, *Chancellorsville*, 211.
22. Furgurson, *Chancellorsville*, 129–30.
23. Furgurson, *Chancellorsville*, 130.
24. United States Congress, *Report of the Joint Committee on the Conduct of the War, at the Second Session Thirty-Eighth Congress—Chancellorsville (1865)*, 68.
25. *Official Records*, vol. 25, pt. 2, Correspondence, 328.
26. United States Congress, *Report of the Joint Committee* (1865), 66.
27. *Official Records*, vol. 25, pt. 2, Correspondence, 328.
28. Sears, *Chancellorsville*, 212.

29. Abbot, *From Schoolboy to Soldier*, 200.
30. Freeman, *Lee's Lieutenants*, 472.
31. Freeman, *Lee's Lieutenants*, 474–75.
32. Sears, *Chancellorsville* (Boston: Houghton Mifflin, 1996), 239.
33. "Lee's Report," *Official Records*, vol. 25, pt. 1, 798.
34. Lee to Davis, May 2, 1863, *Official Records*, pt. 2, p. 765.
35. Ibid., 765.
36. Robertson, *Stonewall Jackson*, 714.
37. Robertson, *Stonewall Jackson*, 714.
38. Robertson, *Stonewall Jackson*, 715.
39. Furgurson, *Chancellorsville*, 141.

Chapter 3

1. "Howard's Report," *Official Records*, vol. 25, pt. 1, 628.
2. James S. Pula, *Under the Crescent Moon with the XI Corps in the Civil War*, vol. 1, *From the Defenses of Washington to Chancellorsville, 1862–1863* (El Dorado Hills, CA: Savas Beatie, 2017), 121.
3. *Official Records*, vol. 25, pt. 2, Correspondence, 351.
4. *Official Records*, vol. 25, pt. 2, Correspondence, 362.
5. J. H. Van Alen to Howard and Slocum, May 2, 1863, 9:30 a.m., *Official Records*, vol. 25, pt. 2, 360–61.
6. Sears, *Chancellorsville*, 270.
7. "Schurz's Report," *Official Records*, vol. 25, pt. 1, 651–52.
8. Pula, *Under the Crescent Moon*, 1:120.
9. Pula, *Under the Crescent Moon*, 1:124.
10. "Sickles Report," *Official Records*, vol. 25, pt. 1, 386.
11. Pula, *Under the Crescent Moon*, 1:124–25.
12. Robertson, *Stonewall Jackson*, 328.
13. Robertson, *Stonewall Jackson*, 710–11.
14. Miller, *Mapping for Stonewall*, 115.
15. Robertson, *Stonewall Jackson*, 722.
16. Matthew W. Lively, *Calamity at Chancellorsville* (El Dorado Hills, CA: Savas Beatie, 2013), 48–49.

17. Miller, *Mapping for Stonewall*, 115.
18. Richard E. Wilbourn, "An Eyewitness Account of Stonewall Jackson's Wounding." Virginia Museum of History & Culture, copyright 2024, https://virginiahistory.org/learn/historical-book/chapter/eyewitness-account-stonewall-jacksons-wounding.
19. *Official Records*, vol. 25, pt. 2, *Correspondence*, 769.
20. Freeman, *Lee's Lieutenants*, 487–89.

Chapter 4

1. Dudley Pendleton, Fredericksburg-Spotsylvania National Military Park Bound Volume 84-25. Fredericksburg-Spotsylvania National Military Park Bound Volume Collection. Fredericksburg & Spotsylvania National Military Park, Fredericksburg, Virginia.
2. Freeman, *Lee's Lieutenants*, 496.
3. Freeman, *Lee's Lieutenants*, 496.
4. Freeman, *Lee's Lieutenants*, 497.
5. William Barksdale, *Richmond Daily Dispatch*, May 21, 1863, page 1, column 4, Fredericksburg-Spotsylvania National Military Park Bound Volume 137-07. Fredericksburg-Spotsylvania National Military Park Bound Volume Collection. Fredericksburg & Spotsylvania National Military Park, Fredericksburg, Virginia.
6. Barksdale, *Richmond Daily Dispatch*, May 21, 1863, page 1, column 4, Fredericksburg-Spotsylvania National Military Park Bound Volume 137-07.
7. Compiled Service Records of Confederate Soldiers Who Served in Organizations from the State of Mississippi, 1861–1865, Catalog ID: 586957, Record Group 109, Mississippi, Roll 0268, National Archives, Washington, DC, accessed through Fold3.
8. "Barksdale's Report," *Official Records*, vol. 25, pt. 1, 841–43.
9. "Barksdale's Report," *Official Records*, vol. 25, pt. 1, 841–43.
10. Chris Mackowski and Kristopher White, *Chancellorsville's Forgotten Front: The Battles of Second Fredericksburg and Salem Church* (El Dorado Hills, CA: Savas Beatie, 2013), 201.
11. Mackowski and White, *Chancellorsville's Forgotten Front*, 201.
12. William H. Moore to his mother, May 10, 1863, Fredericksburg-Spotsylvania National Military Park Bound Volume 336-12. Fredericks-

burg-Spotsylvania National Military Park Bound Volume Collection. Fredericksburg & Spotsylvania National Military Park, Fredericksburg, Virginia.

13. William Barksdale, *Richmond Daily Dispatch*, May 21, 1863, page 1, column 4, Fredericksburg-Spotsylvania National Military Park Bound Volume 137-07.

14. *Official Records*, vol. 25, pt. 2, Correspondence, 362–69.

15. *Official Records*, vol. 25, pt. 2, Correspondence, 365–66.

16. *Official Records*, vol. 25, pt. 2, Correspondence, 558.

17. *Official Records*, vol. 25, pt. 2, Correspondence, 559.

18. Abraham Titus Brewer, *History, Sixty-First Regiment Pennsylvania Volunteers, 1861–1865* (Pittsburgh, Art Engraving & Printing Co.,1911), 54.

19. Mackowski and White, *Chancellorsville's Forgotten Front*, 199–200.

20. Nelson V. Hutchinson, *History of the Seventh Massachusetts Volunteer Infantry in the War of the Rebellion of the Southern States against Constitutional Authority* (Taunton, MA: Regimental Association 1890), 126.

21. "Sedgwick's Report," *Official Records*, vol. 25, pt. 1, 559.

22. Furgurson, *Chancellorsville*, 268.

23. Charles Marshall, *An Aide-de-Camp of Lee: Being the Papers of Colonel Charles Marshall, Sometime Aide-de-Camp, Military Secretary, and Assistant Adjutant General on the Staff of Robert E. Lee, 1862–1865* Edited by Sir Frederick Maurice. (Boston: Little, Brown,1927), 172–73.

Chapter 5

1. Ezra J. Warner, *Generals in Blue: Lives of Union Commanders* (Baton Rouge: Louisiana State University Press, 1996), 446; James A. Hessler, *Sickles at Gettysburg* (El Dorado Hills, CA: Savas Beatie, 2009).

2. "Sickles Report," *Official Records*, vol.25, pt 1, 386.

3. Hessler, *Sickles at Gettysburg*, 55–56.

4. "Sickles Report," *Official Records*, vol. 25, pt. 1, 390.

5. John Bigelow Jr., *Chancellorsville* (New York: Smithmark, 1995), 327.

6. Edward Porter Alexander, *Fighting for the Confederacy: The Personal Recollections of General Edward Porter Alexander*, ed. Gary W. Gallagher (Chapel Hill: University of North Carolina Press, 1989), 204.

7. Bigelow, *Chancellorsville*, 342.

8. "Sickles Report," *Official Records*, vol. 25, pt. 1, 391.
9. Bigelow, *Chancellorsville*, 348.
10. "Sickles Report," *Official Records*, vol. 25, pt. 1, 391.
11. United States Congress, "Sickles Report," *Report of the Joint Committee (1865)*, 7.
12. Sue Chancellor, "Recollections of Chancellorsville," *Confederate Veteran Magazine* 29 (1921): 213–15.
13. Jonathan Letterman, *Medical Recollections of the Army of the Potomac* (Appleton, 1866), 137.
14. United States Congress, "Sickles Testimony," *Report of the Joint Committee (1865)*.
15. "Couch's Report," *Official Records*, vol. 25, pt. 1, 307.
16. United States Congress, "Birney's Testimony," *Report of the Joint Committee (1865)*, 35.
17. United States Congress, "Birney's Testimony," *Report of the Joint Committee (1865)*, 36–37.
18. Charles S. Wainwright, *A Diary of Battle: The Personal Journals of Colonel Charles S. Wainwright, 1861–1865*, ed. Allan Nevins (New York: Da Capo, 1998), 193.
19. *Official Records*, vol. 25, pt. 2, Correspondence, 378.
20. United States Congress, "Hancock's Testimony," *Report of the Joint Committee (1865)*, 70.
21. United States Congress, "Birney's Testimony," *Report of the Joint Committee (1865)*, 36–37.
22. United States Congress, "Sickles Testimony," *Report of the Joint Committee (1865)*, 10.
23. Wainwright, *Diary of Battle*, 193–94.
24. Warner, *Generals in Blue*, 242.
25. United States Congress, "Hunt's Testimony," *Report of the Joint Committee (1865)*, 92–93.
26. United States Congress, "Hunt's Testimony," *Report of the Joint Committee (1865)*, 92–93.
27. "Hunt's Report," *Official Records*, vol. 25, pt. 1, 252.
28. "Hunt's Report," *Official Records*, vol. 25, pt. 1, 252.
29. "Hunt's Report," *Official Records*, vol. 25, pt. 1, 250.

30. "Hunt's Report," *Official Records*, vol. 25, pt. 1, 250.
31. "Hunt's Report," *Official Records*, vol. 25, pt. 1, 250.

Chapter 6

1. Edward F. Hopkins, Fredericksburg-Spotsylvania National Military Park Bound Volume 319-12. Fredericksburg-Spotsylvania National Military Park Bound Volume Collection. Fredericksburg & Spotsylvania National Military Park, Fredericksburg, Virginia.
2. Edward F. Hopkins, Fredericksburg-Spotsylvania National Military Park Bound Volume 319-12.
3. Edward F. Hopkins, Fredericksburg-Spotsylvania National Military Park Bound Volume 319-12.
4. Bigelow, *Chancellorsville*, 416.
5. Bigelow, *Chancellorsville*, 416.
6. United States Congress, "Hooker's Testimony," *Report of the Joint Committee* (1865), 133–34.
7. *Official Records*, vol. 25, pt. 2, *Correspondence*.
8. *Official Records*, vol. 25, pt. 2, *Correspondence*, 407.
9. *Official Records*, vol. 25, pt. 2, *Correspondence*, 407.
10. *Official Records*, vol. 25, pt. 2, *Correspondence*, 410.
11. United States Congress, "Hooker's Testimony," *Report of the Joint Committee* (1865), 134–35.
12. United States Congress, "Hooker's Testimony," *Report of the Joint Committee* (1865), 134–35.
13. Sears, *Lincoln's Lieutenants*, 517.
14. *Official Records*, vol. 25, pt. 2, *Correspondence*, 419.
15. *Official Records*, vol. 25, pt. 2, *Correspondence*, 435.

Chapter 7

1. Alexander, *Fighting for the Confederacy*, 213.
2. Alexander, *Fighting for the Confederacy*, 214.
3. "Lee's Report," *Official Records*, vol. 25, pt. 1, 802.
4. *Official Records*, vol. 25, pt. 2, *Correspondence*, 779.

5. "Lee's Report," *Official Records*, vol. 25, pt. 1, 802.
6. Freeman, *Lee's Lieutenants*, 509–10.
7. "Lee's Report," *Official Records*, vol. 25, pt.1, 888.
8. Alexander, *Fighting for the Confederacy*, 215.
9. Stephen W. Sears, *Chancellorsville* (Boston: Houghton Mifflin Harcourt, 2014), 430.
10. Carl Wickesberg, Fredericksburg-Spotsylvania National Military Park Bound Volume 353-27. Fredericksburg-Spotsylvania National Military Park Bound Volume Collection. Fredericksburg & Spotsylvania National Military Park, Fredericksburg, Virginia.
11. Stephen Pingree, Fredericksburg-Spotsylvania National Military Park Bound Volume 279-07. Fredericksburg-Spotsylvania National Military Park Bound Volume Collection. Fredericksburg & Spotsylvania National Military Park, Fredericksburg, Virginia.
12. Warren B. Persons, Fredericksburg-Spotsylvania National Military Park Bound Volume 283-09. Fredericksburg-Spotsylvania National Military Park Bound Volume Collection. Fredericksburg & Spotsylvania National Military Park, Fredericksburg, Virginia.
13. Sears, *Lincoln's Lieutenants*, 520–24.
14. *Official Records*, vol. 25, pt. 1, *Reports*, 171.
15. *Official Records*, vol. 25, pt.1, *Reports*, 171.
16. *Official Records*, vol. 25, pt. 1, *Reports*, 171.
17. Sears, *Lincoln's Lieutenants*, 522–23.
18. John M. Cate, Fredericksburg-Spotsylvania National Military Park Bound Volumes 183-4 and 251-1. Fredericksburg-Spotsylvania National Military Park Bound Volume Collection. Fredericksburg & Spotsylvania National Military Park, Fredericksburg, Virginia.
19. Stephen W. Sears, *Chancellorsville* (Boston: Houghton Mifflin Harcourt, 2014), 475–501.
20. John O. Casler, *Four Years in the Stonewall Brigade* (1906), 151.
21. Stephen W. Sears, *Chancellorsville* (Boston: Houghton Mifflin Harcourt, 2014), 433.
22. Stephen W. Sears, *Chancellorsville* (Boston: Houghton Mifflin Harcourt, 2014), 442.
23. Haley, April 9, 1863, 141–42.

Appendix I. Battlefield Guide to the Critical Decisions at Chancellorsville

1. Noel G. Harrison, *Chancellorsville Battlefield Sites* (Lynchburg, VA: H. E. Howard, 1990), 24.

2. A. L. Peel Diary, April 30, 1863, Fredericksburg-Spotsylvania National Military Park Bound Volume 336-10. Fredericksburg-Spotsylvania National Military Park Bound Volume Collection. Fredericksburg & Spotsylvania National Military Park, Fredericksburg, Virginia.

3. "Richard Anderson's Report," *Official Records*, vol. 25, pt. 1, 850.

4. "George Sykes's Report," *Official Records*, vol. 25, pt. 1, 525.

5. Harrison, *Chancellorsville Battlefield Sites*, 16–17.

6. Francis Adams Donaldson, *Inside the Army of the Potomac: The Civil War Experience of Captain Francis Adams Donaldson*, ed. J. Gregory Acken (Mechanicsburg, PA: Stackpole Books, 1998), 232.

7. Martin W. Brett's Memoirs, Fredericksburg-Spotsylvania National Military Park Bound Volume 26-10. Fredericksburg-Spotsylvania National Military Park Bound Volume Collection. Fredericksburg & Spotsylvania National Military Park, Fredericksburg, Virginia.

8. T. M. R. Talcott, July 19, 1886, Fredericksburg-Spotsylvania National Military Park Bound Volume 375-24. Fredericksburg-Spotsylvania National Military Park Bound Volume Collection. Fredericksburg & Spotsylvania National Military Park, Fredericksburg, Virginia.

9. Benjamin B. Carr, "Sketch of the Battle of Chancellorsville," Fredericksburg-Spotsylvania National Military Park Bound Volume 2-03. Fredericksburg-Spotsylvania National Military Park Bound Volume Collection. Fredericksburg & Spotsylvania National Military Park, Fredericksburg, Virginia.

10. Darwin D. Cody, May 9, 1863,Fredericksburg-Spotsylvania National Military Park Bound Volume 37-7. Fredericksburg-Spotsylvania National Military Park Bound Volume Collection. Fredericksburg & Spotsylvania National Military Park, Fredericksburg, Virginia.

11. "Rodes Report," *Official Records*, 941.

12. James P. Smith, "Stonewall Jackson's Last Battle," in *Battles & Leaders of the Civil War* (1887), 3:211.

13. "James Ewell Brown Stuart's Report," *Official Records*, vol. 25, pt. 1, 887.

14. James E. Kelly, edited by William B. Styple, *Generals in Bronze:*

Interviewing the Commanders of the Civil War (Kearny, NJ: Belle Grove, 2005), 122.

15. Albert M. White, May 16, 1863, Fredericksburg-Spotsylvania National Military Park Bound Volume 455-14. Fredericksburg-Spotsylvania National Military Park Bound Volume Collection. Fredericksburg & Spotsylvania National Military Park, Fredericksburg, Virginia.
16. Harrison, *Chancellorsville Battlefield Sites*, 99–102.
17. "Stephen D. Ramseur's Report," *Official Records*, vol. 25, pt.1, 995–97.
18. Henry Morhous, Reminiscences of the 123d Regiment, Fredericksburg-Spotsylvania National Military Park Bound Volume 319-8. Fredericksburg-Spotsylvania National Military Park Bound Volume Collection. Fredericksburg & Spotsylvania National Military Park, Fredericksburg, Virginia.
19. Harrison, *Chancellorsville Battlefield Sites*, 11–15.
20. "Winfield S. Hancock's Report," *Official Records*, vol. 25, pt. 1, 314–15.
21. Captain Charles Bowers, May 4, 1863, Fredericksburg-Spotsylvania National Military Park Bound Volume 280-12. Fredericksburg-Spotsylvania National Military Park Bound Volume Collection. Fredericksburg & Spotsylvania National Military Park, Fredericksburg, Virginia.
22. William H. Moore, May 10, 1863, Fredericksburg-Spotsylvania National Military Park Bound Volume 336-12. Fredericksburg-Spotsylvania National Military Park Bound Volume Collection. Fredericksburg & Spotsylvania National Military Park, Fredericksburg, Virginia.
23. Bailey Smith, Pocket Diary Entries, May 3, 1863, Fredericksburg-Spotsylvania National Military Park Bound Volume 364-20. Fredericksburg-Spotsylvania National Military Park Bound Volume Collection. Fredericksburg & Spotsylvania National Military Park, Fredericksburg, Virginia.
24. Harrison, *Chancellorsville Battlefield Sites*, 161–62.
25. "Robert E. Lee's Report," *Official Records*, vol. 25, pt. 1, 801.
26. Fred H. West, May 5, 1863, Fredericksburg-Spotsylvania National Military Park Bound Volume 372-23. Fredericksburg-Spotsylvania National Military Park Bound Volume Collection. Fredericksburg & Spotsylvania National Military Park, Fredericksburg, Virginia.
27. "John Sedgwick's Report," *Official Records*, vol. 25, pt. 1, 559–60.
28. Edwin Buckman, May 9, 1863, Fredericksburg-Spotsylvania National Military Park Bound Volume 399-4. Fredericksburg-Spotsylvania

National Military Park Bound Volume Collection. Fredericksburg & Spotsylvania National Military Park, Fredericksburg, Virginia.
29. "George Gordon Meade's Report," *Official Records*, vol. 25, pt. 1, 508.
30. Abbott, *Fallen Leaves*, 176–78.

Appendix II. Chancellorsville and the Lost Cause

1. Caroline E. Janney, *Remembering the Civil War: Reunion and the Limits of Reconciliation* (Chapel Hill: University of North Carolina Press, 2013), 103–20.
2. Jeffry D. Wert, "James Longstreet and the Lost Cause," in *The Myth of the Lost Cause and Civil War History*, ed. Gary W. Gallagher and Alan T. Nolan, (Bloomington: Indiana University Press, 2000), 135.
3. Gary W. Gallagher and Alan T. Nolan, editors, *The Myth of the Lost Cause and Civil War History*, "The Immortal Confederacy" by Lloyd A. Hunter (Bloomington: Indiana University Press, 2000), 198.
4. Mackowski and White, *Chancellorsville's Forgotten Front*, 200–203.
5. Mackowski and White, *Chancellorsville's Forgotten Front*, xxvi–xxvii
6. Gary W. Gallagher, "Jubal A. Early, the Lost Cause, and Civil War History," in *The Myth of the Lost Cause and Civil War History*, ed. Gary W. Gallagher (Bloomington: Indiana University Press, 2000), 49.

BIBLIOGRAPHY

Collections

Fredericksburg-Spotsylvania National Military Park Bound Volume Collection. Fredericksburg & Spotsylvania National Military Park, Fredericksburg, Virginia:

William Barksdale, *Richmond Daily Dispatch*, Bound Volume 137-07

Charles Bowers, Bound Volume 280-12

Martin W. Brett, Bound Volume 26-10

Edwin Buckman, Bound Volume 399-4

Benjamin B. Carr, Bound Volume 2-03

John M. Cate, Bound Volumes 183-4 and 251-1

Darwin D. Cody, Bound Volume 37-7

Charles Engel, Bound Volume 419-15

Edward F. Hopkins, Bound Volume 319-12

William H. Moore, Bound Volume 336-12

Henry Morhous, Bound Volume 319-8

A. L. Peel Diary, Bound Volume 336-10

Dudley Pendleton, Bound Volume 84-25

Warren B. Persons, Bound Volume 283-09

Stephen Pingree, Bound Volume 279-07

John F. Reynolds, Bound Volume 466-05

Bailey Smith, Bound Volume 364-20

T. M. R. Talcott, Bound Volume 375-24

Fred H. West, Bound Volume 372-23

Albert M. White, Bound Volume 455-14

Carl Wickesberg, Bound Volume 353-27

Joseph Hooker Military Papers. The Huntington Library, San Marino California.

Primary Sources

Accounts

Chancellor, Sue. "Recollections of Chancellorsville." *Confederate Veteran Magazine* 29 (1921): 213–15.

Smith, James P. "Stonewall Jackson's Last Battle." In *Battles & Leaders of the Civil War*, Volume 3, edited by Robert Underwood Johnson and Clarence Clough Buel. Century Company, 1887.

Wilbourn, Richard E. "An Eyewitness Account of Stonewall Jackson's Wounding." Virginia Museum of History & Culture. Copyright 2024. https://virginiahistory.org/learn/historical-book/chapter/eyewitness-account-stonewall-jacksons-wounding.

Compilations

Compiled Service Records of Confederate Soldiers Who Served in Organizations from the State of Mississippi, 1861–1865. Catalog ID: 586957, Record Group 109, Mississippi, Roll 0268. National Archives, Washington DC. Accessed through Fold3.

United States Congress. *Report of the Joint Committee on the Conduct of the War, at the Second Session Thirty-Eighth Congress—Chancellorsville.* 1865.

United States War Department. *Official Records.* Vol. 21, pt. 1, *Reports.*

United States War Department. *Official Records.* Vol. 21, pt. 2, *Correspondence.*

Books

Abbot, Edward Stanley. *From Schoolboy to Soldier: The Correspondence and Journals of Edward Stanley Abbot, 1853–1863.* Edited by Quincy S. Abbot. West Hartford: Quincy Abbot, 2013.

Abbott, Henry Livermore. *Fallen Leaves: The Civil War Letters of Major Henry Livermore Abbott.* Edited by Robert Garth Scott. Kent, OH: Kent State University Press, 1991.

Alexander, Edward Porter. *Fighting for the Confederacy: The Personal Recollections of General Edward Porter Alexander.* Edited by Gary W. Gallagher. Chapel Hill: University of North Carolina Press, 1989.

Brewer, Abraham Titus. *History, Sixty-First Regiment Pennsylvania Volunteers, 1861–1865.* Pittsburgh, Art Engraving & Printing Co., 1911.

Casler, John O. *Four Years in the Stonewall Brigade.* Appeal Publishing Company, 1906.

Donaldson, Francis Adams. *Inside the Army of the Potomac: The Civil War Experience of Captain Francis Adams Donaldson.* Edited by J. Gregory Acken. Mechanicsburg, PA: Stackpole Books, 1998.

Haley, John W. *The Rebel Yell & The Yankee Hurrah: The Civil War Journal of a Maine Volunteer.* Edited by Ruth L. Silliker. Camden, ME: Down East Books, 1985.

Hutchinson, Nelson V. *History of the Seventh Massachusetts Volunteer Infantry in the War of the Rebellion of the Southern States against Constitutional Authority.* Taunton, MA: Regimental Association, 1890.

Kelly, James E. *Generals in Bronze: Interviewing the Commanders of the Civil War.* Edited by William B. Styple. Kearny: Belle Grove, 2005.

Letterman, Jonathan. *Medical Recollections of the Army of the Potomac.* New York: Appleton, 1866.

Lincoln, Abraham. *Lincoln: Speeches and Writings, 1859–1865.* Edited by Roy P. Balser. New York: Library of America, 1989.

Marshall, Charles. *An Aide-de-Camp of Lee: Being the Papers of Colonel Charles Marshall, Sometime Aide-de-Camp, Military Secretary, and Assistant Adjutant General on the Staff of Robert E. Lee, 1862–1865.* Edited by Sir Frederick Maurice. Boston: Little, Brown, 1927.

Taylor, Walter H. *Four Years with General Lee.* Edited by James I. Robertson Jr. Bloomington: Indiana University Press, 1996.

———. *Lee's Adjutant: The Wartime Letters of Colonel Walter Herron Taylor, 1862–1865.* Edited by R. Lockwood Tower. Columbia: University of South Carolina Press, 1995.

Wainwright, Charles S. *A Diary of Battle: The Personal Journals of Colonel Charles S. Wainwright, 1861–1865.* Edited by Allan Nevins. New York: Da Capo, 1998.

Secondary Sources

Bigelow, John, Jr. *Chancellorsville.* New York: Smithmark, 1995.

Conner, Albert Z., Jr., and Chris Mackowski. *Seizing Destiny: The Army of the Potomac's "Valley Forge" and the Civil War Winter That Saved the Union.* El Dorado Hills, CA: Savas Beatie, 2016.

Cozzens, Peter. *Shenandoah, 1862: Stonewall Jackson's Valley Campaign.* Chapel Hill: University of North Carolina Press, 2008.

Freeman, Douglas Southall. *Lee's Lieutenants: A Study in Command.* Abridged to one volume by Stephen W. Sears. New York: Scribner, 1998.

Furgurson, Ernest B. *Chancellorsville, 1863: The Souls of the Brave.* New York: Vintage House, 1992.

Gallagher, Gary W., and Alan T. Nolan, eds. *The Myth of the Lost Cause and Civil War History.* Bloomington: Indiana University Press, 2000.

Harrison, Noel G. *Chancellorsville Battlefield Sites.* Lynchburg, VA: H. E. Howard, 1990.

Hennessy, John J. *The First Battle of Manassas: An End to Innocence, July 21, 1861.* Rev. ed. Mechanicsburg, PA: Stackpole, 2015.

———. *Return to Bull Run: The Campaign of Second Manassas.* Norman: University of Oklahoma Press, 1993.

Hessler, James A. *Sickles at Gettysburg.* El Dorado Hills, CA: Savas Beatie, 2009.

Janney, Caroline E. *Remembering the Civil War: Reunion and the Limits of Reconciliation.* Chapel Hill: University of North Carolina Press, 2013.

Lively, Matthew W. *Calamity at Chancellorsville.* El Dorado Hills, CA: Savas Beatie, 2013.

Mackowski, Chris, and Kristopher White. *Chancellorsville's Forgotten Front: The Battles of Second Fredericksburg and Salem Church.* El Dorado Hills, CA: Savas Beatie, 2013.

McPherson, James. *The Battle Cry of Freedom: The Civil War Era.* Oxford: Oxford University Press, 1988.

Miller, William J. *Mapping for Stonewall: The Civil War Service of Jed Hotchkiss*. Washington, DC: Elliott and Clark, 1993.

O'Reilly, Francis Augustin. *The Fredericksburg Campaign: Winter War on the Rappahannock*. Baton Rouge: Louisiana State University Press, 2006.

Pula, James S. *Under the Crescent Moon with the XI Corps in the Civil War*. Vol. 1, *From the Defenses of Washington to Chancellorsville, 1862–1863*. El Dorado Hills, CA: Savas Beatie, 2017.

Robertson, James I., Jr., *Stonewall Jackson: The Man, the Soldier, the Legend*. New York: Simon and Schuster, 1997.

Sears, Stephen W. *The Landscape Turned Red: The Battle of Antietam*. Boston: First Mariner Books, 1983.

——. *Chancellorsville*. Boston: Houghton Mifflin Company, 1996.

——. *Lincoln's Lieutenants: The High Command of the Army of the Potomac*. New York: Houghton Mifflin Harcourt, 2017.

Warner, Ezra J. *Generals in Blue: Lives of Union Commanders*. Baton Rouge: Louisiana State University Press, 1996.

INDEX

Abbot, Stanley, 40, 41, 44, 50
Abbott, Henry L., 25, 31, 50, 192
Adams, R. H. T., 170
Alexander, Edward Porter, 134, 135, 221
Allen, Thomas, 97
American Battlefield Trust, xx, 143, 153, 154
Anaconda Plan, 3
Anderson, Richard, 35, 40, 79, 100, 151–52, 220
Anderson's Division, 24, 37, 40, 44, 55, 99, 102, 106, 134, 151, 185, 220
Antietam, Battle of, 7, 16, 17, 19, 121–22, 230, 247
Antietam Plan, 196
Appomattox Court House, 194
Aquia Landing, 28–29
Army of Northern Virginia, xiii, 6–7, 9–11, 19–26, 32–33, 38, 50, 55, 79, 84, 89, 140, 142, 147, 192, 219; headquarters, xiv, 24, 34, 50, 79, 80, 133, 135, 148
Army of Northern Virginia Corps; First Corps, xvi, 7, 19–25, 21–22, 35, 44, 134, 140, 147, 151, 152, 182, 186–87, 219; Second Corps, xvi, 22–23, 33–34, 36, 50, 55, 57, 59, 68, 71–81, 99, 104, 112–13, 134, 140–41, 168, 170–71, 222
Army of the Cumberland, 3
Army of the Potomac, 5–12, 15–18, 28, 32–33, 37, 114, 118, 120, 135–42, 192, 199; artillery, 120, 124; headquarters, xiii, xiv, 13, 19, 44, 60, 92, 100, 114–15, 119, 121–24, 136, 145, 147, 156–58, 160, 175; rebuilding the, xvi, 18–19, 25–27, 136, 145–47
Army of the Potomac Corps; First Corps, 14, 17, 60, 63, 92, 102, 112, 119, 128, 199; Second Corps, 31, 41, 44–46, 48, 66, 92–93, 109, 116–17, 128, 136, 178, 192, 201; Third Corps, 41, 45, 48, 62–63, 65, 92, 108–10, 112–13, 115, 118, 128, 171, 172, 174–75, 204; Fifth Corps, 17, 41–47, 102, 112, 115, 117, 119, 128, 153–54, 157, 160, 178, 190–91, 206; Sixth Corps, 15–16, 31, 87, 92–94, 101, 106, 136–37, 181,

Army of the Potomac Corps (cont.)
183, 187, 190, 209; Eleventh Corps, 41, 45, 48, 60–69, 71–72, 74, 99, 107, 110, 113, 128, 136, 138, 147, 156–58, 165–66, 168, 172, 178, 192, 197, 211; Twelfth Corps, 31, 41–42, 44–48, 109, 128, 156, 160, 175, 176, 213
artillery, 44, 51, 62, 69, 80, 83, 94, 100–1, 107, 109–12, 147, 159, 174, 176; ammunition, 94, 113, 118, 122, 124, 135, 159, 177; Confederate, 20–21, 46, 54, 68, 73, 84, 86, 88, 90, 98, 110, 113, 132, 134, 156, 165, 181, 183, 186; Union, 9, 14, 28, 37, 45, 65, 67, 71, 96, 104, 109–10, 112, 118–26, 135, 141–42, 150, 153–55, 158–59, 166, 172, 174–75, 178, 180
Atlantic Ocean, 150

Balloon Corps, 26, 27, 41, 44, 92,
Banks' Ford, 13, 121, 122, 129, 131–34, 180, 187–91
Barksdale, William, 84, 86–92, 220
Barksdale's Brigade, 40, 86–88, 91, 98–99, 151, 182, 220
Berry-Paxton Drive, 174, 177
Birney, David B., 110, 115, 118, 204
Blue and Gray Parkway, 180, 184
Boswell, James Keith, 68, 73–74, 161, 169
Bowers, Charles, 178
Bowling Green Road, 93
Bragg, Braxton, 3
Bragg Road, 189
Brett, Martin W., 158
Brewer, Abraham Titus, 94
Brock Road/Route 613, 161
Brompton House, 84, 181
Brooks, W. T. H., 15, 209
Buckman, Edwin, 190
Buel, Don Carlos, 3
Bullock, Oscar, 177
Bullock House Site, 115, 177–78, 180
Bullock Road, 128, 149, 167, 170, 177

Bull Run, First Battle of, 1
Bull Run, Second Battle of, 7, 13. *See* Manassas, Second Battle of
burial of the dead, 89, 91, 114, 139, 183
Burnside, Ambrose, 12–15, 25; and Battle of Fredericksburg, 8–9; removed from command, 15–18, 146
Buschbeck Line, 69, 165,
Butterfield, Daniel, 92–93, 116, 129, 132, 157

Calder, William, 40
cannon, xiii, 14, 54, 63, 84, 92, 96, 98, 113–14, 120, 122, 125, 134–36, 156, 171, 173–75, 180–81, 183, 190. *See also* artillery
Cape Fear River, 24
Carr, Benjamin B., 162
casualties, 3, 7, 9; at Chancellorsville 97, 134, 138–140, 191, 194, 230
Cate, John M., 138
Catharine Furnace, 48, 51, 63, 65–66, 109, 157, 163, 171
Catharine Furnace Road, 160
cavalry, 44; Confederate, 20, 23, 27–28, 34, 38, 51–52, 54–55, 68, 79, 152, 160–62; Union, 20, 26, 28, 30–31, 62–63, 65–66, 109, 112, 137, 147, 153–54, 171–72
Cedar Mountain, Battle of, 6, 22
Chancellor, Frances, 156
Chancellor Family, 44, 174
Chancellorsville, Battle of. *See* decisions
Chancellorsville, First Day Battlefield, 153–55, 160
Chancellorsville Battlefield Visitor Center, 145, 147, 149, 167–68, 170–71, 195
Chancellorsville Clearing, xiii, 46, 51, 63, 119, 154
Chancellorsville Crossroads, xiii, xvi, 35–36, 41–42, 44–46, 48, 51, 59, 69, 72, 74, 80, 100–101, 107, 110–11, 114,

133, 135, 140, 142, 155–56, 164, 166, 170, 172–76, 181
Chancellorsville House, 42, 44, 60, 100, 113–15, 142, 156–57, 159–60, 171, 175–76
Chancellorsville House Site, xiii, 155–56, 158, 160
Chancellorsville monuments, 170, 174, 195–96. *See also* Fredericksburg National Cemetery; Salem Church monuments
Chantilly, 7, 22
civilian, 6, 9, 23, 51, 53, 68, 114, 145, 150, 178, 194
Civil Rights, 194
Cochrane, John, 15
Cody, Darwin, 166
Colston, Raleigh, 104, 225
Couch, Darius, 48, 115–17, 119, 128–31, 136, 201
Coup, 13, 136
court-martial, 13
Crane, Stephen, 196–97
cross fire, 88, 113, 181, 190
Culpeper, 27

Davis, Jefferson, 5, 55, 134
decisions (chronological); critical decisions defined, xiv-xvii, 9–11, 144–45; critical decisions results, 133–42; Lincoln appoints Hooker, xvi, 11, 12–19, 32, 140, 145–47; Lee sends Longstreet's Corps away, xvi, 11, 19–25, 32, 140, 147–49; Hooker determines his offensive strategy, xvi, 11, 25–32, 140, 145–47; Lee decides to turn and fight, xvi, 33, 34–40, 140, 149–56; Hooker Pulls Back, xvi, 33, 40–50, 140, 153–60; Lee allows Jackson to initiate a flank attack, xvi, 33, 50–57, 140, 160–67; Hooker decides the Confederates are retreating, xvi, 59, 60–67, 140–41, 156–60, 165–67; Jackson plans to cut off the Federals from US Ford, xvi, 59, 67–74, 141, 165–71; Lee Puts J. E. B. Stuart in command of the Second Corps, xvi, 59, 74–81, 141, 167–74; Griffin grants a temporary truce, xvi, 83, 84–92, 141, 180–85; Sedgwick's Troops move forward, xvi, 83, 92–98, 141, 180–85; Lee Divides His Army Again, xvi, 83, 99–106, 141, 185–92; Hooker orders Sickles to abandon Hazel Grove, xvi, 107, 108–13, 141, 171–77; Union Officers do not replace Hooker after his injury, xvi, 107, 114–19, 141, 156–60, 174–80; Hooker brings hunt from the rear, xvi, 107, 119–26, 141, 177–80; Hooker retreats, xvi, 127, 128–32, 141, 177–80, 189–92
defensive position, 23, 36, 38, 113, 135; at Chancellorsville, 45–50, 53, 62–63, 66, 107, 110–11, 113, 119, 140, 156, 159–60, 163, 165, 175, 177; at First Fredericksburg, 8–9, 22; at Salem Church, 101, 151; at Second Fredericksburg, 38, 87, 181; during retreat, 122, 124–25, 141, 177–79. *See also* Hooker's Last Line
Department of Virginia and North Carolina, 23
dictatorship, 17
Donaldson, Francis Adams, 157
Dowdall's Tavern, 74, 113

Early, Jubal, 38, 55, 57, 79, 86–87, 92, 98, 99–102, 106, 134, 224
Early's Division, 40, 55, 224
earthworks, 45, 48, 61, 128, 132, 135, 150–51, 168, 172, 174–75, 178
Eastern Theater, 5, 9, 12, 28, 196
Ely's Ford, 35, 41, 80
Ely's Ford Road, 119, 128, 149, 155–56, 160, 177, 179–80
Emancipation Proclamation, xiv, 9, 11, 12, 16, 23, 194

Engel, Charles, 12, 14, 19
engineer, 35, 48, 53, 68, 73, 78, 129, 152, 155, 169
England, 7
Europe, 1, 5, 9, 11, 19, 61

Fairview, xiii, 48, 51, 110–13, 156, 171–77
Fairview Cemetery, 156, 174
fires, 7, 139, 159
flank attack, 33, 50–57, 59, 67–69, 72, 79, 99, 106, 108–9, 138, 140–41, 158, 160–68, 196
Fort Donelson, 3, 5
Fort Henry, 3, 5
Fort Pulaski, 3
France, 7
Franklin, William B., 13–18
Fredericksburg, 9, 20, 22, 26, 28, 30–31, 34–39, 41, 45–46, 50, 55, 57, 104, 106, 132, 134, 148–52, 186, 189
Fredericksburg, First Battle of, 9, 12–13, 16, 19, 23, 27, 98, 121–22, 185, 196
Fredericksburg, Second Battlefield, 143, 145, 180–85, 196
Fredericksburg, Second Battle of, 79, 83–99, 107, 112, 122, 136, 138, 141, 147, 188, 192, 195
Fredericksburg Battlefield Visitor Center, 180, 184
Fredericksburg National Cemetery, 183–84
friendly fire, 73–74, 195
Furnace Road, 160, 163

General Orders No. 8, 14
General Orders No. 20, 18
General Orders No. 49, 137
General Semmes Road, 184, 189
10th Georgia Infantry, 187, 219
12th Georgia Infantry, 158, 224
51st Georgia Infantry, 186–87, 219
German American, 60–61, 136, 138, 166, 197

Germanna Ford, 34, 41
Gettysburg, Battle of, 22, 113, 140–42, 195–97
Gibbon, John, 93, 202
Gods and Generals, 197
Gordonsville, 30, 62, 172
Grant, Ulysses S., 3
Griffin, Thomas, xvi, 83–84, 89–92, 98, 181–82, 191
gunboat, 28

Haley, John, 1, 10, 142
Halleck, Henry, 13, 15
Hamilton's Crossing, 147–49
Hancock, Winfield S., 48, 178, 201
Harpers Ferry, 7, 16
Harrison Road, 149
Hawkins Farm, 62
Hays's Brigade, 86–87, 225
Hazel Grove, xiii, xvi, 48, 80, 99, 108–14, 141–42, 156, 171–77
Hill, A. P., 73–76, 169–70, 222
Homefront; Northern, xvi, 9, 10, 16; Southern, 20
Hooker, Joseph, 36–40, 54–57, 99–100, 106, 148, 160, 219; appointed to command, xvi, 12–19, 140, 145–47; brings Hunt back to command, xvi, 107, 119–26, 141, 177–79; conflicts with officers, 13, 17, 46–48, 119–20, 136–38; council of war, 127, 129–31; decides the Confederates are retreating, xvi, 59, 60–67, 140–41, 156–60, 165–70; offensive strategy, xvi, 25–32, 33, 52, 140, 145–47; Fighting Joe (nickname), xiii, 17, 24, 100; orders Sickles to abandon Hazel Grove, xvi, 107, 108–13, 141, 171–77; pulls back to Chancellorsville, xvi, 40–50, 140, 153–60; rebuilds Army of the Potomac, 18–19, 25–26, 140, 146–47; relying on Sedgwick, 83, 92–96, 98, 129,

Index

181, 183; responds to defeat, 136–38, 141; retreats, xvi, 72, 100–101, 127, 128–32, 134–35, 138, 141, 177–79, 187–88, 189–92; wounded, xvi, 107, 113–19, 141, 156–60, 174–79. *See also* Army of the Potomac
Hooker's Last Line, 177–79, 187
Hopkins, Edward F., 128, 132
Hotchkiss, Jedidiah, 35, 53
Howard, Oliver O., 60–61, 65, 67, 109, 129–30, 136–38, 211
Hunt, Henry J., xvi, 107, 119–26, 141–42, 177–80, 216
Hutchinson, Nelson, v, 97

immigrants, 61, 197
Innis House, 181, 183
interior lines, 17, 38
interpretive panels, 147, 149, 164, 167, 174, 185
interpretive trail, xiii, 147, 149, 153, 155, 168, 170, 174, 177–78,

Jackson, Thomas J. "Stonewall," 5–9, 22–23, 34–36, 147–48, 222; death, 140; plans and leads Flank Attack, 50–55, 59, 140–41, 160–62. *See also* Jackson's Flank March and Flank Attack; plans to cut off Federals from US Ford, 59, 67–74, 80; wounding, 73–76, 99, 140, 168–70, 194–97; at Zoan Church Ridge, 36–44, 86, 150–53
Jackson's Flank March (historic), 55–57, 62, 162–63. *See also* Flank Attack
Jackson's Flank March (roads). *See* Jackson Trail West and Jackson Trail East
Jackson Trail East, 163
Jackson Trail West, 163
James River, 6, 13, 227
Johnston, Joseph E., 5
Johnston, S. R., 152

Joint Committee on the Conduct of the War, 13, 113, 118

Kelly's Ford, 30, 31, 34, 41
Kelly's Ford, Battle of, 20, 26
Killer Angels, The, 197

Lacy, Beverly Tucker, 53, 196
Lafayette Boulevard, 180, 184
Lee, Fitzhugh, 79, 228
Lee, Robert E., 5–9, 67, 72, 113; and decisions, 140–41; and decisive victory, xiii, 9, 19–20, 141–42; allows Jackson to initiate a Flank Attack, 50–57, 59, 68, 160–64, 164–68; decides to turn and fight, 33–40, 86, 147–49, 149–53, 153–60; divides his army again, 83–84, 99–106, 185–88; excerpts of report, 185–86; Hooker's strategy against, 26–32, 33, 45–46, 49–50, 60, 63, 66, 92–93, 131, 183; puts Stuart in command, 74–81, 168–70, 171–75; reaction to Chancellorsville, 132–35, 191, 194–95; sends Longstreet's Corps away, 19–25, 147–49
Lee Drive, 149
Lee Drive Extended, 149
Lee-Jackson Bivouac Site, 160, 163, 164
Lee's Hill, 87, 94, 98–99, 181
Letterman, Jonathan, 114–15, 117, 139
Lick Run, 153
Lincoln, Abraham, 5–7, 9, 28, 139; changes war aims, xiv, 8, 11, 194; and Hooker, xvi, 12–19, 31, 116, 132, 136, 138, 140–41, 145; reviews troops, 1, 146
Logistics, xiv–xvi, 19–20, 31, 34, 68, 72, 115, 120, 123, 142, 147, 181
Longstreet, James, 7, 9, 19–24, 26–27, 32, 38, 55, 147
Lost Cause, 193–197
Lowe, Thaddeus, 41

Mahone, William, 35, 106, 220
17th Maine, 1, 142, 204
Manassas, First Battle of. *See* Bull Run, First Battle of
Manassas, Second Battle of, 19, 21–22, 23, 38, 52. *See* Bull Run, Second Battle of
Marye's Heights, 106, 180–84, 195–96; during First Fredericksburg, 8, 13, 17; during Second Fredericksburg, 83–98, 99, 138, 141, 185
Maryland, 7, 209, 213, 216, 225, 228; Campaign 7–8, 16, 22, 52
20th Massachusetts, 25, 192, 203
32nd Massachusetts, 178, 207
33rd Massachusetts, 138, 212
Maxwell, Ron, 197
McClellan, George B., 5–8, 13, 16, 18–19, 26
McGee Ridge, 44, 154, 160
McLaws, Lafayette, 100, 104, 106, 152, 185, 219
McLaws's Division, 24, 37–38, 40, 44, 55, 79, 87, 99, 102, 104, 106, 134, 151, 182, 185–86, 219–20
Meade, George G., 47–48, 115, 117, 119, 129–30, 141–42, 190, 206
Memory (historical), 74, 131–32, 133, 142, 191, 193–97
Mesnard, Luther, 67
Milroy, Robert, 22
Mineral Spring Road, 128
Mine Road, 36, 131
18th Mississippi Infantry, 88–91, 98, 220
19th Mississippi Infantry, 151, 221
21st Mississippi Infantry, 91, 182, 220
Mississippi River, 3
Moore, William H., 182
morale, 14, 16, 18, 20, 25, 28, 42, 60, 78, 118, 128, 130, 133, 140, 146, 192
Morhous, Henry, 176
Mott's Run Boat Launch, 189
Mountain Road, 73, 167–70

Mount Hope Church Road, 147
Mud March, 12, 14, 19
Murphy, Audie, 197

Nashville, 3
National Park Service, xiii, 143, 148, 161, 163–64, 185, 195
15th New Jersey Infantry Monument, 189
23rd New Jersey Infantry Monument, 188–189
New Orleans, 3
Newton, John, 15, 210
36th New York, 97, 211
64th New York, 136, 202
123rd New York, 176, 213
137th New York, 12, 19, 214
149th New York, 128, 132, 201
North Anna River, 23, 38
North Carolina, 23, 24
2nd North Carolina, 40, 224
4th North Carolina, 173, 224
18th North Carolina, 74, 170, 222
20th North Carolina, 162, 224

offense (strategy), xvi, 5, 11, 16, 23–24, 25–32, 34–40, 42, 46, 59, 67, 79, 101–2, 107, 110, 112–13, 140, 147. *See also* Hooker's plan and decisions
1st Ohio Artillery, 166, 206
55th Ohio Infantry, 67, 212
Old Plank Road, 153, 160, 164, 177
Old Salem Church Road, 184, 189
Orange Court House, 62
Orange Plank Road, 42, 44–45, 48, 68, 152, 155, 160, 165
Orange Turnpike, 34, 42, 44–45, 48, 63, 65–66, 68–69, 71, 73, 87, 109, 111, 113, 150, 153, 156, 165, 168, 169, 175
Overland Campaign, 142
Owen, T. H., 152

Parker's Battery, 184, 221
parking/parking lots, 145, 149, 152–53,

Index

155, 160, 163–64, 167–68, 171, 174, 177, 180, 184–85, 189
Paxton, Elisha F., 196, 225
Peel, A. L., 151
Pender, William Dorsey, 135, 222
Pendleton, Alexander S., 75–76, 78
Pendleton, Dudley, 84, 88
Peninsula, Rappahannock, 28
Peninsula, Virginia, 5–7, 13, 16–17, 26
8th Pennsylvania Cavalry, 44, 65, 215
61st Pennsylvania Infantry, 94, 211
98th Pennsylvania Infantry, 190, 211
118th Pennsylvania Infantry, 157, 207
Perryville, Battle of, 3
Person, Warren, 136
Pingree, Stephen, 136
Pitzer, Andrew, 99
Plank Road/Route 3, 149, 152, 155, 160, 163–65, 167, 171, 177, 180, 189
Pleasonton, Alfred, 172, 215
politics, xiv, 1, 5, 9–10, 13, 15–19, 25, 108, 118, 131–33, 136, 138, 141
pontoon bridges, 9, 14, 26, 30, 34, 41, 87, 93, 114, 128–29, 132, 135, 189–91
Pope, John, 6–7, 19
Porter, Fitz John, 13,
Posey, Carnot, 35, 151,
preservation, battlefield, 143, 196
prisoners, 92, 98, 134–35, 186
Prospect Hill, 148–49

railroad, 6, 23–24, 28, 30–31, 38, 62–63, 68, 138
Railroad, Richmond, Fredericksburg & Potomac, 8, 147–48
Railroad, Unfinished, 84, 87, 98
Ramseur's Brigade, 173, 175, 224
Ramseur, Stephen D., 175–76, 223
Rapidan River, 26, 31, 34, 41, 72,
Rappahannock River, 6, 13, 23, 26, 116, 122, 127, 141–42, 147, 150; and crossing before Second Fredericksburg, 34, 36, 45, 55, 92–93, 148; during First Fredericksburg, 9, 12; during March to Chancellorsville, 26–31, 34, 41, 147; and Hooker's Retreat, 59–60, 71–72, 102, 112, 128, 131, 134, 138, 177–80; and Sedgwick's Retreat, 106, 128–29, 138, 187, 189–92
Red Badge of Courage, The, 196–97
Republican Party, 16, 194
Reynolds, John F., 14, 60, 129–30, 199
Richmond, 5–9, 11, 13, 16, 19, 22–24, 26–31, 52, 55, 67, 86–88, 134, 137, 147, 188
rifle pits, 62, 94
Right Cause, 194
River Road, 42, 47, 101, 131, 151
River Road/Route 618, 151, 189
Rodes, Robert, 68, 75–76, 78–80, 167, 222
Roebling, Washington A., 46–47
Rosecrans, William, 3, 5

Salem Church, 104, 151, 185–86
Salem Church Battlefield, 134, 143, 145, 184, 187
Salem Church, Battle of, 83–84, 97, 106–7, 129, 134, 180, 185–86, 192
Salem Church monuments, 188–89
Salem Church Road/Route 639, 184, 189
Savannah River, 3
Schurz, Carl, 62, 212
Sedgwick, John, 48, 87, 116, 126, 137–38, 157, 209; crosses river and waits, 31, 36–41, 45–47, 50, 55, 57, 60, 148; attacks at Fredericksburg, 66, 83–86, 92–99, 181, 183; fights at Salem Church, xvi, 101–6, 107, 112–13, 127, 184–88; retreats across Rappahannock, 128–36, 180, 189–91
Seven Days Battles, 6, 16, 22, 54
Shaara, Jeff, 197
Shaara, Michael, 197
Shenandoah Valley, 5, 21–23
Shiloh, Battle of, 3
Sickles, Daniel, 62, 108–9, 129–31, 142, 157, 204; Ordered to withdraw from Hazel Grove, xvi, 108–13, 119,

255

Index

Sickles, Daniel (*cont.*) 171–74; Notices Hooker's wounding, 119
Sigel, Franz, 61
slavery, xiv, 8–9, 11, 194
Slocum Drive, 177
Slocum, Henry, 46–47, 109, 129–30, 136, 155, 213
Smith, Bailey, 183
Smith, Edmund Kirby, 3
Smith, James Power, 168–69, 196
Smith, William "Baldy," 13
Smith, W. P., 152
Spotsylvania, Battle of, 184
Spotsylvania County, 147, 149
Spotsylvania County Museum, 153
staff officers, 19, 46, 53, 63, 67–69, 73, 76, 79, 101, 109, 114–18, 134, 170, 195–96
Stafford Civil War Park, 146–47
Stafford County, 25, 44, 92, 135–36, 145–46
Stafford Heights, 37
Stanton, Edwin, 14–15, 31
Stephens House, 181
Stoneman, George, 30–31, 65, 137–38, 215
Stoneman's Raid, 31, 65
Stones River, Battle of, 3
Stonewall Brigade, 139
Stuart Drive, 171, 174
Stuart, James Ewell Brown "Jeb," 44, 52, 54–55, 102, 128, 131, 134–35, 161–62, 222, 227; reports information, 34, 50–54, 160; takes command of the Second Corps, xvi, 74–81, 99–101, 111, 113, 140–41, 168–71, 177
Suffolk, 21–24, 26, 38, 55
Sumner, Edwin V., 13, 18
Sunken Road, 180–84; During First Fredericksburg, 88; During Second Fredericksburg, 83, 88, 90–91, 94, 97–98

supplies, 7, 14, 21, 30, 116, 124, 147
Sykes, George, 41, 47–48, 50, 154–55, 207

Talcott, T. M. R., 161–62
Tally Farm, 62
Tammany Hall, 108
Taylor, Walter H., 19, 24, 75
telegraph, 24, 27, 44, 116, 132, 157
Telegraph Road, 87, 98, 181
Tennessee River, 3
traffic light/signal, 145, 149, 155–56, 160, 163–65, 171, 175, 177, 180, 184, 187, 189
trail. *See* Interpretive Trail
trailhead, 168, 177
trenches, 40, 48, 50, 60, 62, 69, 71, 73, 80, 99, 109, 111, 118, 128, 132, 135, 151–52, 178–79. *See also* earthworks
truce, xvi, 83–84, 89–92, 94, 141, 181–82, 195–96

Underwood, Adin, 62
University of Mary Washington, 181
United States Ford, 31, 35, 41, 72, 125, 127–32, 134–35, 178, 190; Jackson wants to attack, xvi, 67, 72–73, 104, 165, 168
17th US Infantry, 40, 208

4th Vermont, 136, 210
6th Vermont, 183, 210
veterans, Civil War, 193–97
Vicksburg, 3
3rd Virginia Cavalry, 152
30th Virginia Infantry, 177
Virginia Military Institute, 78
Virginia, xiii, 3, 5, 8–11, 13, 15, 19, 21, 23, 37, 51, 68, 137, 145, 196; central, xiv, 6, 20, 22–23, 26, 35–36, 51, 63, 134, 147. *See also* Army of Northern Virginia and Peninsula, Virginia

Wainwright, Charles S., 119–20, 122, 125
Warren, Gouverneur K., 48, 129, 155
Washington, DC, 5–7, 9, 14, 19, 23, 26, 28, 30, 116, 146; defenses of, 28
weather, 13, 30, 44, 134
Wellford, Charles, 53
Western Theater, 3, 5, 22
West, Fred H., 186–87
West Point, 79
Whipple, Amiel W., 110, 206
White, Albert M., 173
Wickesberg, Carl, 136
Wilbourn, Richard E., 74–75
Wilcox, Cadmus, 104, 152, 185–87, 220
wilderness, xiv, 31, 33, 37–38, 40–42, 46–55, 62, 71, 79, 83, 86, 109, 122, 125, 134, 136, 142, 150–52, 154, 157, 160, 165, 174, 185, 197
Wilderness, Battle of, 184, 196
William Street, 94
Willis Hill, 183
Winchester, 22–23, 68
winter of 1862–63, xiii, 1, 9, 13, 17, 19–26, 108, 136, 145–148, 151
5th Wisconsin Infantry, 97, 211
26th Wisconsin Infantry, 136, 213

Yerby Plantation, 34

Zoan Church, 131, 150–51
Zoan Church Ridge, 36–37, 40–42, 92, 99, 101, 149–53

www.ingramcontent.com/pod-product-compliance
Lightning Source LLC
Chambersburg PA
CBHW030513080526
44586CB00011B/179